Social Stress

SOCIAL

STRESS

Sol Levine
  and
Norman A. Scotch
The Johns Hopkins University

Aldine Publishing Company

First published 1970 by
Aldine Publishing Company
529 South Wabash Avenue
Chicago, Illinois 60605

Library of Congress Catalog Card Number 68-8159
SBN 202-30066-8
Printed in the United States of America

To ALICE AND FREDA
gentle experts in the management of stress

Preface

WHILE preparing and conducting our research on stress and coronary heart disease in the Framingham Heart Studies, our exhaustive search of the literature turned up many thoughtful conceptual papers and important empirical findings. We were particularly impressed with the work of Selye, Janis, Mechanic, Caudill, Basowitz, Dohrenwend, and Scott and Howard. Nowhere in the literature, however, were we able to find in one volume a thorough and systematic discussion of the conceptual and methodological issues of the sources and consequences of social stress. Accordingly, we set about preparing this volume in the hopes that it would fill this void in the literature and meet a special need in stress research by spanning several disciplines, including medicine, sociology, physiology, and psychology.

In acknowledging our debts to others we wish first to thank our contributors for the fine quality of their work and for their willing cooperation. The overall design and plan of the volume benefited from discussions with Elliot Mishler, George Vlasak, Gordon Cader, Paul White, Tom Bice, and a number of other F.O.L.'s. Paul White, in particular, was extremely helpful in editing several chapters, especially the two by the editors. We wish to thank Warren Strauss and Frances Feinerman for their assistance in reviewing the extensive literature. Finally, it is not possible to convey in print the debt we owe our secretary, Susan Spencer, who with intelligence and serenity withstood the intermittent stress of our impatience and badgering.

S.L.
N.A.S.

Contents

PART ONE
Introduction

1. Social Stress

SOL LEVINE AND
NORMAN A. SCOTCH

WHEN a man suffers a coronary heart attack or other acute life-threatening episode, the alert physician providing medical care almost invariably attempts to collect a social as well as a medical or physical history. In particular the physican is interested in any evidence that the patient has experienced "unusual psychological trauma or distress." But he is rarely quite sure what to do with such information. Should the patient recover, the physician may very likely caution him to "try to avoid" psychological upsets in the future, even though both physician and patient know how difficult it is to avoid the stress so often built in to the lives of members of modern society. Even in the absence of reliable, systematic data, many distinguished physicians believe that some sort of social or psychological threat or insult, which for the moment we may term stress, contributes to the risk of developing heart disease, and indeed any number of other serious and trivial diseases. While there are some physicians who maintain considerable skepticism regarding

Sol Levine is chairman and professor, and Norman A. Scotch is professor, Department of Behavioral Sciences, The Johns Hopkins School of Hygiene and Public Health. They are co-editors of this volume.

1

stress, few rule it out altogether as important in contributing to disease.

Physicians are not alone in their concern with stress. Other professionals, such as psychologists and social workers, invoke stress to explain social pathology, for example, alcoholism, suicide, and drug abuse. They are joined by many lay people (whatever their experience or sophistication regarding health and illness) in implicating stress in the development of disease. Indeed, conventional wisdom includes the notion that to worry, or to be tense, or to take things hard, is to increase one's vulnerability to disease.

THE NATURE OF THE EVIDENCE

At least five major kinds of evidence can be identified that support the notion that stress is related to and even contributes to physiological dysfunction, disease, mental disorder, and socially pathological behavior. The five types of supporting evidence are: (1) clinical impressions, (2) laboratory studies, (3) variation in prevalence of the "disorder," (4) empirical, epidemiological studies, and (5) "logic and common sense." Let us briefly examine each of these.

1. *Clinical impressions.* From time immemorial, it seems, physicians have observed that patients suffering from different diseases appear to have special life histories, peculiar vulnerabilities, or distinctive personalities. In addition, episodes of physical illness often seem preceded by situational "shocks," such as the loss of a job or the death of a loved one. These same histories, vulnerabilities, and personalities have also been noticed among the mentally ill and the socially deviant. These observations have led some to take the next step and to study and record these special characteristics. The medical literature is filled with retrospective case studies of patients suffering a particular disorder and possessing this or that personality characteristic. Much of this literature has been based on small numbers of patients, often less than twenty or even ten.

Despite the insights and suggestive value of some of these studies, by far the majority fail to pass the minimal requirements of scientific inquiry. Rudimentary scientific procedures — sampling, controls, etc., — are nearly always violated. It would not be easy to dispose quickly of decades of observations by thoughtful and intelligent men, were it not that these observations are often at odds with one another, and the characteristics alleged to be associated with one disease by one practitioner are conspicuously ignored by another. At best, this class of evidence remains suggestive.

2. *Laboratory studies.* Dating back to Selye's brilliant and trail-blazing studies of the effects of stressful stimuli on laboratory animals, there have been hundreds of inventive experiments on human and animal subjects demonstrating that both the threat and the actual use of either psychic or physical stressors produce physiological reactions in vital organs. Indeed, it was Selye who first brought the concept of stress and its concomitant general adaptation syndrome (GAS) into prominence (Selye, 1956). It is simple to alter the vital signs of a human being (e.g., blood pressure, heart beat) in the laboratory; the stimuli necessary range from relatively mild physical stimuli such as electric shocks and immersion of hands in ice water to psychological fear of failure or group disapproval. Indeed, almost every physician has observed that the simple psychological "threat" of the taking of blood pressure of a patient "causes" the pressure to rise. Almost invariably, as the patient becomes more familiar with the experience and presumably less threatened, there is a subsequent drop in pressure reading as it is taken at five-minute intervals. Accordingly, the second reading is generally lower than the first, a third lower than the second, until a plateau is reached.

Closely related to this class of data are the findings that have emerged from studies of natural disasters. Studies conducted of soldiers entering combat (Ehrstrom, 1945) have revealed increases in blood pressure and other vital signs associated with Selye's GAS, and other studies indicate that the prevalence of hypertension increases for civilians under war-time conditions (Graham, 1945).

All of these studies offer consistent support to the belief that both artificial and real stresses lead to alterations in body state involving preparation for "fight" or "flight." Nevertheless, a number of questions remain unanswered. There is the problem, for example, of to what degree artificial laboratory stresses tend to be milder than those encountered in real life. To overcome laboratory distortion, sophisticated monitoring devices are currently being developed to track changes in bodily functioning of the individual as he carries on his "normal" daily activities.

One general question posed by both laboratory and natural disaster studies is, "How permanent are bodily changes that are caused by temporary stresses?" Very little is known in this area. More specifically, "What is the relation of temporary rises in blood pressure to the development of hypertensive heart disease?" Theories abound but factual data are scarce.

3. *Variations in prevalence.* The distribution of virtually all physiological or behavioral "disorders" varies by social as well as biolog-

ical characteristics. It is difficult to think of a single disorder—from cancer and asthma to drug addiction and juvenile delinquency—that does not distribute unequally among different segments of the population. Even seemingly pure biological criteria for grouping populations such as age and sex have powerful psychological and social concomitants. Thus cancer, heart disease, tuberculosis, juvenile delinquency, suicide, alcoholism, and homosexuality vary by country, region, ethnic group, religion, age, sex, social class, and other social parameters.

Differential prevalence of a disease or differential distribution among various social groups should provide some general clues for ascertaining etiology and the possible effects of stress. For example, when we find that economically deprived persons suffer from an unusually high prevalence of nutritional disorders, it is easy to hypothesize that lack of money leads to lack of food, or that persons without money are often without education and are therefore unlikely to be familiar with the notion of a balanced diet. In the case of chronic diseases, similar reasoning may be employed. If we find among a group of high-level business executives that those with only a high school education have a higher prevalence of coronary heart disease than those with a college education we have to ask, "Why the discrepancy?" (Hinkle and others, 1968). An answer might be postulated in terms of the stresses associated with "role incongruence," implying that a high degree of social mobility entails considerable psychological costs. Executives who have only a high school education often have to deliberate whether their behavior is correct (are they using the proper fork at dinner? are they talking correctly to the president of a firm?, etc.), unlike the college graduate who has presumably learned his etiquette at an earlier age and finds it and all aspects of life at the top considerably less disruptive and threatening.

It is frequently found that there are demographic variations in the prevalence of disorder. Urban areas often exhibit a higher prevalence of a particular condition (e.g., hypertension) than rural areas. A frequent interpretation of this phenomena is to assume that stress is associated with the development of hypertension, and then to reason that stress is associated more with urban than with rural living. It is not difficult to make a convincing argument and to conclude tautologically that stress increases hypertension. Example: more hypertension in the city. More stress in the city; evidence: overcrowding, noise, greater competition, etc. Therefore: more stress, more hypertension. The trouble with this kind of reasoning is that it is often just as easy to "prove" the opposite. Example: "We found a mistake in our data. Actually the prevalence of hypertension is higher in rural than in urban areas." Long pause. "Well," it will then be argued, "there is actually more stress in rural areas." Evidence: great social isolation in the country, anxiety brought about by the lack of medical care facilities, lack of anonymity and privacy, and the punitive nature of gossip and social control. Only a lack of an imagination limits the extent to which social conditions found to be associated with a disorder can be interpreted as being stressful. One conspicuous example in this regard is the higher prevalence of hypertension among Negroes (Comstock, 1957; Geiger and Scotch, 1963; Scotch and Geiger, 1963). It can easily be reasoned that since Negroes have greater stress than do whites, they therefore experience higher prevalence of hypertension, but closer examination enables us to take a more circumspect position on the kinds of possible relationships that may actually exist between social stress and a particular disorder. It has been found consistently that Negroes do, indeed, have a higher prevalence of hypertension than do whites. The question that immediately must be posed is: In what ways do Negroes differ from whites? Heredity, diet, constitution, and the "quality" of their lives are primary differences. Finding differences between the races means that the epidemiologist must collect data that will permit more refined observations and, it is hoped, testable hypotheses. In comparing the lives of Negroes with whites, it is hard to refute the observation that Negroes do indeed suffer from greater stress than whites. Differential treatment and experience of Negroes in a whole range of American institutions would tend to support this. We can agree that Negroes suffer from more stress experiences and also have a higher prevalence of hypertension. Unfortunately it is at this point that epidemiologists—at least until recently—have failed to pursue the question and to test the relationship of stress experiences to the development of hypertension, or to demonstrate a dynamic association between the two.

The hypothesized relationship between stress and hypertension, then, may be a promising starting point, but it is only a starting point. If an investigator could devise measures of stress applicable to a Negro population and then determine whether or not highly stressed Negroes had significantly more hypertension than those with less stress, especially if constitution and diet could be held constant, the proposition that stress is related to hypertension would be supported. The same type of investigation should, of course, be conducted for whites, or for specific ethnic groups. In addition, we should have to distinguish between types of stress (e.g., episodic versus chronic) or between life areas in which stress may be present (e.g., work, family, social relations) and ascertain whether variations in stress have differential relationships to hypertension. Only by pursuing the leads presented by differential prevalence can real progress be made.

4. *Epidemiological studies.* Epidemiological studies attempt to go beyond the casual observation and impressionistic interpretation of gross relationships; they are more purposively designed, more systematically executed, and more rigorously analyzed. In the past few years there has been a small but growing number of epidemiological studies that have produced on accumulating body of evidence linking stress to disorder. For example, studies of accountants at tax deadlines, students at examination time, and Pentagon officials about to testify before congressional committees indicate significant changes in blood pressure, cholesterol values, and blood-clotting time. Among the various other investigations that form an increasing body of evidence in this area are the studies of heart disease among lawyers, the studies of personality and heart disease by Jenkins, Rosenmen, and Friedman (1968), and others by Rosenmen and associates (1968), and the work by Syme and others on social mobility and hypertension.

These studies represent a significant advance over previous studies in that they begin to offer specific clues to the dynamic relationship between stress and disease. They provide some information concerning the differential "power" of stress, as indicated by personality and social group membership, in affecting the status and behavior of human populations.

5. *Logic and common sense.* For some observers the question should not be, "Does psychosocial stress lead to disorder?" To them the existence of a relationship is obvious. Who has not under moments of considerable stress experienced a pounding heart, a racing pulse, perspiration, or the urge to urinate? If a person experiences stress chronically or frequently, will not his heart "pound" and his pulse race more than others? How long can this continue without causing physiologic alterations and, finally, morbidity and mortality? Proponents of this position do not feel impelled to demonstrate that a relationship does indeed exist.

If membership in particular social groups with particular cultural beliefs and practices influence how people behave, what they think and what they perceive, it stands to reason, those who hold this position argue, that social events will have some effect on physiology, whether or not this will be mediated through mental processes. The position is exemplified in the following statements from students of different fields.

Disease and its treatment are only in the abstract purely biological processes. Actually such facts as whether a person gets sick at all, what kind of disease he acquires and what kind of treatment he receives depend largely upon social factors (Akerknecht, 1947).

Religion, philosophy, education, social economic conditions—whatever determines a man's attitude towards life—will also exert great influence on his individual disposition to diseases and the importance of these cultural factors is still more evident when we consider the environmental causes of disease" (Sigerest, 1943).

If it is granted that physical, social and cultural factors combine to make a man a whole person, it is equally imperative to consider their potential effects in his *undoing*, whether this takes place through illness, accidents, or other illfated happenings" (Simmons and Wolff, 1954).

These then are the types of evidence or reasoning that support the hypothesis that psychosocial stress is a contributing factor in specific disorders. We have tended to take our examples from medicine, where the "disorder" appears as "disease." Other disorders could also have been considered, such as mental illness, suicide, or criminal behavior. Yet, although more data are being collected on these disorders than ever before, and present methods of study are superior to those of the past, one still has to conclude that the evidence is far from conclusive. There are simply no consistent findings.

WHY SO LITTLE RESEARCH?

In view of the importance attached to stress as a possible contributing factor to every unfortunate physical and behavioral "outcome," from disease to drug use, one is struck by the slightness of the evidence that links stress to disorder and, more important, that describe the nature of the relationship, its processes, and mechanisms. The simple, obvious explanation is that very little research has been conducted in this area.

It is, in fact, not easy to conduct such research. Much sophistication is needed to measure not only stress itself but the various physiological parameters as well. When physicians conduct research on social factors in the etiology of various diseases—arthritis, for example,—they may have sufficient familiarity with the disease, but they often find that it is difficult to conceptualize and measure social stress. Similarly, sociologists may know how to make assessments of social stress but may be relatively ignorant about the disease. Fortunately, recent collaborative research between experts in the various areas has tended to improve the work being done: Ostfeld and Lebovits, 1964; Jenkins, Rosenman, and Friedman, 1967; Rosenman, Jenkins, and Friedman, 1968; Rosenman, Jenkins, Friedman, and Bortner, 1968.

In addition to the problems of cross-disciplinary research, there are major conceptual and methodological problems that tend to adhere to the independent and dependent variables under investigation. These problems deserve our attention, for they must be solved before significant progress can occur. Let us turn first to problems associated with the concept of stress, the independent variable, and later consider disorders, the dependent variable of the equation.

STRESSORS — THE INDEPENDENT VARIABLE

Although the idea of stress has been utilized with considerable frequency,[1] it remains to a large extent a vague and ambiguous concept, and one frequently used without explicit definition. Sometimes the general meaning is assumed to be known and a specific, narrow, operational definition is provided (Hurvitz, 1960; Thomas and Murphy, 1958); or a writer will define stress in the broadest possible terms and fail to make explicit its particular use in the study at hand (Barrabee and Mehring, 1953). Even writers who complain about the vagueness of the concept often proceed to present their empirical finding without themselves explicitly defining the concept (Scotch, 1960).

When defined, either explicitly or implicitly, stress has been employed by different investigators to refer to divergent dimensions or processes. For example, definitions may be given in terms of stimuli, or stressors (such as electric shock, or loss of a loved one), that lead to changes in the organism (Basowitz and associates, 1955; Gordon and others, 1961; Haggard, 1943; Hanfmann, 1950; Hill, 1958; Janis, 1958; Schein, 1957; Thomas and Murphy, 1958; Winokur and others, 1960). Or the definition may refer to the outcome from such stimuli (hyperventilation, increased blood pressure levels, personality disintegration: Dohrenwend, 1961; Fox and associates, 1957; Notterman and Trumbull, 1959; Janis, 1958). In some cases the reference is to

The discussion on these pages, 8–10, is taken from "Toward a Theoretical Model." 1967, Levine and Scotch.

the emotional state or the emotional experience accompanying a changing personal or social situation (anxiety, frustration: Barrabee and Mehring, 1953; Mechanic and Volkart, 1961).

Accompanying such definitional difficulties are a number of unwarranted assumptions about stress: (1) that all unpleasant situations or occurrences are stressful; (2) that what is stressful for one will inevitably be stressful for another; (3) that events stressful for an individual must lead to disruptive or pathological consequences (Levine and Scotch, 1967).

Research also tends to be plagued by methodological errors or inadequacies. Research in which the measures of the independent variable are not kept separate from the dependent variable are common. In addition, specific indicators, or measures of stress, are often highly questionable (e.g., loneliness, culture change, etc.: Alexander and Anderson, 1957; Mechanic and Volkart, 1961; Pearlin, 1959). Specific types of stress are rarely distinguished and time sequences may be either ignored or obscured, so that one is not always certain whether the event causes the stress, or the stress the event (Hurvitz, 1960; Pearlin, 1959). All of these difficulties have undoubtedly contributed to problems in interpreting findings purporting to measure stress and its effects. As a result, interpretations of the relationship of stress to outcome tend to be circular, and the value of the concept as a guide to research is undermined (Levine and Scotch, 1967).

There are a number of possible explanations for this situation. First, the idea of stress has been employed by specialists with widely divergent interests from a broad range of different disciplines (sociology, psychology, psychiatry, medicine, and engineering). These disciplines vary not only in their subject matters and respective methodologies, but also in the degrees to which they are committed to making explicit the phenomenon they are discussing. Second, within the social sciences, stress has received more initial attention from the clinically oriented than the more quantitative and methodologically oriented students, who typically are more prone to define concepts in clear operational terms. Third, the idea of stress is rooted strongly in contemporary intellectual parlance and used freely as a given. Fourth, clarity is obscured further in that the word "stress" lends itself to different usages. The phrase being "under stress," for example, may have reference to the operation of some outside stimulus or stressor, or it may refer to the processes experienced by the individual who is stressed. This confusion permits writers to engage in a careless discourse and to move cavalierly from one level of data to another (Levine and Scotch, 1967).

A number of researchers have begun to address themselves to

these difficulties and have tried to keep the measures of stress independent of the measures of outcome. Caudill (1961), among others, has noted the importance of the meaning of the potentially stressful event, and has pointed out that man is unique in that he actively seeks stress. Caudill (1961) has also developed the model of the linked-open systems (the physiological, the psychological, the social, etc.), where stress in one system has ramifications in another. Dohrenwend (1961), too, has attempted to add clarity to the process by contributing the notions of internal and external constraint to point up the essential interplay of inner and outer stimuli as they are screened in a particular context. Basowitz and others (1955) have pointed out that although the ultimate measure of stress rests with outcome, stimuli can be discussed in terms of the *probabilities* that they will be stressful.

DISORDERS — THE DEPENDENT VARIABLE

If the reader has been impressed with the magnitude of the problems associated with attempts to measure the independent variables (stressors), he should not entertain high hopes that the situation will prove more promising in attempting to measure the dependent variables (disorders). Although it is a popular article of faith that measurements are easier and more precise in the biological than the social areas of life, the facts indicate that confusion, disagreement, and lack of precision are by no means unique in any one field. In some areas, notably the mental disorders (especially schizophrenia), the problems of measurement, diagnosis, and prognosis are formidable.

Systematic reviews of the literature in three such diverse fields as rheumatoid arthritis, hypertension, and schizophrenia attest to the difficulties in defining the disease phenomenon and in developing appropriate diagnostic criteria. Let us review, for example, the problems entailed in the study of rheumatoid arthritis:

> Despite agreement on the 1958 American Rheumatism Association revisions, a formidable problem of diagnosis and diagnostic criteria remains. The 1958 outline established not one but four categories of rheumatoid arthritis, "classical," "definite," "probable" and "possible." Assignment of a case to one of these categories is based on eleven criteria. Of these, one (morning stiffness) is subjective; five (involving joint tenderness, two parameters of joint swelling, symmetry of lesions, and presence of subcutaneous nodules) require observation and judgment—according to poorly

defined criteria for such rubrics as "swelling" or "tenderness" — by an observer; one involves X-ray changes, which must similarly be interpreted; and four involve laboratory methods or pathological examination. Satisfaction of the criteria for any of the four diagnostic categories may be negated by the presence of any of twenty other factors (indicative of lupus, gout, etc.) which similarly require physician judgments, laboratory tests, or both. These complexities are hardly unique to rheumatoid arthritis — indeed, the diagnostic problems in many other chronic diseases seem more difficult — but they have, nevertheless, serious implications for epidemiological and cross-cultural studies. They suggest that fairly wide variations in diagnosis will continue to exist and that, in any case, diagnosis will require extensive medical and laboratory facilities which may not be available in many areas of the world. Cobb (2) has discussed the problems of a committee attempting to establish precise diagnostic criteria and the need for continuing concern with reliability and validity of diagnostic judgment (Scotch and Geiger, 1962, p. 1038).

The problems of defining and measuring schizophrenia are equally if not more perplexing. The task of achieving reliability in studies of schizophrenia is particularly difficult. As one review noted:

It would appear from the few papers dealing with the reliability of diagnosis that variation between even experienced clinicians is so great that comparisons between groups used by different investigators are subject to large error. In one study, three psychiatrists agreed in only 20 per cent of their cases and had a majority agreement in only 48 per cent. Another study revealed that the widest disagreement occurred among the most experienced clinicians. (Mishler and Scotch, 1963).

The problem of specifying, delineating, and operationalizing the dependent variable, of course, is not limited to disease entities but obtains for a whole range of social phenomena. Let us consider, for example, the study of crime. One measure of crime is whether a person has, in fact, been adjudicated for committing a crime. While the criterion here is explicit, we are confronted with variations in the behavior and effectiveness of arresting personnel, in the recording procedures, and in the adjudication processes. Even more fundamental problems occur when we question the essential definition of crime. It may be argued, as Sutherland (1940) did so eloquently, that a crime is a violation of the law, irrespective of whether the person committing the crime is apprehended and prosecuted. This reconceptualization of the meaning of crime ushers in a wide range of

behavioral phenomena which were excluded by our previous definition. Thus, for example, we are now confronted with a vast array of
white collar crime including embezzlement, fraudulent medical
practices, income tax evasion, and a host of other forms of institutionalized deviation.

It might appear that we can escape from these definitional and
methodological difficulties if we focus on what is presumably a more
definitive phenomenon like suicide. Suicide seems to be definite
and final. The classic student of suicide, Emile Durkheim, was attracted to the study because it appeared to meet established sociological criteria and avoided the kinds of definitional and methodological problems encountered other social phenomena. But as Hyman (1955) points out:

> Durkheim himself insists that the sociologist must take as the
> object of his research groups of facts clearly circumscribed, capable
> of ready definition, with definite limits, and adhere strictly to them.
> He then notes that one of the reasons for his choice of the problem of
> suicide was that among the various subjects that we have had occa-
> sion to study in our teaching career few are more accurately to be
> defined. Yet a few pages later, there is a detailed treatment of the
> difficulties of defining the phenomenon appropriately in which it takes
> Durkheim approximately 5 pages to examine alternative methods of
> defining his problem for study and to arrive at a definition that he
> regards as satisfactory (Hyman, 1955, p. 69).

The problem of properly conceptualizing the phenomenon of suicide becomes conspicuous when one attempts to specify the time
order or sequence pattern among variables. Suicide appears to be an
end product, or the "culmination" of previous life processes. As
Hyman states, ". . . no variable would appear to have greater finality
than committing suicide. It is by definition the final point in the
entire life sequence of the individual. Thus, any relationship of
suicide as a phenomenon to individual characteristics such as marital
status, occupation, military experience, class, etc., would appear to
have a determinate time order" (1955, p. 195). Similarly, one would
seem to be on safe ground in relating previous life stress experience
to suicide. But, as Hyman adds, ". . . this is only true if suicide be
seen as a unitary act. If one introduces the notion of process, of
tendency, of predisposition, of incipient suicide, it becomes perfectly possible to see the time order as the reverse. . . ." For example,
Durkheim's finding that married people tend to commit suicide less
frequently than single people might possibly be construed so that
the tendency to suicide is viewed as preceding a decision to marry.

Similarly, if we attempt to ascribe a relationship between stress and suicide, we would have to rule out a tendency for suicide types to seek more stressful lives.

THE PURPOSE OF THIS BOOK

In this introduction we have tried to emphasize the degree to which professionals and laymen use the concept of stress to explain various human conditions and disorders. We have also discussed the kinds of evidence employed to support the hypothesis that stress influences the state and behavior of the organism, and we have pointed to some of the serious semantic, conceptual, and methodological barriers to the study of stress, per se, as well as to the investigation of its relation to other variables. Most of the illustrations we have used emerge from the general field of social epidemiology, where the interests and methods of medicine and social science converge. Thus, one of our paramount interests is in how stress may produce physical, psychological, or behavioral pathology for the individual. This general rubric embraces a wide range of empirical concerns, including how social factors may be related to such specific conditions as heart disease, mental illness, suicide, alcoholism, and delinquency. It is also important, however, to realize that social stress may itself be the object of study as a dependent variable. Thus, for example, it may be desirable to ascertain the relationship between varying social contexts and the degree of stress experienced by different individuals. More specifically, to what extent do various work and organizational settings engender stress for various occupants? To what degree does upward and downward social mobility create stress? What are the effects of family disruptions—death, divorce or desertion—upon the psychological state of the individual? Whether we focus upon stress, per se, its origins and its management, or upon its relationship to individual pathology and behavior, it is necessary to appreciate its complexity and its various dimensions. First of all, there are a number of different sources of stress—the family, the work setting, social class position, and degree of urbanization. Second, the impact of stress may be manifested on a number of different levels—physical, psychological, and social. Finally, the conceptual rubric of stress contains several specific components—the nature of the stressor, its perception or meaning for the individual, his mode of coping with the stressor, and the resultant strain or deformation produced by the stress experience.

This book has been organized to present a clearer and more comprehensive picture of the phenomena encompassed within the conceptual rubric of stress and to explicate such specific levels or dimensions as the sources of stress, its management, and its consequences. The authors of the various chapters include researchers from the fields of sociology, anthropology, psychology, and medicine. The editors have deliberately not tried to structure the content of each chapter nor have they required each author to accept a working definition of stress. With the state of the field as it is presently constituted, it was felt that it would be more fruitful for each author to organize his material in his own way, using that definition of stress he finds most useful. The persistent and uniform themes and data that pervade the various chapters are made explicit in the final chapter.

REFERENCES

ACKERKNECHT, E. H. 1947. "The Role of Medical History in Medical Education." *Bulletin of the History of Medicine,* 21:135–45.

ALEXANDER, T., and ANDERSON, R. 1957. "Children in a Society under Stress." *Behavioral Science,* 2 (January): 46–55.

BARRABEE, P., and MEHRING, O.V. 1953. "Ethnic Variations in Mental Stress in Families with Psychotic Children." *Social Problems,* 2 (October): 48–53.

BASOWITZ, H.; PERSKY, H., KORCHIN, S., and GRINKER, R. R. 1955. *Anxiety and Stress.* New York: McGraw-Hill.

CAUDILL, W. 1961. "Effects of Social and Cultural Systems in Reacting to Stress." *New York Social Science Research Council,* 26:51–58.

COMSTOCK, G. W. 1957. "An Epidemiologic Study of Blood Pressure Levels in a Biracial Community in the Southern United States." *American Journal of Hygiene,* 65:271.

DOHRENWEND, B. P. 1961. "The Social Psychological Nature of Stress." *Journal of Abnormal and Social Psychology,* 62:294–302.

EHRSTROM, M. C. 1945. "Psychogenic Hypertension in Wartime." *Acta Medica Scandinavica,* 122:546–70.

FOX, H. M., GIFFORD, S., MURAWSKI, B. J., RIZZO, N. D., and KUDORAUSKI, E. N. 1957. "Some Methods of Observing Humans under Stress." *Psychiatric Research Report,* 7 (April): 14–26.

GEIGER, H. J., and SCOTCH, N. A. 1963. "The Epidemiology of Essential Hypertension. A Review with Special Attention to Psychologic and Sociocultural Factors. I. Biologic Mechanisms and Descriptive Epidemiology." *Journal of Chronic Diseases,* 16:1151–82.

GORDON, R., SINGER, M. B., and GORDON, K. K. 1961. "Social Psychological Stress." *Archives of General Psychiatry,* 4 (May): 53–64.

GRAHAM, J. D. P. 1945. "Blood Pressure after Battle." *Lancet,* 1:239–40.

HAGGARD, E. A. 1943. "Some Conditions Determining Adjustment during and Readjustment following Experimentally Induced Stress," in Silvan S. Tomkins, ed., *Contemporary Psychopathology*. Cambridge, Mass.: Harvard University Press.

HANFMANN, E. 1950. "Psychological Approaches to the Study of Anxiety," in Paul H. Hoch and Joseph Zubin, eds., *Anxiety*. New York: Grune and Stratton.

HILL, R. 1958. "Generic Features of Families under Stress." *Social Casework*, 39:139-50.

HINKLE, L. E., WHITNEY, L. H., LEHMAN, E. W., DUNN, J., BRY, B., KING, R., PLAKUN, A., and FLEHINGER, B. 1968. "Occupation, Education, and Coronary Heart Disease." *Science*, 161 (July): 3838:238-46.

HURVITZ, N. 1960. "The Measurement of Marital Strain." *American Journal of Sociology*, 65 (May):610-16.

HYMAN, H. 1955. *Survey Design and Analysis*. New York: Free Press.

JANIS, I. L. 1958. *Psychological Stress*. New York: John Wiley.

JENKINS, C. D., ROSENMAN, R., FRIEDMAN, M. 1967. "Development of an Objective Psychological Test for the Determination of the Coronary Prone Behavior Pattern in Employed Men." *Journal of Chronic Diseases*, 20(June):371-9.

LEVINE, S., and SCOTCH, N. A. 1967. "Toward the Development of Theoretical Models: II." *Milbank Memorial Fund Quarterly*, 45:2:163-74, pt. 2.

MECHANIC, D., and VOLKART, E. 1961. "Stress, Illness Behavior, and the Sick Role." *American Sociological Review*, 26:51-58.

MISHLER, E. G., and SCOTCH, N. A. 1963. "Sociocultural Factors in the Epidemiology of Schizophrenia." *Psychiatry*, 26:315-61.

NOTTERMAN, J. M., and TRUMBULL, R. 1959. "Note on Self-Regulating Systems and Stress." *Behavioral Science*, 4:324-27.

OSTFELD, A. M., LEBOVITS, B. Z. 1964. "A Prospective Study of the Relationship between Personality and Coronary Heart Disease." *Journal of Chronic Diseases*, 17 (March):265-76.

PEARLIN, L. I. 1959. "Social and Personal Stress and Escape Television Viewing." *Public Opinion Quarterly*, Vol. 23, Summer 255-59.

ROSENMAN, R. H., JENKINS, C. D., and FRIEDMAN, M. 1968. "Replicability of Rating the Coronary Prone Behavior Pattern." *British Journal of Preventive Social Medicine*, 22 (January):16-22.

ROSENMAN, R. H., JENKINS, C. D., FRIEDMAN, M., and BORTNER, R. W. 1968. "Is There a Coronary-Prone Personality." *International Journal of Psychiatry*, 5 (May):427-29.

SCHEIN, E. H. 1957. "Reaction Patterns to Severe Chronic Stress in American Army Prisoners-of-War of the Chinese." *Journal of Social Issues*, 13:21-30.

SCOTCH, N. A. 1960. "A Preliminary Report on the Relation of Sociocultural Factors to Hypertension among the Zulu." *Annals of the New York Academy of Sciences*, 84 (December):1000-9.

SCOTCH, N. A., and GEIGER, H. J. 1962. "The Epidemiology of Rheumatoid Arthritis." *Journal of Chronic Diseases*, 15:1037-67.

1963. "The Epidemiology of Essential Hypertension. A Review with Special Attention to Psychologic and Sociocultural Factors. II. Psychologic and Sociocultural Factors in Etiology." *Journal of Chronic Diseases*, 16:1183-1213.

SEYLE, H. 1956. *The Stress of Life.* New York: McGraw-Hill.

SIGERIST, H. E. 1943. *Civilization and Disease.* New York: Phoenix.

SIMMONS, L. W., and WOLFF, H. G. 1954. *Social Science in Medicine.* New York: Russell Sage.

SUTHERLAND, E. H. 1940. "White Collar Criminality." *The American Sociological Review*, (February):VI-12. pp. 2-5.

SYME, S. L., HYMAN, M. M., and ENTERLINE, P. E. 1965. "Cultural Mobility and the Occurrence of Coronary Heart Disease." *Journal of Health and Human Behavior*, 6 (Winter):178-89.

THOMAS, C. B., and MURPHY, E. A. 1958. "Further Studies on Cholesterol Levels in the Johns Hopkins Medical Students: The Effect of Stress at Examinations." *Journal of Chronic Diseases*, 8:661-68.

WINOKUR, G., STERN, J. A., and GRAHAM, D. T. 1960. "Stress as an Inhibitor of Pathological Processes." *Psychiatric Research Report*, 12 (January):73-80.

PART TWO
Sources of Stress

2. The Family as a Source of Stress

SYDNEY H. CROOG

AMONG the many controversies that center around the concept of stress, one of the least resolved concerns the relation of stress to the institution of the family. Since a large segment of social science literature about the family touches on problem situations, crises, stresses, and dysfunctions in one way or another, it would appear on superficial view that this literature presents a rich and bountiful resource of scientific information pertaining to stress and the family. Numerous classifications have been developed specifying types of crisis, problem, or stressor situations that occur in families, some of which develop from external sources, some of which originate in the family itself (Burgess and others, 1963; Farber, 1964; Hill, 1958; Hill and Hansen, 1962; Spiegel, 1957). Perhaps the most systematic work has been concerned with problems of reaction, adjustment, and adaptation. Many efforts have been made at delineating the nature of response patterns, the processes of functional and dysfunctional adaptation, and variables associated with differential types of response by the family to stress (Farber, 1964; Hansen and Hill, 1964).

Sydney Croog is associate professor of sociology in the Harvard University School of Public Health, Boston.

In addition, many practitioners in the "helping professions" have been endeavoring to refine procedures that can be employed for intervening in family crisis for therapeutic ends or for assisting family members in adaptation to stress (Ackerman, 1966; Caplan, 1961; Jackson, 1962; Leslie, 1964). Nevertheless, as some critics have observed in reviewing the literature on family response pattern and adjustment to stress, a great deal of systematic work remains to be done in conceptual clarification and specification (Hansen and Hill, 1964, pp. 815–16).

One aspect that has received comparatively less systematic attention is the role of the family as a *source* of stress. In various forms the problem has long been a favored theme in the creative arts, and the image of man suffering because of his family is mirrored in the history of Oedipus, Romeo and Juliet, Anna Karenina, and the son of the late George Apley, among countless others. Research workers, theorists, and lay critics of society have produced a substantial body of literature in which many types of negative consequences have been traced back to stressful family situations or to particular types of family structures. These include mental illness, psychosomatic disease, delinquency, economic dependency, political radicalism, and immorality (Chen and Cobb, 1960). While this work has led to many major contributions of both a theoretical and empirical nature, it would appear that the role of the family as a stress source is even less clearly understood than the aspect of the family in response to stress or crisis.

In what ways is the family a source of stress? Among the various problems, conflicts, and crises to which individuals may be subjected during life in complex society, what are the kinds of stresses that may be traced to the family as an institution and as a social context? Can the procedure of examining the family as a stress source be a productive one in theoretical and practical terms? It would seem that many of the problems inherent in the study of the family in relation to stress might be considerably relieved if the nature of the initial stimulus, the family as a source of stress, could be clarified.

This chapter, focusing primarily on the family as a source of stress, first presents a brief review of some of the conceptual and methodological issues that must be systematically dealt with. In addition, it offers some illustrative examples of directions of research that are concerned in part with problems of how stresses may originate with the family. The section on directions of research is first concerned with the examination of family forms and structures of various types in terms of their functions as possible stressors. Attention then shifts to another area, that of value conflicts within the family. Stressors associated with the normal life cycle of individuals in the family and then of the family itself are next considered, and problems of role conflict situations in the family context are reviewed. Next, some patterns of interaction and interpersonal relationships are examined, with particular emphasis on their role in the etiology of illness. Finally, consideration is given to ways in which adaptive responses to stress within the family may themselves serve as stressors. Although family stressors may have consequences for other major social institutions, for formal organizations, and for other structures within a society, the focus in this chapter is devoted to consideration of stressors in relation to individuals.

These materials constitute only a small selection from a broad range of published empirical reports, theory, and speculation. They are presented as one means of drawing together concepts and findings regarding stressors that researchers and theorists have touched upon, though their own concerns may not touch directly on the family as a source of stressors.

The family and stress: problems of definition and conceptualization. Consideration of the family as one source of stress leads inevitably into areas of substantial conceptual and methodological difficulties. Some of these relate to problems of definition; others concern the logic of the approach; still others concern problems of measurement and of interpretation.

One of the most immediate problems in considering the family as a source of stress is that stress itself is elusive and difficult to define. For our present purpose, stress will be considered as "a condition of tension within an individual which occurs as a response to one or more stressors." Adapting the definition of Howard and Scott (1965), a stressor can be defined as any problem condition that is posed to the individual or organism for solution. As a point of departure we assume that the family itself can be seen as a source of stress insofar as it produces stressors that trigger off tension responses.

Examination of ways in which the family is a source of stressors is complicated by problems of the nature of the stressor variable itself. Stressors in the family vary greatly not only in form and severity but in degree of continuity. While some consist of brief crises, others are long-term and persisting contributors to situations of conflict. While some are clearly delineable as events, others are more subtle, such as structural arrangements in the family or long-term patterns of interpersonal conflict rarely verbalized and perhaps scarcely recognized. A particular family phenomenon may be a stress source, and it may also constitute a response to stress. Hence, the family stressor variable can be both an independent and a dependent variable at the same time. It may also operate as a mediating variable, however. In these conditions the problem of identification and clear definition of stressor source may be a difficult one.

Another kind of problem, one that has often been noted by students of stress, is that of the delineation and measurement of the stressor element. Many of the complexities of the issue are described in this volume in other contexts, but two particular problems appear to occur in the case of behavioral or social phenomena viewed as stressors. One relates to the sheer difficulty of delineation of the stressor element, the other to assessment of the level of force or level of severity of the stressor. The specification of even an explicit situation of conflict as a stressor has manifold difficulties if any attempt is made to measure it with high precision, using tools currently available. Substantial problems of measurement are involved in the assessment of differential degrees of stress in such variables as marital conflict, family structure, marital skew, sibling rivalry, or child-rearing practices.

Mechanisms of suppression of conflict may also serve to disguise the nature of stressors operative within the family, hampering the prospects of measurement. It is possible that hostilities which arise between members may be made obscure by their being expressed to other persons and in situations outside the family system. The conflict instead may emerge at work, at school, in peer groups, or in illness behavior seemingly unrelated to family stress. Such a mechanism serves to maintain a situation of apparent peace within the family, helping assure the continuing maintenance of functions. However, this phenomenon of displacement outside the family lends added complexities to tasks of identifying stressors within the family and measuring differential levels of power of concurrent stressors within it.

The phrase "one man's meat is another man's poison" sums up another problem aspect of definition of family stressors. An element that may serve as a stressor in some family contexts may not be a stressor for others. Further, stressor elements within the same family context do not operate equally for all members. Hence, to identify stressors it is often necessary to do so in terms of their effects. Seen in these terms, virtually anything in family life may be potentially traced back as a stressor. The common use of tautological reasoning in identification of family stressors makes for an undesirable condition in the scientific analysis of these phenomena.

An examination of stressors that may be considered as stemming from the family inevitably leads to problems of consideration of ultimate causes. Many stressors can be traced to elements either external to the family or only peripherally related in the most precise sense, but a question arises as to whether it is the family itself that is a source of stress. Stresses that appear to be centered in the family and to have their roots within it may actually be a displacement phenomenon, with the stresses arising from situations or developmental factors outside the family. For example, a situation of interpersonal conflict in a marriage relationship may be described at one level as a source of stress for the children of the family, but the problem of marital incompatibility may have its roots in personality problems of the individuals involved and may thus antedate the marriage relationship by decades. Further, immediate sources of the marital conflict may lie in difficulties in the work situation that the husband is experiencing, and his tension there may be given expression in ways that lead to marital conflict.

In addition, there are questions of ultimate causes that are complicated by the fact of interrelationship of elements within a social system. Leighton, for example, has hypothesized that the nature of interpersonal relationships, including those stressful enough to be pathogenic, may be a reflection of the level of integration or disintegration of the social system within which subunits such as the family exist. In reports on the Stirling County studies in Nova Scotia, he has suggested that these pathogenic elements within subsystems such as the family may be altered by inducing change in the level of integration of the social system (Hughes and others, 1960; Leighton, 1959, 1965). Theorists and researchers in the area of basic personality structure or modal personality, furthermore, have indicated ways in which elements within the family, such as child-rearing practices, are linked to norms and values outside the family system itself. Thus, some of the more stressful aspects of child-care practices, it has been postulated, may be associated with elements in the economic institutions, religious systems, and other areas of social structure (Kardiner, 1939; Kardiner and others, 1945; Whiting and Child, 1953). The Moynihan report on the Negro family in the United States, in defining the nature of a problem for action, also takes an approach that emphasizes the relationship between stress factors within the family and external sources. Moynihan notes the existence of a cycle involving family stability, male employment, and educational achievement. The way to reduce the problem aspects of the family, such as the number of welfare-dependent children, therefore, means breaking into the cycle at some point, whether within or outside the family (Moynihan, 1965, p. 47).

Other difficulties involve the delineation of that entity which presumably produces the stressors: the family. In the literature pertinent to the problem, the family is conceptualized in many ways: as a societal institution, as a situational context, as a particular kind of structure such as "nuclear" or "extended," as an interaction system, as a household unit, and as a set of persons related by marriage ties or kinship. Development of information on "the family as a source of stressors" is also complicated by the fact that many conclusions drawn by researchers in regard to "the family" can only in a limited sense be classified as relevant to this particular system. Vincent, for example, refers to "the quasi-family orientation of family therapies (1967, p. 33)." He points out that among studies dealing with mental illness and the family, as well as with family therapies, "the vast majority of research projects" are oriented not to the family so much as to "the pathological elements or members involved in the mental or physical stress." Hence, the loose focus of the literature itself leads to easy and erroneous generalizations in regard to stressors that are formally identified as deriving from the family but which actually have their roots in other sources.

Complicating the problem of identification of stressor elements in family life is the fact that current methods of spotting these elements have a built-in bias. Those most readily apparent are those with negative consequences, and the more striking those consequences, the more easily can one point to ostensible sources. Not all stressors have negative consequences, however. Many of the most constructive and creative acts of human beings—if adequate measures were developed—might be traced back to the operation of stressor situations in the family context. The intervening effects of stressors in family life have often been noted; for example, in their effects upon the creative productions of such persons as Elizabeth Barrett Browning, Chagall, Gauguin, and Hemingway (Baker, 1969, Chagall, 1960). In the social science literature, however, there appears to be a tendency to avoid the analysis of normal, nondeviant, or creative behavior as a response to stressors, while following the favored analytic procedure of tracing back the clearly negative forms to stressful situations. Since a large segment of creative behavior and of "normal" life patterning is not readily identifiable as related to stress, the stressors behind it are overlooked.

Although virtually any stressor situation that seems rooted in the family can be traced back to causes that clearly lie outside the family,

is it still worthwhile to look at the family as a stress source? While
the issue of origins may lead to questions, the family does provide a
setting in which individuals experience stressors of multiple types.
In fact, the family setting is, in many instances, the sine qua non by
which these stresses are experienced. Though the family may not in
itself be the source, in another sense it can at least be seen as a
crystallizing entity within which these stressors emerge and exert
their impact.

STRESSORS AND THE FAMILY: SOME AREAS OF INQUIRY

Family forms and structures. Studies of family forms and structures have for many years provided a major perspective on ways in
which the family as an institution and a social context may constitute
a source of stressors. A large body of research and theory has identified as stressful: (1) common family forms, (2) particular substructural
aspects of common forms, (3) situations of family forms in the process
of transition, and (4) family structures that are either overtly broken
in structure or are broken in a functional sense. While this literature
has constituted a core of support for many of the common assumptions concerning the family and stress, it is limited by problems of
inadequate definition, vague criteria, and a readiness on the part of
investigators to assume association between variables without ample
review of additional explanatory phenomena. Aside from providing
the substance for major assumptions concerning the family as stressor, however, it has also furnished a rich series of questions for
investigators to resolve through empirical work.

One line of interest has led to the identification of such common
forms as the extended and the nuclear families as stress sources.
Although widely current, both kinds of families have been described
in some instances as dysfunctional for individual members and for
the society as a whole. The extended family, for example, has been
described as usually having an authoritarian power structure that
restricts the freedom of individual members. In many societies the
extended family system provides direction on such matters as choice
of marriage partner, selection of occupation, and location of residence. In varying degrees the devices of control cause frustrations
for individual members who wish to make their own choices.

On the other hand, the nuclear family system also constitutes a
source of problems for individual members as well as for the society
as a whole (Parsons, 1959; Parsons and Fox, 1952; Sussman, 1959).

The autonomy, independence, and freedom that characterize nuclear family systems also have their costs. For example, there tends to be high emotional commitment between members of the small, relatively isolated nuclear family, and when disruption occurs because of death or divorce, the consequences may be severe for individual members. Further, the nuclear family is less able to provide support and resources for its members than is the extended family, and hence the aged, infirm, and ill are especially vulnerable in the nuclear family system. Guilt and recrimination may afflict family members who are unable or unwilling to provide care for the aged or disabled parent or relative.

In addition, particular substructural features of the family system, though these are essential arrangements for orderly functioning, may be sources of stress for individual members. Principles of authority, the system of inheritance and descent, as well as even the formation of the conjugal family itself, are among the many aspects of the family to which stressful consequences have been traced. These features have been illustrated in many cross-cultural contexts. For example, as Linton has described the situation among the Tanala of Madagascar, there is a strong emphasis on a patriarchal family system, with the father maintaining authority and control over property of the sons even after formation of their conjugal families. With the death of the father, a rearrangement of authority becomes necessary, as well as changes in the system of control over property. While the younger sons may for a time be willing to remain under the authority of an older brother, eventually they may move to form their own patriarchal extended unit, and issues of allocation of property may arise (Linton, 1939). With the formation of new units comes a period of decisions and possible disagreements regarding timing of the move, allocation of property, and the breaking away from the control of the elder sons. In a quite different setting, that of traditional rural Ireland, the system of primogeniture in the extended family has been identified as linked to deferral of marriage, delay in attainment of adult status, and decline in the birth rate. It has been suggested that these elements, coupled with emigration, have had complex and somewhat dysfunctional effects on the character of family life, personality development of young family members, and the economy of the nation (Arensberg and Kimball, 1940).

Even the social restructuring that accompanies the normal processes of marriage formation has been identified as a source of stressors. The normal integration of consanguine and conjugal family structures may suffer negative consequences by virtue of the fact that siblings develop many mutual ties during their period of residence within the consanguine family (Linton, 1959). These relationships persist after the formation of conjugal families, and they constitute a source of division of loyalties between the consanguine and conjugal systems. The possibilities of conflicts have been so marked, that in order to minimize stresses, societies have apparently found it necessary to specify with considerable clarity the separate functions of consanguine and conjugal families. Radcliffe-Brown has also suggested that the formation of the conjugal family, certainly a virtually universal phenomenon, constitutes a stressor situation in the sense that it requires a "rearrangement of social structure." He refers to marriage as producing "a temporary disequilibrium situation," and he notes that among its other consequences, marriage creates particular points of tension in the relationship between each spouse and his in-laws (Radcliffe-Brown, 1950, p. 43 ff.).

In societies that are in situations of rapid cultural change, the extended family system is being displaced by the nuclear family type, a condition that has been a source of many problems and conflicts for individuals within both types of structures. Choice of the nuclear family as the preferred norm constitutes a deviation from traditional ways, and common stressor situations arise as individuals break away from the extended family and the ways of their elders.

Some of the problems of personal and social conflict occurring with these developments have been documented in many contexts, including the new nations of Africa and developing countries of southeast Asia and the Middle East. In American society these conflicts have been seen as immigrant families, attempting to maintain the extended family system of the Old World in the United States, have watched children and grandchildren break away in conforming to the American pattern (Campisi, 1948; Kluckhohn, 1968; Lantz, 1958). With the attempt of revolutionary governments to intervene in the process and to create immediate change through legal means and government decree, these problems have been particularly exacerbated. While fragmentary evidence is available on the upsets in parent-child relations, authority systems, and the economy of the family, few systematic studies have been made of the pervasive consequences of the stresses that ensue from alteration of family forms in such nations as Nazi Germany, China, Cuba, and the Soviet Union (Goode, 1961; Schlesinger, 1949; Timasheff, 1946; Vallier, 1962; Yang, 1959).

As indicated earlier, the nature of the stress concept is such that virtually any aspect of the family can be cited as a stressor or source of problems, and few analysts have been unable to identify negative consequences and some of the processes which lead to them. While this type of examination has resulted in many fruitful ways of conceptualizing areas, forms, and structures as stressors, it leaves many questions for ultimate resolution. In each of the areas cited, there is need for further specification of the range of individual situations in which the particular form or substructure is operating as a stressor. Other questions relate to the various levels of stress initiated by particular forms. Thus far there has been inadequate attention paid to the degree of variability of particular stressors and the elements that influence this variability. Another area of importance is that of the compensatory mechanisms that intervene, affecting the levels of stress to which individuals are subjected. Still other basic questions relate to definition of the initiating variable.

Many of the assumptions reported in the literature, while they may be valid initial observations, can be considerably strengthened through empirical testing. For example, some stressful consequences involving the nuclear family are widely assumed to be valid and even self-evident. Let us examine the simple generalization that the Scandinavian nuclear family unit is not as stressful for individuals as is the American nuclear family, a type of generalization that derives from reasoning and descriptive evidence common to this field. As the author of one family text points out, both the Scandinavian and the American nuclear family share the common characteristic of detachment from a larger circle of relatives, but the strains are less for Scandinavians (Blitsten, 1963). This condition of lesser strain in Scandinavian nuclear families is reported as related to their "political, economic, religious, and educational organizations, and to the size and homogeneity of their populations" (Blitsten, 1963, p. 169).

This example sums up both the opportunities and problems that stem from such an observation about the nuclear family as stressor. Is the nuclear family unit of Scandinavia actually less stressful than the American? A first issue here is the dimensions of the phenomena being measured in each context. A second issue is whether appropriate controls are made in order to ensure comparability in terms of social class, historical period, and other conditioning factors. Another set of issues concerns the actual degree of stress that the nuclear family induces in each country. Resolution of these issues, however, depends on the handling of another problem, the question of adequacy of the tools and techniques to be used in the measurement of differential stress in each setting. A related appropriate area for investigation is the mediating role of political, economic, and religious institutions and of other societal structures and organizations. The issue as to whether these really are related to the level of effect of the stressor then leads to such additional questions as how one may measure the influence of these systems, the kinds of observational units to be employed, the specification of comparison groups, and the use of controls.

The critical stance necessitated by the research itself might also encourage others to be aware of the relevant criteria and issues before making broad generalizations and then accepting them uncritically. Moreover, some useful side effects might emerge which at the least might aid the reformulation of the initial research questions. Some recent empirical work on the consequences of traits of the nuclear family provides a useful illustration here. Several investigators, in examining the support structure of the nuclear family, have indirectly clarified considerably the role of this family as stressor. They found evidence that the American nuclear family is less isolated than it may appear, that there are networks of relationships that provide support, and that easy communication and transportation may aid greatly to offset apparent physical isolation. In fact, as some have suggested, the nature of the data is such that it might be most profitable to reformulate notions of the nuclear family itself, to consider the American type as a "modified extended family" (Litwak, 1960; Sussman, 1959; Sussman and Burchinal, 1962).

Skewed structures: the broken family and related forms. Another type of family form of some concern is one whose structure has been disrupted by events such as death, divorce, separation, or desertion. Numerous reports have maintained that from the broken family stem a variety of problems, including crime, delinquency, mental illness, and a heterogeneous mass of ills afflicting individuals, institutional systems, and societies as a whole. The fact that partial family structures appear to be differentially distributed in particular groups in American society has furnished investigators with important clues for explaining deviant behavior of many types in groups with high broken family rates, notably the lower class and the Negro population (Beiser, 1969; Chen and Cobb, 1960; Spiegel and Bell, 1959).

In addition to the true "broken family," there is a common family form characterized by functional disruption, often brought about by minimal participation of key family members in their expected roles (Hughes and others, 1960; A. H. Leighton, 1959; D. C. Leighton and others, 1963). In such cases there is inability or unwillingness to meet traditional role responsibilities. Examples are the incapacitating illness of a parent, absence of the wife from the home because she is regularly employed, absence of a father whose job responsibilities keep him from home for long periods, and the self-isolation of a parent who may be physically present at home but who is a minimal participant in family life. In these quasi-broken family forms may also be found many of the problems of family integration, socialization of children, and minimal fulfillment of roles that have been reported as characteristic of families broken by specific events of marital dissolution.

Research reports that deal with the broken family as stressor present a picture of heterogenous mixture in terms of method and conceptualization. Many of these reports basically consist of descriptions of some of the multitudinous negative consequences that coexist with broken family structure and that are assumed to be related to it or to derive from it directly. The more systematic efforts in this research have attempted to identify and trace the processes of adjustment and to explore the relationship of social, psychological, and other variables to differential patterns of response. Among the many lines of inquiry with which investigators have been concerned have been the influences of this type of family structure upon (1) socialization process and personality development, (2) the mental health and social adjustment of individuals, and (3) the integration and social competence of families as a whole (Burton and Whiting, 1961; Minuchin and others, 1967; Nye, 1957; Wardle, 1961).

In the case of research on the broken family, though the individual stressor variables are relatively proscribed in contrast to family forms and structures, a continuing problem has been one of specification. Indicating that the stressor is the death of a particular family member, a divorce, or a formal separation designates a relatively clear-cut event, but it provides only minimal information concerning the dimensions and power of the event as a stress source. What is required for appropriate analysis is not just a simple classification by type of stressor but, rather, a series of auxiliary data dealing with both objective and subjective phenomena. The stressor input of death of a relative, for example, varies according not only to the kinship classification, age of the deceased, and circumstances of death, but also according to the subjective meaning of that person for individuals within the family context. Thus, a study of response to bereavement on the part of family members should specify the independent variable in terms of such characteristics as sex, identity, age, circumstances of death, and previous subjective meaning of that person for those in the study population. A lack of such items of identification really means studying response to a stressor whose form and dimensions are relatively diffuse.

In a report on the aftermath of divorce, Goode (1956) has provided some direct empirical evidence that may serve to illustrate the contingencies in which the relative influence of this type of marital disruption may have differential effects. It is not the simple fact of divorce alone that is stressful, but rather the particular total circumstances within which it occurs. The amount of stress experienced varies in relation to such factors as the age and sex identity of the divorced person, the degree of family disapproval, the presence of children, and the level of ambivalence in the divorced person about the decision. Hence, a study of the processes of stress that stem from divorce or of the process of adaptation should ideally include identification of the several relevant dimensions of the initial variable.

Many studies of the broken-family variable do indeed recognize the differing influence of the variable as related to contingent circumstances. For example, numerous reports on the influence of the broken family on the socialization process have pointed up the importance of the age level or developmental stage of children in the family. Comparatively few of these studies, however, also consider other contingent variables in the total situation that may either exacerbate or reduce the relative power of the stressor, including the availability of parental substitutes and of other sources of emotional support, attitudes of significant others toward the breakup, the economic situation of the family, or the relative degree of social isolation of its members. Moreover, few of these studies consider the relative power of stressor variables in terms of differences related to social class status, religious identity and commitment, the value system of the family and its cultural setting, ethnic origins, or regional setting. If the relative power of the initiating stressor is to be a significant element in the analysis, it would seem essential to define the variable in sufficient terms so that the basic factors characterizing the stressor may be included. Such procedures could then lead, depending on the interests of the investigator, to the classification of stressor by relative strength, and to the institution of appropriate controls while carrying out the analysis (Ausubel and Ausubel, 1967; Kaffman, 1965; Mead, 1966).

A closely related problem in analysis of the broken home as stressor is that, as indicated earlier, family-based stressors tend to be multiple rather than single phenomena. In families where the home is broken by a specific event, numerous other kinds of stressor conditions may be found, including inadequacy in performance of parental role, unemployment, illness, interpersonal conflict, improper nutrition, and sexual misconduct. These conditions of multiple family pathologies serve to obscure the role of the broken family variable itself as an initiating stressor (Myers and Roberts, 1959; Rogler and Hollingshead, 1965; Stein and Susser, 1967).

Many studies of mental and physical illness have pointed to the existence of these multiple, coexisting phenomena and to their possible role in etiology and in the maintenance of continuing pathology (Beiser, 1965). The presence of these additional conditions opens the way for a more specialized series of studies of broken-home phenomena. Thus it becomes possible to classify the broken home in terms of multiple stressor criteria, comparing, for example, the homes broken by bereavement alone with those broken by bereavement plus a series of other stressor situations. This approach, therefore, may lead to development of theory in which the relative stressor effect of particular combinations of multiple pathologies can be rated in terms of their power and influence.

One particularly interesting study that casts light on the role of differing types of broken home situations as stressors is the Langner and Michael study of residents of an area of Manhattan (Langner, 1963, pp. 158ff). By examining the mental health status of respondents in relation to differing types of variables in their family histories, the authors provide perspectives on elements that are associated with degrees of mental health and current problem situations. Thus, the authors found that levels of "mental health risk" relating to the broken home in childhood varied according to cause of the break up and according to socioeconomic status of the respondent. The mental health risk associated with death of a mother, they report, is particularly high among respondents of low socioeconomic status. Among respondents of high socioeconomic status, however, there was little difference in mental health risk between persons from unbroken as compared with broken homes. For reasons which remain to be fully explained, the stresses of loss of mother may perhaps have greater impact upon the mental health of persons of lower social status in particular. Another finding was that those respondents who came from a home marked by the stresses of divorce, separation, or desertion of a parent were themselves more likely to have broken marriages, as compared with respondents from stable parental homes. While this study relies on retrospective data, tracing consequences of events which began many years previously, it constitutes one of the few systematic efforts to distinguish between different types of broken homes in terms of their relative power as stressors.

A central issue in the consideration of the "broken home" as stressor is the problem of exactly how this phenomenon operates to produce negative consequences. Numerous explanations have been offered. Miller, for example, attempts to trace the behavior of lower-class men back to family relationships that are themselves one consequence of family breakup (Miller, 1958, 1959). He points out that in the true "lower-lower" class, high proportions of homes are broken, most commonly with the father absent. The lack of a male figure raises problems for the sex identification of the children. When the mother is the primary figure for identification, Miller contends, this produces conflicts in the male children about their own masculinity. In a process of reaction formation they come to emphasize toughness and aggressiveness. Moreover, as Miller contends, such lower-class males develop feelings of self-hatred, having absorbed the mother's resentment toward men in general. This self-hatred in turn leads to problems later in the boy's own marriage, rendering him more vulnerable to disruption of that marriage. Thus a cycle is set up extending over generations, carrying along feelings of bitterness, recrimination, and anxieties over masculinity.

Such attempts to account for the processes by which the broken family produces its effects have typically taken the broken family or some component aspect as a "given" or as a starting point. There has been only minimal concern with clarifying the nature of the initiating event itself. Such attempts, however, bear promise for clarifying considerably the stressor variable itself. They present opportunities, for example, for examining and comparing differing types of broken family situations as initiating stressors. Thus, work on stress indicators in lower-class families leads to questions as to whether the same phenomena operate in families with other social status characteristics. What are the communalities of the process, and what are the factors related to variation within it? With the use of case-study techniques and speculative generalization, it may then be possible to move to controlled empirical studies which, though centering on consequences, will also contribute to a knowledge of a key dimension in the total stress process, the initiating variable.

Have there been variations over time in the degree to which the family has served as a source of stress? Both the lay and professional literature are replete with statements, based on conjecture, that the family of today is "in trouble," that there are more stressors within it than at other times in history. As indicated earlier, the methodological and conceptual problems in such assessments are formidable; but, through reference to data on broken family structures it is possible to trace the relative frequency of some stress indicators.

Thus, through secondary sources such as census materials, record studies by insurance companies, and reports of government agencies, it is possible to estimate the relative frequency of occurrence of those circumscribed events which disrupt family structure. For example, such records on divorce permit us to trace historical trends in frequency of divorce among various segments of the population. Studies by insurance companies have pointed out that the frequency of orphanhood has declined radically since the turn of the century. Because of advances in public health and medical care, the extension of length of life has resulted in the fortunate circumstance that fewer children than in earlier times have had to suffer the stressful consequences which are usually associated with death of one or both parents or of siblings. Similarly, parents have had to deal with death of a child with decreasing frequency over time.

These records do not, of course, tell the whole story of total stress effects of broken family occurrences, nor do they indicate the impact of these events nor the total number of persons involved. They are inadequate as empirical measures of such phenomena as desertion or informal separation. However, in regard to at least some types of family stressors, they provide useful empirical measures of historical trends in frequency. They provide hard evidence that can be employed in developing correlational studies on relationships between types of stressors and other current, possibly associated phenomena.

Value conflicts. Among the many elements that give form, direction, and meaning within the family but which also act as sources of stress are the cultural values that are internalized by family members. In the large volume of literature dealing with this subject, the conflicts perhaps most frequently described are those that arise when two or more family members hold differing values on a particular issue or when a family member follows a course of behavior consistent with his own values but inconsistent with those held by others. Another major source of stress develops out of incompatibilities of internalized values pertinent to family situations, such as those relating to child-rearing, kinship obligations, marital choice, dominance-submission in the husband-wife relationship, and sexual behavior (Bradburn and Caplovitz, 1965, pp. 29 ff.; Burgess and Wallin, 1953; Kirkpatrick, 1963, pp. 90 ff). During the socialization process individuals are expected to learn opposing values and to resolve the incompatibilities between them. On some issues intrapsychic stress ensues, and guilt concerning the resolution of these dilemmas may form a core of neurotic conflict (Fromm, 1947; Horney, 1937; Leighton, 1959).

Since the number of individual values held by family members within even a single culture can be enormous, the potential for conflict between value is obviously large. Which of these value conflicts are severe enough or frequent enough to deserve attention as significant stressors within the family? Although little systematic study has been carried out in this area, some relevant data are available in reports on patterns of disagreement between spouses. While these studies are based on limited populations in American settings, they do provide some indication of the possible patterning of value conflicts, their frequency of occurrence, and their distribution within subpopulations (Bowerman, 1964; Farber, 1957; Mitchell and others, 1962).

A study by Blood and Wolfe (1960), for example, presents data on disagreements reported by 909 wives in a study population located in urban and rural areas of Michigan. The three areas of disagreement between husband and wife most frequently mentioned were indicated as money matters, child-rearing, and recreational activities. A heterogeneous category of "personality clashes" ranked fourth. Further, there are some marked variations according to educational level of the wife in frequency of reporting disagreements. One or more were reported by 92 percent of the women with college-level education, by 89 percent of those with some high school, and by 73 percent of those who had completed no more than eight grades.

The patterning of specific disagreements varied by stage of the life cycle. For example, disagreement in regard to money matters was most frequently reported by women with pre-school children, and it was least frequently mentioned by those in the early stages of the marriage (i.e., those childless and who had been married for less than four years). On the issue of raising children, the frequency of conflict reported was highest among those with adolescent children. Some indication of the relative severity of these disagreements as stressors has also been furnished by Blood and Wolfe. They indicate that a very small proportion of the wives (2 percent) stated that they were unable to reach agreement or compromise with their husbands when arguments occurred.

A study of marital conflict employing somewhat different methods (Croog and others, 1969) obtained results congruent in several respects with the Blood and Wolfe work. The study population consisted of families in which the husbands had recently suffered a myocardial infarction. Main attention in the research was focused on variables associated with differing levels of adaptation to the crisis of the heart attack, and information on level and pattern of marital disagreement in the pre-attack period was collected. Data were obtained through interviews with both spouses, and disagreement was noted if it was reported by either spouse. Among couples with children, the single most frequently mentioned item was disagreement about children. Ranking second were matters of finance, and in third place were disagreements about recreation or use of leisure time. Further, there was a positive statistically significant association between educational level of the husband and total number of disagreement areas reported. Another major empirical finding was that those husbands with high work tension also noted more matters on which they were in conflict with their wives at home. When husbands and wives were questioned about possible disagreements in twelve areas, a direct association between work tension and existence of conflict was found in eleven of the areas.

These findings raise questions concerning a matter mentioned in the introductory section of this chapter—the issue as to the origins of stressors that appear within the family. Why were a higher number of areas of disagreement reported in families with high work stress? Do these families really disagree on a broad number of issues, and is this carried over into the work situation? Or, when there is tension at work, are men likely to come home in a frame of mind such that virtually anything can set off a dispute? Answers to questions such as these would help clarify the extent to which value conflicts in themselves act as stressors and the degree to which disagreements in these areas are in reality a masked expression of stress in other areas of life.

Methodological and conceptual problems place special limits on the interpretation of such findings. For example, the finding of an association between disagreement level and education may be simply a product of differential interest, ability, or willingness of the better educated to assess their home situations and respond in a survey research situation. Some of the more serious or more persisting areas of conflicting values may not have been recognized or reported by respondents because of the operation of mechanisms of repression or shame at talking about them. Further, the studies reflect some of the difficulties in measurement of level of severity of a stressor. Frequency of mention is by no means a measure of level of severity. The most problematic issues may simply be avoided or left unspecified in a family because of the recognition that bringing them into the open may tear the family apart.

The importance of value conflicts as stressors is reflected in other types of data, though these too bear limitations that prevent generalizations about frequency or severity. For example, data on frequency of divorce provides at least one type of indication of populations within which value conflict may have played a severe role as stressor. These data do not, of course, provide any general indication about the severity of value conflict in the population that is not divorced. Further, studies of factors in marital success indicate that homogeneity in background, implying homogeneity in values, is associated with stability in marriage, whereas studies of marital breakup among couples from mixed religious, racial, or social class origins help point up the possible role of the stressor effects of disparate value systems. While it is tempting to identify the factor of differing cultural backgrounds as a principal element in the dissolution of these marriages, it is possible that other variables often overlooked in empirical research may be operative. For example, those who marry outside the group, insofar as they are willing to resist pressures upon them for conformity, may be more individualistic, more independent, or more rebellious persons than those who marry within. These characteristics in both spouses, assuming that they persist after marriage, may be divisive. The fact that they may disagree in particular value areas may be less important than their basic personality structure in affecting the stability of the family.

Perhaps some of the most seminal work done until now has been concerned with exploration of ways in which value conflicts may lead to emotional illness. This work, while contributing to theories of etiology of mental disease and to ego psychology, has also served to clarify the role of value incompatibility as stressor. One recent study, for example, centers on the context of a single family and attempts to outline ways in which the mediation of value conflicts may be related to the genesis of psychoneurotic disorder. Cleveland and Longaker identify two conflicting types of value orientation. One emphasizes "striving" or "long-range gratification in individual achievement of material success," while the other emphasizes "being" or gratifications deriving from "adjustment to one's environment in a manner emphasizing the pleasurable rhythms of nature and the immediacy of gratifications (Cleveland and Longaker, 1957, p. 171)." Employing a case study technique, the authors attempt to show how problems of resolving these incompatibilities during the socialization process within the family can contribute to the development of a neurotic maladaptation process which they term "disparagement." They suggest that the individuals examined, failing to arrive at a satisfactory psychic adjustment of the conflicting values, resolve the situation through neurotic patterning that consists in part of self-deprecation or extreme self-devaluation. Cleveland and Longaker offer the clinical impression, furthermore, that the use of this mechanism is also linked to the disparagement of others. While this suggestion deserves more ample exploration, it constitutes an interesting attempt to indicate a chain of stressor influences stemming from value conflict in the family, leading through neurotic response, and linking to other types of conflict among family members involved in the disparagement situation.

The family context and the life cycle. In the course of the normal life cycle, individuals move into new roles, passing out of others, within the family setting. Certain "normal" stresses and tensions occur as individuals meet and master tasks at each stage. Movement from infancy into childhood, from adolescence into adulthood, from·maturity into old age involves types of physical, social and emotional adaptation to new circumstances and problems (Erikson, 1959; Hess and Handel, 1959). Some of the common stressors that accompany such transitions have been described in formulations that deal with the developmental tasks that must be mastered by a normal personality, the role tasks that face newly married couples, and the problems of adjustment to parenthood (Dyer, 1963; Erikson, 1959; LeMasters, 1957; Rapoport and Rapoport, 1964).

In a sense, the family unit as a whole appears to pass through a life cycle of its own, during which at its various stages the individuals within it are coping with the normal stressors of their own continuing life course (Duvall, 1962; Glick, 1955; Hill and Rodgers, 1964; Lansing and Kish, 1957). These stress situations have often been described, but they have rarely been given systematic treatment in research or in theoretical formulations. One of the most ample statements on the family life cycle explicates the phases in terms of goals dominant at each point, citing such categories as adjusting to living as a married pair, adjusting to pregnancy, reorganization of the unit around the needs of infants and pre-school children, etc. (Hill and Rodgers, 1964, p. 188).

What types of stressors are associated with each phase of the family life cycle? Simple specification of an initial stage, the formation of the family through marriage, brings into relevance the vast literature that describes the various kinds of stress situations and problems in relation to marriage that typically face individuals, families, and social structures. As virtually every textbook on marriage and the family indicates, the general picture of problems associated with each stage of the family life cycle can be readily sketched in. Moreover, many empirical studies, though not formally concerned with the problem, can be classified as casting light on *individual* phases of the family life cycle, insofar as these are concerned with the family with adolescent members, the problems of the aged, differential types of child-rearing techniques in families with young offspring, and similar topics. While these formulations, descriptions, and empirical findings may be useful for providing a general picture of stressors at each stage of the family life cycle, they do not as yet permit conclusions about some of the more fundamental aspects of the family life cycle as a whole. One problem here is that little empirical research has been carried out in terms of a framework of the *total* family life cycle.

Among all families that have passed into the child-rearing stage of their cycle, one of the most stressful actual or potential occurrences is the death of a child. Yet both the immediate and long-term effects of this stressor vary, depending in part on the cultural meaning of the event. In the rural family of India or Egypt, for example, the passing of a single male child has a somewhat different meaning than it does in a rural American family. For rural Indian or Egyptian parents, the death of a male child may portend further economic difficulties in the future, since a source of labor and future income is gone. It portends the loss of one source of support in their old age. In a family with few sons, the pride and social standing of the father is threatened by the loss of his boy. In the American rural family at present, the emotional impact of the loss is perhaps greater than the economic, supportive, and status implications.

As these families in their different settings proceed through the life cycle, the long-term stressor effects for each of them vary greatly, and in pragmatic as well as affective ways. Though differences such as these may be sketched in their general terms, it is not possible at present to make precise assessments of the relative power of the stressor on the basis of data currently available. Thus many questions remain unanswered: What do particular types of family life cycle patterns do to the individuals who live within them? Are some especially productive of the mentally ill, the depressed, the deviant? Are others especially productive of creative, independent, or emotionally stable personalities? Are there shifts between generations in the pattern of stressors in the family life cycle, shifts that may be responsible to a degree for changing the character of a total society or region? These are some of the kinds of questions that more intensive attention to the family life cycle and its stressor effects might serve to answer. Without ample and basic information on the nature of the family life cycle as stressor, researchers may be severely handicapped in studies of the effects of this type of phenomenon.

Some indications of the continuing flow of stressors during the course of family life over an extended period may be seen in the rich biographical materials furnished by Lewis (1961, 1966) on family life in Mexico and Puerto Rico. These life histories of individual members of families, when taken together, form a dramatic and rich account of major segments of family life cycles, and they portray the patterning of stressors that appear at each stage, their interrelations within the lives of the various members, and their reappearance and submersion over the course of time. While these life history materials do not codify, process, or classify stages, they provide useful insights into the processes and problems over time involving new marriages, births, child-rearing, family migration, marital conflict, and changing relationships between generations. A series of such reports, drawn from differing cultures and from differing social status groups within the same society, could provide basic secondary materials with which students of stress could proceed in more intensive analysis in the measurement of stressors, and their strength, and their effects.

Roles in the family. In a burgeoning literature, numerous studies refer to the stressor aspects of roles within the family. Types of conflict situations in families involving role demands and expectations have often been traced in terms of their relationship to other structures and situations. Although few attempts have been made to quantify the frequency with which particular patterns of conflict arise from specific types of role problems, at least some generic types of conflict patterns have been made plain and can be offered for brief illustration here.

Incompatibilities between role demands, the conditions under which they arise, their effect on the socialization process, and other consequences have often been reviewed. The fact that children are expected both to be independent of parents and to be dependent on them for guidance and control constitutes one of the most pervasive types of role conflict. All children in the course of socialization must resolve conflict between conformity and independence, and different subcultures may stress one or the other. Variations between families in pattern of emphasis and timing of training children for dependence-autonomy have been found to be associated with many types of social variables including factors of social class, religion, ethnic origins, and type of employment of the father (Erikson, 1963; Kohn, 1963; McClelland, 1961; Miller and Swanson, 1958; B. Whiting, 1963). However, differentiation and measurement of the relative severity of this type of stressor in each of the socialization contexts remains as a major problem for empirical study.

The organization of role obligations within different types of extended families has also been cited as a source of stress for individuals. In a study of Jewish families, Leichter and Mitchell (1967) examined the frequency of conflicts between those holding particular reciprocal kinship statuses, hypothesizing that the organization of the roles may lead to these conflicts. They found that the type of kin relationship most frequently the subject of marital discord was the relationship with the husband's kin, particularly the husband's mother. A common problem was that of divided loyalties on the part of the husband, relating to his need to fulfill role obligations as both a husband and a son. Young and Wilmott point out that in England the relationship of the wife to her relatives, particularly her mother, is a source of conflict, in contrast to the situation involving the husband's mother as seen in the American Jewish families (Young and Wilmott, 1957).

One type of role conflict situation that has received relatively extended attention is that of the employed wife. A basic stressor stems from the conflicting demands of the wife-mother and the economic provider roles. However, associated with the occurrence of this conflict, as numerous investigators have suggested, are many other types of stresses that pervade areas of family life and roles. Though many of the reports of empirical research in this area are inconsistent, it has been shown that the involvement of wives in gainful occupations may have disruptive effects upon family integration, socialization of children, and the fulfillment of traditional obligations of providing companionship, performance of household tasks, and other functions. It may also lead to emotional distress in the woman as to whether she is following the appropriate feminine role. It has been identified as related to the incidence of delinquency, adjustment of adolescent members, school performance, and the level of dependence-independence among children (Blood and Wolfe, 1960; Douvan, 1960; Glueck and Glueck, 1957; Hoffman, 1963; Nye, 1958).

Ironically, one product of the sizable research effort that has been concerned with the employment of the wife has been controversy and conflicting evidence regarding the exact nature of the stressor and of its effects. As has often been the case in the past, empirical studies of the problem have demonstrated that easy assumptions and armchair conceptualizations have tended to oversimplify an extremely complex phenomenon. Thus, a series of recent empirical studies and critiques of research has pointed up the fact of variation in the level of stress related to employment of women, showing the importance of considering such intervening variables as social class of the family, ideologies of the spouses, and personality factors.

Some excellent reviews of this mass of studies on the employment of the wife have performed an important service, insofar as they help clarify what needs to be known concerning this variable as stressor (Nye and Hoffman, 1963; Stolz, 1960). For example, Hoffman suggests that the concept "maternal employment" is too broad and needs further definition in order to be used productively in studies of its effects on the socialization of children. Further, Hoffman underlines the importance of the principle that "we understand precisely what aspects of maternal employment are important, what its specific effects on the child are, and the process by means of which these effects take place" (1963, pp. 210-11). These same comments presumably would hold for the studies of this stressor in other areas of family life as well.

Finally, some mention should be made of the situation of serious illness in a family, where role conflicts may take various forms. The most common conflict stems from incompatibilities between the demands of the sick role and the demands of the usual life roles in which the sick person has been engaged (Parsons, 1951; Parsons and Fox, 1952). The situation of a man who is a father and head of a household is frequently made difficult because the sick role requires dependency and reliance upon others. Conflict arises when he is unwilling to relinquish even temporarily the exercise of his former roles, since he views the attempt of other family members to take over his responsibilities as a threat to his self-image. His emotional problems in resolving the incompatibilities between roles may exacerbate the effects of his illness.

Visotsky and others (1961) are among those who have pointed out another type of conflict, in which during protracted illness other persons take over aspects of the role of the ill person. As recovery takes place, they refuse to surrender the prerogatives and power they have acquired in their new roles. Thus, a wife or a son may take over the authority of the husband of the family, may become responsible for economic support and may bear responsibility for decision-making in regard to the management of children and the use of family funds. Then, as recovery occurs, the father may come into conflict with the others as he strives to reassert himself. Along with overt conflict, there may occur guilt among family members about their actions in keeping the father in a subordinate sick role, although this may be accompanied by rationalizations about the necessity for maintaining control in order to help keep the father well.

These are only two aspects of the varied types of situations involving conflict regarding roles that may occur in the case of the widespread phenomenon of serious illness in families. One of the most important questions in regard to this problem concerns the degree to which differing levels of severity of conflict affect the course of recovery, its length, and the ultimate level of adjustment by the patient. The matter is not only of interest to the student of stress for its theoretical implications; it also has relevance to medical practitioners, hospital personnel, planners of health agencies, and others concerned with aspects of the management of illness and provision of therapies.

Interpersonal relationships, interaction patterns and pathogenic stressors. In the long search for causes of illness and other forms of deviance, numerous investigators have pointed to interpersonal relationships or patterns of interaction in the family that appear to be pathogenic. While consideration of the relationships and patterns necessarily overlaps with some of the classes of stressor sources indicated earlier, they deserve at least brief attention here by themselves insofar as they are concerned with a special class of problems: linkages between internal dynamics within the family and pathological outcomes. Many of the studies in this area owe much to the pervasive influences of psychoanalytic concepts and frames of reference (Levine and Scotch, 1968).

Particular positions within the family structure have been identified as likely to involve individuals in networks of interaction or with role dilemmas sufficiently stressful to lead to deviance or illness behavior. For example, the position of being the first-born in the family has been hypothesized as involving special vulnerabilities, some of which derive from the fact that parents are still in the process of learning their own roles in child-rearing. Others derive from the fact that to some extent the older child is inevitably displaced with the arrival of a sibling. Not only may he feel rejected but there may also be guilt reactions to his own feelings of hostility toward the newcomer. Caudill and Schooler (1968), in a study of mental patients in Japan, found that the number of first-born males among the patient population was higher than could be expected by chance, and they suggest that role obligations in the Japanese family system may be particularly stressful for the oldest sons. Whatever the underlying basis, various empirical studies have found the first child to differ in personality traits from his siblings, as well as in apparent susceptibility to various physical and mental diseases (Chen and Cobb, 1960; McArthur, 1956; Sears and others, 1957).

It has often been suggested that other kinds of normal statuses in the family may involve individuals in stressful interaction, and the youngest, "middle," and the "only" child have all been studied from this standpoint (Gregory, 1958; Hawkes and others, 1958). A notable feature of the literature bearing on ordinal position and its stressor effects is the volume of contradictory and inconsistent findings. Thus, while one study reports first children to be somewhat more aggressive than their siblings, another study using different techniques of research reports them to be less aggressive (Sears, 1951; Sears and others, 1957).

In addition, individuals may be informally assigned positions within the family that increase their vulnerability. As Vogel and Bell and others have pointed out, a disturbed child in the family may be given the role of "scapegoat." As such, he serves to relieve the personality tensions of the parents, and he thus may aid in the maintenance of family solidarity (Vogel and Bell, 1968). The consequences for the emotional state of the disturbed child himself, however, may be severe.

The quality of interpersonal relations, as numerous investigators have demonstrated, may also constitute a source of stressors. Findings in this area have been so numerous and the phenomenon is so well known that only brief mention is necessary here. Neurotic conflict between parents, parental rejection of children, inconsistent punishment, and coldness and hostility in family relationships are among the many factors that have been commonly cited as sources of difficulty in families, and these have been identified as being among the roots of specific types of mental disorders, marital conflicts and dissolutions, aggressive and withdrawn behavior, as well as delinquency, criminality, drug addiction, and other forms of deviant behavior. One line of research effort has been concerned with isolating the variables associated with the manifestation of those types of relationships that are ego-damaging and productive of deviance. A common course of inquiry in this research on family relationships is the examination of a study population of individuals distinctive for some form of deviance, sometimes comparing these with a control group, then tracing back and usually finding some forms of stressful interpersonal family environment or some particularly critical mechanism (Beiser, 1969; Dager, 1964).

In a study comparing schizophrenic and "neurotic" individuals from lower-class and lower-middle–class backgrounds, Myers and

Roberts (1959) report apparent differences in the quality of parent-child relationships. They found in the family backgrounds of lower-class schizophrenics, for example, such stressor factors as "the disorganized home, parental neglect, lack of parental guidance and control, lack of familial affection, and harsh but inconsistent punishment," and they suggest that these elements may promote "feelings of defensiveness, isolation, neglect, rejection, and fear" in the patients. Among schizophrenic patients of lower-middle–class origins, these investigators found a different patterning in quality of relationships in the parental home. They found rigid protectionism on the part of the mothers, the withholding of affection as a device of social control, and problems relating to the place of the father as a masculine figure within the home. These features, they suggest, led to particular patterns of withdrawal, dependency, and problems of sex identity in the case of male patients.

Finally, according to some investigators, within the family unit there may appear specific stressor mechanisms of interaction and communication that may be related to the occurrence of a particular illness. For example, Bateson and his co-workers have examined the influence of the "double bind" pattern upon the etiology of schizophrenia (Bateson and others, 1956). In the mother-child relationship in the families of schizophrenics, they hypothesize, the child is presented with incongruent expectations, and these are of such a nature that no matter which one the child fulfills, he is subjected to punishment. The child is held in a situation in which he must respond in one way or another, and if he is to avoid punishment, the only solution is to avoid understanding of the meaning of the mother's demands.

The terms "marital schism" and "marital skew" have been employed by Lidz to characterize particular types of interaction situations he has found in the families of schizophrenic patients (Lidz and others, 1957). In the first, there is severe marital discord, with competition between parents for the loyalty and affection of the children. In the second, there is relative equilibrium in the relationship between parents, but relationships in the family are distorted by the psychopathology of one parent. In such families the mother is usually the dominant partner, while the father is passive. Along similar lines, other investigators have designated types of family interaction, role structures, and communication patterns that are associated with mental illness (Fisher and Mendell, 1956; Haley, 1959; Jackson, 1960; Mishler and Waxler, 1965).

One ironic aspect of the role of the family in regard to stress is that in performing stress-reduction for some members, it may also con-

tribute to stressor situations for others. In industrial society the family setting is frequently a locus in which members may express emotional tensions that originate in other contexts but that cannot be
freely expressed there (Schelsky, 1966). One negative consequence
of this phenomenon, however, is that the release of these emotions
may in themselves create tension situations that have the effect of
stressors as far as other family members are concerned. This may
lead to disturbances in role relationships and in the emotional tone
of the family, as well as to the use of defense mechanisms such as
withdrawal or counter-aggression on the part of the individual family
members. These mechanisms in turn may have long-term deteriora-
tive and pervasive effects.

When the family unit as a whole responds to crises, such as natural
disaster, illness of a member, or unemployment, the adaptation may
itself become a source of continuing stress (Kellner, 1966). In some
instances the stressful effects of the "adjustment" may be more pervasive and perhaps more damaging than the original threat. While
crisis can on the one hand lead to solidarity and cohesion, some
types of response that are adaptive at a superficial level may also be
essentially disruptive, leading to isolation, recrimination and deviant
behavior. In reports of parental response to brain-damaged children
or to those afflicted by polio, it has been shown, for example, that
such parents may become over-protective and may also reduce social
interaction outside the family (Davis, 1963; Farber, 1959; Holt, 1958;
Zuk, 1959). The need to make adaptations may also lead to negative
reactions, however, so that parents come to express both open and
latent hostility toward the child. In turn, these reactions tend to
exacerbate the emotional problems of the child, leading to further
response on the part of the parents.

CONCLUSION

In a period when increasing attention is being given to the nature of
the stress process in relation to the family, it appears that some
fundamental issues still remain for clarification. Much research has
focused on the stress process within the family, on the consequences
of stress, and upon the delineation of adaptive responses. This chapter has centered on one aspect of the total process, the ways in which
the family may function as a source of stressors. In particular, it has
been concerned with such aspects as structure, roles, values, and
interaction patterns, drawing together some materials in the social
science literature in these areas which may serve to outline ways in

which stressors may originate in the family. As this review has indicated, much remains to be accomplished in regard to questions of conceptualization, method, and basic empirical information.

A primary problem, as has been seen, is the identification and delineation of stressors, for in the family context, as in other social contexts, there are pervasive phenomena that are extremely difficult to measure. A second problem is that basic work remains to be done in distinguishing those stressors that truly originate in the family from those that have their origins in other contexts but have thus far been loosely identified as having their origins in the family. The development of theories in the area of stress, particularly those that relate to the family, would seem to demand clear distinction of family and nonfamily stressors.

A third issue is the problem of the utility of conceiving of family stressors. For purposes of development of knowledge concerning the total stress process, it may indeed be useful to examine the family institution as a source of stress, but many of the stress phenomena in the family context can be regarded in terms of other frames and concepts. While the examination of these phenomena in terms of a family frame of reference can provide useful leads, there are many areas that might perhaps more economically be examined through other means. For example, concepts of role, culture, stratification, social process in small groups, and personality dynamics may provide more convenient approaches to some of the stressors that occur in the family context.

A fourth problem is that of the paucity of basic empirical information in regard to the identification of specific stressor phenomena and the degree of severity they may possess in differing social and cultural contexts. As has been seen, former easy assumptions about the degree of stress engendered by the nuclear family structure or by passage into parenthood have required reformulation on the basis of empirical research. Many of the beliefs current about particular elements that have been identified as stressors will also undoubtedly be altered as systematic studies examine, measure, and clarify phenomena through empirical research. Thus far, the assessment of data on stressors is handicapped by the nature of many of those empirical studies of the family that deal with problems pertinent to stress issues. Small samples, minimal use of controls, lack of standardized and validated instruments point up the need for caution in arriving at generalizations about stressors.

Though the tasks ahead are numerous and difficult, at least two benefits may derive from efforts to identify and measure stressors that originate in the family. Such efforts can promote the refinement of theories of stress insofar as they can clarify the conditions and elements that comprise the first stage in the stress process—the origination of stressors. In addition, there are more immediate benefits, particularly for those in the "helping" professions who are engaged in developing and using modes of intervention or therapy. As more precise assessments of the nature and power of particular family stressors become available, such information can considerably assist them in deciding upon the points at which to intervene and the areas toward which therapies can most profitably be directed.

REFERENCES

ACKERMAN, N. W. 1966. *Treating the Troubled Family.* New York: Basic Books.

ARENSBERG, C. M., and KIMBALL, S. T. 1940. *Family and Community in Ireland.* Cambridge, Mass.: Harvard University Press.

AUSUBEL, D., and AUSUBEL, P. 1967. "Ego Development among Segregated Negro Children," in J. I. Roberts, ed., *School Children in the Urban Slum,* New York: Grune and Stratton.

BAKER, C. 1969. *Ernest Hemingway: A Life Story.* New York: Scribner's.

BATESON, G., JACKSON, D. D., HALEY, J., and WEAKLAND, J. 1956. "Toward a Theory of Schizophrenia." *Behavioral Science,* 1:251–64.

BEISER, M. 1965. "Poverty, Social Disintegration and Personality." *Journal of Social Issues,* 21:56–78.
1969. "The Etiology of Childhood Psychiatric Disorder: Sociocultural Aspects," in B. W. Wolman, ed., *Manual of Child Psychopathology.* New York: McGraw-Hill.

BLITSTEN, D. R. 1963. *The World of the Family.* New York: Random House.

BLOOD, R. O., JR. and WOLFE, D. M. 1960. *Husbands and Wives: The Dynamics of Married Living.* Glencoe, Ill.: Free Press.

BOWERMAN, C. E. 1964. "Prediction Studies," in H. T. Christiansen, ed., *Handbook of Marriage and the Family.* Chicago: Rand McNally.

BRADBURN, N. M., and CAPLOVITZ, D. 1965. *Reports on Happiness.* Chicago: Aldine Publishing Company.

BURGESS, E. W., and WALLIN, P. 1953. *Engagement and Marriage.* Philadelphia: Lippincott.

BURGESS, E. W., LOCKE, H. J., and THOMES, M. M. 1963. *The Family from Institution to Companionship.* New York: American Book.

BURTON, R. V., and WHITING, J. W. M. 1961. "The Absent Father and Cross-sex Identity." *Merrill Palmer Quarterly,* 7:85–95.

CAMPISI, P. J. 1948. "Ethnic Family Patterns: The Italian Family in the United States." *American Journal of Sociology,* 53:44–49.

CAPLAN, G., ed. 1961. *Prevention of Emotional Disorders in Children.* New York: Basic Books.

CAUDILL, W., and SCHOOLER, C. 1968. "Symptom Patterns and Background

Characteristics of Japanese Psychiatric Patients," in W. Caudill and T. Lin, eds., *Mental Health Research in Asia and the Pacific*. Honolulu: East-West Center Press.

CHAGALL, M. 1960. *My Life*. New York: Orion Press.

CHEN, E., and COBB, S. 1960. "Family Structure in Relation to Health and Disease: A Review of the Literature." *Journal of Chronic Diseases*, 12:544–67.

CLEVELAND, E. J., and LONGAKER, W. D. 1957. "Neurotic Patterns in the Family," in A. H. Leighton, J. A. Clausen, and R. N. Wilson, eds., *Explorations in Social Psychiatry*. New York: Basic Books.

CROOG, S. H., LIPSON, A. G., and LEVINE, S. 1969. "Patterns of Marital Conflict." *Heart Patient Study: Report No. 7*, mimeo.

DAGER, E. Z. 1964. "Socialization and Personality Development in the Child" in H. T. Christiansen, ed., *Handbook of Marriage and the Family*. Chicago: Rand McNally.

DAVIS, F. 1963. *Passage Through Crisis: Polio Victims and their Families*. Indianapolis: Bobbs-Merrill.

DOUGLAS, J. W. B., and BLOMFIELD, J. M. 1958. *Children under Five*. London: Allen and Unwin.

DOUVAN, E. 1960. "Sex Differences in Adolescent Character Process." *Merrill Palmer Quarterly*, 6:203–11.

DUVALL, E. M. 1962. *Family Development*, rev. ed. Philadelphia: Lippincott.

DYER, E. D. 1963. "Parenthood as Crisis: A Re-study." *Marriage and Family Living*, 25:196–201.

ERIKSON, E. H. 1959. "Identity and the Life Cycle." *Psychological Issues*, 1:1–171.

FARBER, B. 1957. "An Index of Marital Integration." *Sociometry*, 20:117–34.
1959. "Effects of a Severely Mentally Retarded Child on Family Integration." *Monographs of the Society for Research in Child Development*, 24, serial no. 71.
1964. *Family: Organization and Interaction*. San Francisco: Chandler.

Fisher, S., and MENDELL, D. 1956. "The Communication of Neurotic Patterns over Two or Three Generations." *Psychiatry*, 19:41–46.

FROMM, E. 1947. *Man for Himself*. New York: Holt, Rinehart and Winston.

GLASER, P., and NAVARE, E. 1965. "Structural Problems of the One-parent Family." *Journal of Social Issues*, 21:98–109.

GLICK, P. C. 1955. "The Life Cycle of the Family." *Marriage and Family Living*, 17:3–9.

GLUECK, S., and GLUECK, E. 1957. "Working Mothers and Delinquency." *Mental Hygiene*, 41:327–52.

GOODE, W. J. 1956. *After Divorce*. Glencoe, Ill.: Free Press
1961. *World Revolution and the Family*. Glencoe, Ill.: Free Press.

GREGORY, I. 1958. "An Analysis of Familial Data on Psychiatric Patients: Parental Age, Family Size, Birth Order, and Ordinal Position." *British Journal of Preventive and Social Medicine*, 12:42–59.

HALEY, J. 1959. "The Family of the Schizophrenic: A Model System." *Journal of Nervous and Mental Diseases*, 129:357–74.

HANSEN, D. A., and HILL, R. 1964. "Families Under Stress," in H. T. Christiansen, ed., *Handbook of Marriage and the Family*. Chicago: Rand McNally.

HAWKINS, G. R., BURCHINAL, L., and GARDNER, B. 1958. "Size of Family and Adjustment of Children." *Marriage and Family Living*, 20:65–68.

HESS, R. D., and HANDEL, G. 1959. *Family Worlds: A Psychosocial Approach to Family Life*. Chicago: University of Chicago Press.

HILL, R. 1949. *Families under Stress*. New York: Harper.

———. 1958. "Generic Features of Families under Stress." *Social Casework*, 39:139–50.

HILL, R., and HANSEN, D. A. 1962. "The Family in Disaster," in G. Baker and D. Chapman, eds., *Man and Society in Disaster*. New York: Basic Books.

HILL, R., and RODGERS, R. H. 1964. "The Developmental Approach," in H. T. Christiansen, ed., *Handbook of Marriage and the Family*. Chicago: Rand McNally.

HOFFMAN, L. W. 1963. "Effects on Children: Summary and Discussion," in F. I. Nye and L. W. Hoffman, *The Employed Mother in America*. Chicago: Rand McNally.

HOLT, K. S. 1958. "The Home Care of the Severely Mentally Retarded." *Pediatrics*, 22:744–55.

HORNEY, K. 1937. *The Neurotic Personality of Our Time*. New York: W. W. Norton.

HOWARD, A., and SCOTT, R. A. 1965. "A Proposed Framework for the Analysis of Stress in the Human Organism." *Behavioral Science*, 10:141–60.

HUGHES, C. C., TREMBLAY, M. A., RAPOPORT, R. N., and LEIGHTON, A. H. 1960. *People of Cove and Woodlot*. New York: Basic Books.

JACKSON, D. D., ed. 1960. *The Etiology of Schizophrenia*. New York: Basic Books.

JACKSON, D. D. 1962. "Family Therapy in the Family of the Schizophrenic," in M. I. Stein, ed., *Contemporary Psychotherapies*. Glencoe, Ill.: Free Press.

JESSOR, R., GRAVES, T. D., HANSON, R. C., and JESSOR, S. L. 1968. *Society, Personality, and Deviant Behavior*. New York: Holt, Rinehart and Winston.

KAFFMAN, M. 1965. "A Comparison of Psychopathology: Israeli Children from Kibbutz and from Urban Surroundings." *American Journal of Orthopsychiatry*, 35:509–20.

KARDINER, A. 1939. *The Individual and His Society*. New York: Columbia University Press.

KARDINER, A., LINTON, R., DuBois, C., and WEST, J. 1945. *The Psychological Frontiers of Society*. New York: Columbia University Press.

KELLNER, R. 1966. *Family Ill Health: An Investigation in General Practice*. Philadelphia: Lippincott.

KIRKPATRICK, C. 1963. *The Family as Process and Institution*, 2nd ed., New York: Ronald Press.

KLUCKHOHN, F. R. 1968. "Variations in the Basic Values of Family Systems," in N. W. Bell and E. F. Vogel, eds., *A Modern Introduction to the Family*, rev. ed. New York: Free Press.

KOHN, M. L. 1963. "Social Class and Parent-child Relationships: An Interpretation." *American Journal of Sociology*, 68:471–80.

LANGNER, T. S. 1963. "Childhood Broken Homes," in T. S. Langner and S. T. Michael, *Life Stress and Mental Health*. Glencoe, Ill.: Free Press.

LANSING, J. B., an KISH, L. 1957. "Family Life Cycle as an Independent Variable." *American Sociological Review*, 22:512–19.

LANTZ, H. R. 1958. *People of Coal Town*. New York: Columbia University Press.

LEIGHTER, H. J., and MITCHELL, W. E. 1967. *Kinship and Casework*. New York: Russell Sage Foundation.

LEIGHTON, A. H. 1959. *My Name is Legion*. New York: Basic Books.

1965. "Poverty and Social Change," *Scientific American*, 212:21–27.

LEIGHTON, D. C., HARDING, J. S., MACKLIN, D. B., MACMILLAN, A. M., and LEIGHTON, A. H. 1963. *The Character of Danger*. New York: Basic Books.

LEMASTERS, E. E. 1957, "Parenthood as Crisis." *Marriage and Family Living*, 19:352–55.

LESLIE, G. R. 1964. "The Field of Marriage Counseling," in H. T. Christiansen, ed., *Handbook of Marriage and the Family*. Chicago: Rand McNally.

LEVINE, S., and SCOTCH, N. A. 1968. "The Impact of Psychoanalysis on Sociology and Anthropology," in J. Marmor, ed., *Modern Psychoanalysis*, New York: Basic Books.

LEWIS, O. 1961. *The Children of Sanchez: Autobiography of a Mexican Family*. New York: Random House.

1966. *La Vida*. New York: Random House.

LIDZ, T., CORNELISON, A. R., FLECK, S., and TERRY, D. 1957. "The Intrafamilial Environment of Schizophrenic Patients: II, Marital Schism and Marital Skew." *American Journal of Psychiatry*, 114:241–48.

LINTON, R. 1939. "The Tanala of Madagascar," in A. Kardiner, *The Individual and his Society*. New York: Columbia University Pres.

1959. "The Natural History of the Family," in R. N. Anshen, ed., *The Family: Its Function and Destiny*, rev. ed. New York: Harper.

LITWAK, E. 1960. "Occupational Mobility and Extended Family Cohesion." *American Sociological Review*, 25:9–21.

LYNN, D. B., and SAWREY, W. L. 1959. "The Effects of Father Absence on Norwegian Boys and Girls." *Journal of Abnormal and Social Psychology*, 59:258–62.

MCARTHUR, C. 1956. "Personalities of First and Second Children." *Psychiatry*, 19:47–54.

MCCLELLAND, D. 1961. *The Achieving Society*. New York: Van Nostrand.

MEAD, M. 1966. "A Cultural Anthropologist's Approach to Maternal Deprivation," in J. Bowlby, ed., *Maternal Care and Mental Health*. New York: Schocken.

MILLER, D. R., and SWANSON, G. E. 1958. *The Changing American Parent.* New York: John Wiley.

MILLER, W. B. 1958. "Lower Class Culture as a Generating Milieu of Gang Delinquency." *Journal of Social Issues,* 14:5–19.

1959. "Implications of Lower Class Culture for Social Work." *Social Service Review,* 33:219–36.

MINUCHIN, S., MONTALVO, B., GUERNEY, B. G., JR., ROSMAN, B., and SCHUMER, F. 1967. *Families of the Slums.* New York: Basic Books.

MISHLER, E., and WAXLER, N. E. 1965. "Family Interaction Processes and Schizophrenia: A Review of Current Theories." *Merrill Palmer Quarterly,* 11:269–315.

MITCHELL, H. E., BULLARD, J. W., and MUDD, E. H. 1962. "Areas of Marital Conflict in Successfully and Unsuccessfully Functioning Families." *Journal of Health and Human Behavior,* 3:88–93.

MOYNIHAN, D. P. 1965. "The Negro Family: The Case for National Action." Washington, D.C.: U. S. Govt. Printing Office.

MYERS, J. K., and ROBERTS, B. H. 1959. *Family and Class Dynamics in Mental Illness.* New York: John Wiley.

NYE, F. I. 1957. "Child Adjustment in Broken and in Unhappy Unbroken Homes." *Marriage and Family Living,* 19:356–61.

1958. *Family Relationships and Delinquent Behavior.* New York: John Wiley.

NYE, F. I., and HOFFMAN, L. W. 1963. *The Employed Mother in America.* Chicago: Rand McNally.

PARSONS, T. 1951. "Illness and the Role of the Physician." *American Journal of Orthopsychiatry,* 21:452–60.

1959. "The Social Structure of the Family," in R. N. Anshen, ed., *The Family: Its Function and Destiny,* rev. ed. New York: Harper & Row.

PARSONS, T., and FOX, R. 1952. "Illness, Therapy, and the Modern Urban American Family." *Journal of Social Issues,* 8:31–44.

RADCLIFFE-BROWN, A. R. 1950. "Introduction," in A. R. Radcliffe-Brown and C. D. Forde, eds., *African Systems of Kinship and Marriage.* London: Oxford University Press.

RAPOPORT, R., and RAPOPORT, R. N. 1964. "New Light on the Honeymoon." *Human Relations,* 17:33–56.

ROGLER, L. H., and HOLLINGSHEAD, A. B. 1965. *Trapped: Families and Schizophrenia.* New York: John Wiley.

SCHELSKY, H. 1966. "The German Family and Opposed Developmental Tendencies in Industrial Society," in B. Farber, ed., *Kinship and Family Organization.* New York: John Wiley.

SCHLESINGER, R., ed. 1949. *The Family in the U.S.S.R.* London: Routledge and Kegan Paul.

SEARS, P. S. 1951. "Doll-play Aggression in Normal Children: Influence of Sex, Age, Sibling Status, Father's Absence." *Psychological Monographs,* 65, no. 6.

SEARS, R. R., MACCOBY, E. E., and LEVIN, H. 1957. *Patterns of Childrearing.* Evanston, Ill.: Row, Peterson.

SPIEGEL, J. P. 1957. "The Resolution of Role Conflict Within the Family." *Psychiatry*, 20:1-16.

SPIEGEL, J. P., and BELL, N. W. 1959. "The Family of the Psychiatric Patient," in S. Arieti, ed., *American Handbook of Psychiatry*, vol. 1. New York: Basic Books.

STEIN, Z. A., and SUSSER, M. 1967. "The Social Dimensions of a Symptom: A Socio-medical Study of Eneuresis." *Social Science and Medicine*, 1:183-201.

STOLZ, L. M. 1960. "Effects of Maternal Employment on Children: Evidence from Research." *Child Development*, 31:749-82.

SUSSMAN, M. B. 1959. "The Isolated Nuclear Family: Fact or Fiction?" *Social Problems*, 6:333-40.

SUSSMAN, M. B., and BURCHINAL, L. 1962. "Kin Family Network: Unheralded Structure in Current Conceptualization of Family Functioning." *Marriage and Family Living*, 24:231-40.

TIMASHEFF, N. S. 1946. *The Great Retreat*. New York: Dutton.

VALLIER, I. 1962. "Structural Differentiation, Production Imperatives, and Communal Norms: The Kibbutz in Crisis." *Social Forces*, 40:233-42.

VINCENT, C. E. 1967. "Mental Health and the Family." *Journal of Marriage and the Family*, 29:18-39.

VISOTSKY, H. M., HAMBURG, D. A., GOSS, M. E., and LEBOVITS, B. Z. 1961. "Coping Behavior under Extreme Stress: Observations of Patients with Severe Poliomyelitis." *Archives of General Psychiatry*, 5:423-48.

VOGEL, E. F., and BELL, N. W. 1968. "The Emotionally Disturbed Child as the Family Scapegoat," in N. W. Bell and E. F. Vogel, eds., *The Family*, rev. ed. New York: Free Press.

WARDLE, C. J. 1961. "Two Generations of Broken Homes in the Genesis of Conduct and Behavior Disorders in Childhood." *British Medical Journal*, 11:349-54.

WHITING, B. B., ed. 1963. *Six Cultures: Studies of Child Rearing*. New York: John Wiley.

WHITING, J. W. M., and CHILD, I. L. 1953. *Child Training and Personality*. New Haven: Yale University Press.

YANG, C. K. 1959. *The Chinese Family in the Communist Revolution*. Cambridge: Technology Press.

YOUNG, M. D., and WILMOTT, P. 1957. *Family and Kinship in East London*. Glencoe, Ill.: Free Press.

ZUK, G. H. 1959. "The Religious Factor and the Role of Guilt in Parental Acceptance of the Retarded Child." *American Journal of Mental Deficiency*, 63:139-47.

3. Work, Organization and Stress

EDWARD GROSS

STRESS is a social–psychological phenomenon—a matter of the relation between the individual and the structure within which he finds himself. Causes of stress can, therefore, lie in the individual or in the structure. For example, Howard and Scott (1965) classify stress-producing "stimuli" as being biochemical (disease germs or hormonal changes in the body), psychological (internal conflicts in the individual personality), physical (serious challenges presented by natural disasters, or by being struck by a heavy weight), or sociocultural. The last is the most complex and will occupy most of my attention here. For example, one part of a culture may be inconsistent with some other part, or may not function adequately, as in the case of some kinds of political conflict or union-management conflict which may require peacemaking mechanisms for resolution. Smelser's (1963) concept of "structural strain" includes four main kinds: inadequacies in the distribution of facilities, in the mobiliza-

Edward Gross is professor of sociology at the University of Washington, Seattle.

tion of motivation, in norms, and in values. Long ago Merton (1949) pointed to "socially structured strain" as a major source of crime: if persons accept the value of success but are prevented from reaching success through legitimate means, they will invent illegitimate means. In that sense, crime is built into the social structure itself.

But whatever the possible causes of stress, I confine my attention to situations in which there are clear *consequences* for the individual. The claim of Basowitz and his associates (1955) that stimuli can be discussed in terms of their presumed or potential effect seems to me to be little more than calling attention to the fact of individual differences: what is stressful to one person may not be to another. But to call any stimulus potentially stressful, there must be evidence that someone or some category finds it so. Otherwise the term seems to me to lose empirical usefulness.

The area of investigation, or what we seek to explain, is the individual under stress. How then do we know that he is under stress? There are two main indicators, called by Lazarus (1966) physiological and psychological. "Physiological" stress refers to forms of stress in which there is some detectable change in the body, such as microbehavioral reactions and biochemical or autonomic disturbances. "Psychological" stress refers to situations in which, in addition to or instead of physiological changes, there are reports of disturbed affects and/or changes in the adequacy of cognitive functioning. The special question of the precise character of "microbehavioral reactions" or "disturbed affects" that are evidence of stress is beyond my competence and, in any case, is dealt with in other chapters in this volume. I shall then take it for granted that adequate methods for the detection of stress are available. But it is always such physiological or psychological consequences that form the object of inquiry. Although such physiological or psychological changes are regarded as consequences of other changes, it is of course possible (and common) for them to become causes in their own right.

DEFINITION OF STRESS

Stress is here defined as "the failure of routine methods for managing threats." There is some resemblance between this definition and that offered by Mechanic (1968, p. 301): "a discrepancy between the demands impinging on a person—whether these demands be external or internal, whether challenges or goals—and the individual's potential responses to these demands." Put that way, however, there are three problems. First, "demands" alone are not enough. Everyone is faced with "demands" but he only pays attention to some of them. For example, a child may make "demands" of his parents without necessarily creating any stress by that token. The demands, in other words, must possess some motivational significance to the individual—he must care about satisfying them, or they must be threatening to him in some way so that failure to satisfy them will entail costly consequences. Mechanic himself later refers to the importance of motivation. Second, put in the way Mechanic does, it can refer to a once-only demand which can be ignored without consequence, or soon forgotten. For example, if a bum stops me, asking for a dime, and I do not, in fact, have any money on me, I am not, therefore, in a state of stress. On the other hand, if it is considered proper to help the poor, and if I regularly do, but because of misfortune cannot afford to this time, then my inability to do so may be stressful indeed. Hence my emphasis on "routine"—that is, I have been able to meet this demand in the past and I cannot now. After all, all first-time demands will give the other at least some reasonable time to get ready. If the person cannot then do it, he may feel stress. Third, the demands must be "reasonable"—that is, involve problems that are, in principle, solvable (or, if not, manageable by explaining that they are insoluble; see Howard and Scott, 1965), and adapted to the person's known or reasonable capabilities (you do not send a boy to do a man's job). They must, then, be demands which, if not met, may well mean the person is undependable or has failed to live up to legitimate standards. It is the failure in *such* situations that is likely to lead to stress.

Mechanic's conception suggests a point in the definition I offer that is implicit but should be spelled out. Stress is a failure of routine methods, as stated, but it may also be one in which the individual never had any routine methods to start with, but it was reasonable to expect that he should have. For example, a senior in a university who is a nuisance in the classroom is felt to be an example of incomplete socialization, and will be felt to be using childish methods for handling the stress of the classroom. If made aware of it (perhaps by sanctions from fellow students), stress is a likely result.

The term "routine" is being used in the sense developed by Garfinkel (1959; 1964; 1967), Sudnow (1967), and other "ethnomethodologists," as well as Glaser and Strauss (1968). As they use the concept of "routine," it refers to the process whereby those persons who have direct concern with some phenomenon not only manage or handle it, but also actually "create" it in the process of dealing with it. Sudnow (1967), discussing the way in which death is managed in a hospital he studied, points out that on closer examination there is no clear definition of what one means by a "dying person." In the view of an existentialist, everyone, once born, is in the process of dying; consequently, one must, within the hospital, decide whom one is going to treat as "dying" and whom as not dying, one key factor being that of how imminent death is assumed to be. This, in turn, is related to the hospital's characteristic way of handling death. Thus a particular routine is involved in labeling various stages a patient may be going through, and a person may be labeled "dying," by a nurse when he is going to die on her shift rather than on the next shift or next week. Death under such circumstances becomes routine and persons inside may not speak of it much at all, but only of unusual situations that come up. In such an atmosphere, should a patient die while being admitted to the hospital, or should someone in the accounting office of the hospital have a heart attack and die at his desk, they are quite as much crises for the hospital as they would be in any other setting, since they have not been organized or fitted into the hospital routine for handling death. The point, then, is not that death itself is routine to a hospital, but rather that the hospital has routine methods for handling persons who are approaching death, methods that only work if persons are fitted into the work flow of the hospital.

In the process of growing up, the individual is faced with a variety of threatening situations. A threatening situation, or simply a threat, I conceive of, following Lazarus (1966), as an imagined possible future deprivation of something one values (valuing being interpreted very broadly to include both learned wants as well as what others might speak of as needs or requirements for life). The individual develops (in time) techniques for managing such threats so that they are no longer threats. The techniques then become a part of a routine, such that a person may even be unaware that he is making use of those techniques. The most obvious of these are those that individuals acquire in the process of growing up, such as ability to communicate one's wishes or needs to others in a position to supply them. But these hardly exhaust those available to him.

In limiting stress only to threat behavior, I am deliberately avoiding making stress behavior into the equivalent of problem-solving. That is too broad and introduces other issues. Nor do I wish to limit the kinds of threat to those situations where action is needed very soon and where there is some expectation or at least belief that something can, *perhaps*, be done. The notion of a time limit might be thought to be useful since otherwise the threat will simply be redefined or not conceived of as a threat if it is in the long-range future. There is an empirical assumption here, however, that persons will only take action or that stress is only of interest in the face of immediate events, and it is true, of course, that those will be the startling ones or those that may have the greatest effect. But it must be recognized that one major mechanism for managing threat is precisely that of trying to reorganize or reconceptualize matters so that one controls the time dimension. It is possible to so redefine the threat that it is seen as not imminent and therefore as *not* being a threat. But surely that is a management technique in its own right, and one worth discussing. If one limits threat only to the imminent or to what cannot be in any way reconceptualized and made more distant, then one excludes this major mechanism or technique of managing threat, and there is no reason to do so.

A similar argument applies to the question of whether we should consider stress as limited only to situations in which there is a threat accompanied by an expectation or belief that something can *perhaps* be done. The reason for such a restriction might be to exclude fatalism such that a phenomenon that is threatening may cease to be threatening, or defined as a nonthreat, by simply being called "the will of God." I do not believe it is desirable to exclude fatalism, for it is a cultural invention for managing threat. If persons are socialized to the belief that certain events are unavoidable, they will go on dying or suffering from whatever it is that is defined as inevitable, but that definition may, perhaps, reduce the severity of the psychological impact.

In order, therefore, not to exclude what is theoretically an interesting set of management strategies, namely, postponements and fatalisms, it seems best not to require that the threat either be imminent or that there be an expectation that something can be done about it.

THE MANAGEMENT OF THREAT

The concept of "management" or "managing" is understood here as involving a great deal more than *individual* devices for handling or "coping with" stress. I wish to be able to include techniques that go far beyond merely coping with threat, and may involve wholly original and highly creative solutions that then become models others may follow. The term "managing" can include those techniques that barely enable one to hold one's head above water (coping techniques), but also may include newly devised and creative solutions, as well as those that eventually become social structures taught to children.[1] For example, Lazarus (1966) provides the following classification of coping techniques available to the individual: attack (with accompanying emotion of hostility or anger), retreat (with accompanying emotion of fear), inaction (with various accompanying feelings, but usually depression), anxiety (in situations where the threat is not easy to locate) and various defense mechanisms (referring to techniques that involve self-deception so that a threat does not appear to be a threat). All of those techniques refer to what the individual may do *in those situations in which he must act alone or on his own resources.* It is of the first importance to recognize that in this chapter we desire to broaden the conception of coping considerably beyond that (hence our desire to use the word "management"). What is threatening to an individual can be handled by the individual's attacking the object and perhaps destroying it, or by retreating from it, with attendant fear. It is a major characteristic of man as distinguished from other organisms, however, that one of his major management techniques is that of developing an *organization* that will handle the threat, or of creating an environment in which the threat simply does not occur. Of course, individuals act, as always, but they are manipulating some type of an organization or structure that has been set up.

By such a means the individual can increase his management (or "coping") ability by an enormous factor, even though he himself may not be changed, or his resources may be no greater than they would be otherwise. In the simplest sort of case, a child's ability to get from one place to another depends ·upon his physical strength, the absence of disease to his body, and so forth. When he reaches an age where he is permitted to and can learn to drive an automobile, however, amount of strength or whatever else is required so far as his physical equipment is concerned may be no different, but his power to move from place to place has been enormously increased.[2]

One of the major management mechanisms or techniques, therefore, that man has available to him is constituted by the organizations or structures he has created to solve what would otherwise be continually recurring threats to his welfare. Consequently, a good deal of

1. Mechanic (1962, chap. 5), while retaining the word "coping," seeks to broaden its meaning to include "dealing with the situation" (as compared to dealing with one's feeling about the situation).
2. In come cases the operation of such a physical mechanism may even require less in the way of physical equipment on the part of the human being. For example, it probably requires less coordination and learning to operate a modern tractor-combine in harvesting wheat than it did in earlier days to drive a team of horses to pull a threshing machine.

the "learning to cope with stress" that occurs in man consists of becoming sophisticated about organizations. One type of such so- phistication consists of learning how to create an organization. This is a complex skill, often not recognized as such. There are more, of course, than merely "skill" elements, including motivation, devel- opment of a conception of one's self as a small businessman, a belief that one can succeed, and the importance in minority groups of a family name that is carried on.

The construction or creation of organizations hardly exhausts the types of strategies or techniques available. Even more important, for most persons, is that of learning to *deal with* organizations, either as clients or as members. In a sense, this is a set of skills and knowl- edges: one learns whom it is one should see, how this person likes to be addressed, how to construct an appropriate vocabulary and rheto- ric, how to acquire appropriate admission symbols and all the rest. Any analysis of the phenomenon of dealing with organizations as a management technique must also take account of the extent to which organizations themselves socialize their clients and their members so that they will make use of only certain approaches — approaches the organization finds acceptable or easy to deal with. For example, the doctor-patient relationship in our society depends very much on the development in the individual of what I have called (Gross, 1964) a "willingness-structure" on the part of the patient. From early child- hood the person is taught to withhold his own feelings and to accept "doctor's orders," so that by the time he reaches adulthood he arrives at the physician's office in a state of willingness to listen and do as he is told. When patients offer resistance, as may be seen in other cultures where clients have not been socialized to those norms, the physician's authority may be much weaker.

It is a central point of our approach here to call attention to the fact that most discussions of stress, in assuming (quite correctly in our view) that stress is an individual phenomenon, assume that the dis- cussion of techniques or strategies for the management of stress must *also* be individual. Although it is always, in the final analysis, indi- viduals who do things and make use of management techniques, it unnecessarily narrows the discussion and omits possibly the most important management techniques that have been developed.

From another perspective, we are talking about something analo- gous to what some anthropologists speak of when they define culture as a "design for living." By that they refer to the extent to which the norms and other aspects of the culture constitute a set of solutions for recurrent problems that do not have to be solved anew by each individual. In effect, they are prescriptions or "recipes" that will take care of the problem when it comes up. On the other hand, the concept of management of stress that I have been developing is broader than that of culture; and culture has, of course, other functions than the management of stress.

The management of human stress includes a set of mechanisms all the way from one extreme—which would consist of individual techniques—to the other extreme—which consists of well-elaborated and institutionalized organizational solutions. These might be classified, under the following headings, along this continuum:

1. *Individual techniques,* such as those described by Lazarus (1966), that the individual engages in when thrown back on his own resources, such as attack, retreat, defensive behavior, anxiety, etc.

2. Various *forms of collective behavior* that, following Smelser (1963, p. 71), may be defined as "uninstitutionalized mobilization through action in order to modify one or more kinds of strain on the basis of a generalized reconstitution of a component of action." Smelser refers to efforts by a group of persons to solve some problem that they are confronted with that is of a highly threatening character and that requires action together. What they will do is a major subject of inquiry in its own right in sociology. What will happen will depend, as Smelser points out, on structural conductiveness (a financial panic can only occur in a society in which there is a money market in which assets can be exchanged freely and rapidly), structural strain, growth and spread of a generalized belief about how the strain may be taken care of, precipitating factors (there may be a predisposition to flee a threatening situation, but something sets this process in action, such as a clash between a white and a Negro in a tense area), mobilization of participants for action, and the operation of various social controls that may prevent the occurrence of an episode or determine how fast, how far, or in what direction the episode may develop.

3. Organized or *regularized methods for the management of stress* that include organizational forms, cultural traits, and other inventions, the development of social identities, and the like. The concern of this chapter falls in this third category, although it is important to note that we are deliberately omitting the forms of management of stress that are comprehended in the other two categories.

A further limitation is that we are interested here only in regularized methods for *doing work;* that is, for obtaining economic goals in a society. The major way of handling stresses associated with work is to form organizations in which such stresses no longer exist.

WORK AND ITS ORGANIZATION

We can define work as "disciplined goal-directed behavior." Persons are said to be doing work when they have some goal in mind they are seeking to obtain in a disciplined manner. "Disciplined" refers to the process of organization of facilities and assemblage of resources according to some type of rational plan for utilizing them so that it is possible for the person to defend the decisions he makes on the utilization of those resources as having a higher probability than any other way of obtaining a goal that the individual has in mind.

When defined in this way it will be seen immediately that work, as such, is not a "coping" method in any direct sense, or—to use the term I prefer—a management strategy. Rather, I would say that, when persons seek to manage stress, they may have to engage in work in the process of doing so. When this is true, then, of course work can be seen in any of the techniques referred to in the above three categories. When a person sets a goal for himself, or pursues a goal he can achieve all by himself (such as digging a hole, or cutting a piece of wood with a saw), then we can see him adjusting his body and his tools in such a way to maximize the probability of attaining the goal, whatever it is. It may be that he is engaging in this behavior in order to protect himself from a threat or to escape from the threat. In that case the work is being used in the service of managing the threat and would fall in the first of the categories that we defined above. It may also be that the person is working in association with others in some form of collective behavior to attack some threat. Thus a mob in the pursuit of some political end may be preparing to attack a government building but finds it must organize its efforts in some sort of a rational manner, such as deciding who will do what and getting tools and implements. Thus some work will be involved.

Our concern, however, and certainly the most remarkable and perhaps the most complex forms that work takes, are those situations that would fall into our third category: those kinds of situations in which work becomes a regularized and dependable way of managing stress when it occurs, or, better, of so arranging things that what would otherwise be a stressful condition simply does not take place at all or is handled or managed before it comes up. I shall concentrate attention mainly on *organized* effort, when a group of persons seek, together, to obtain a group goal and where the discipline consists of the way in which the group itself is organized in order to maximize the probability of group goal attainment.[3]

Such organization has, in modern times in industrialized countries, and increasingly in all other countries as well, taken the form of large-scale organization. A dominant characteristic of modern Western urban industrial society is that it seeks to obtain almost all of its larger goals through large-scale organization. Whether the goals are producing goods, healing the sick, protecting society from criminals, protecting society from foreign enemies, or educating the young, the characteristic approach is to form an organization with goals and a structure. Although many have lamented the cost to the individual of life in organizations (and I shall have something to say about this subject be low), there does not appear to be on the immediate horizon any alternative that is likely to be half as successful as organizations have proven to be. Whenever large-scale formal organizations make their appearance in the modern world they seem to sweep all other forms of organization before them.

The distinctive feature of such organization that accounts for its remarkable power as well as its spread is *the routinization of process*. The goal, whatever it is, is reduced to a flow of goods, services, materials, or people constituting an input, which is then treated routinely so that a predictable output results.

The routinization is both internal and external. Internal routinization is carried out either formalistically or heuristically. Formalistic routinization refers to the process of categorization. The attempt is made to place each case or each item in some type of a category and then to treat all members of the category in the same way, according to some theory about how members of that category behave. In order for this method of routinization to operate, it is necessary that organizational members be willing to accept the categories and treat them in the required way. Persons who work under those conditions must be willing to accept conformity—that is, they must either be willing themselves to be treated as a category or to treat objects in the way

3. "Group goal" refers to some goal the members or participants in the organization seek to achieve by working together and which may not necessarily be the same thing as what each of them separately wants or which constitute their own motives for being there or participating. This individual wishes money; that individual wishes power or seeks the rewards the organization offers to ambitious persons; a third seeks pleasant companionship; a fourth seeks an opportunity to exercise his professional skills. Whatever each seeks from the organization, their common efforts may result in the manufacture of an automobile or the training of a medical student so that he receives his diploma. The latter is the group goal.

required. This may mean that the employees shall have faith in the superior wisdom of the categorizers ("It's no skin off my ass how they run this place; I just do as I'm told"), believe that differences are not important (one unskilled worker is like any other unskilled worker, one automobile is like any other), or perhaps, the employees must accept the sense of themselves as powerless to affect major decisions, particularly policy decisions, and not be too upset by such powerlessness.

Heuristic routinization refers to the use of rules that act as guides to behavior. The rules control the terms of discussion and, in conflict situations, the limits on weapons so that an organizationally relevant solution is forthcoming. This typically assumes a bargaining model in which persons make deals with one another and establish truces that represent their own interests as effectively as possible. The heuristic approach to routinization typically places a lot more faith in the originality and contribution of individuals than does the formalistic process, and typically, then, one finds its use in situations of uncertainty where one is not sure how a routine should be set up which will cover all situations. What one does is to get people who, one feels, can take care of unknown situations when they come up (in accord with rules or guiding policies). This means hiring professionals, knowledgeable persons, or, at least, experienced people. In the simplest case, if a manufacturing firm located in the Northeast decides to expand into the Southwest, it cannot set up a formalistic model since it does not know what kind of a behavior it will encounter or what special problems there may be in the area. The heuristic approach might dictate that they hire men who are familiar with the Southwest area and accept their judgment, providing the men are willing to submit themselves to the general rules of the firm and that a bargain can be struck with them that will be mutually acceptable.

External routinization processes are mainly of three kinds. First there is the control of competitors. This may be attained through rules that all agree to, through mergers, if that is possible, through conflict (the attempt directly to reduce their ability to compete), and through bargaining, so that temporary rules control the process. A second external routinization process has to do with the disposal of output. The organization will seek to legitimize its right to do whatever it is doing in the way that it must do it, and will also attempt to manage the demand for its output. The third type of external routinization process includes procedures for assuring needed input at the appropriate times in appropriate amounts at acceptable prices. This includes purchasing and the attempt to guarantee the permanence of the organization by financing its expansion or continued operation through its own earnings. Or one may attempt to supersede the market through monopoly or monopsony. In economic affairs this may be attained through the economies that occur with very large size such that those who seek to compete find that they simply cannot afford to do so, or, in the case of facilities subsidized out of public taxation, by a similar process whereby the legislature is only able to afford one such facility. For example, most states are unable to afford more than one major public university.

At least since the time Freud (1930 ed.) first described the positive functions of work in the normal healthy personality, many others have pointed to the upsetting effects of lack of work. Christian society has added a grim aspect to the therapeutic view of work by giving the person no choice to do anything else. This attitude appears to be a legacy from Puritanism, with its high evaluation of work and its conception of work as a way of serving God or of proving that one is a member of the elect. In modern times the notion has survived that leisure is free time in the sense that it is time free from the need to be concerned about the need to work, which is related to the means whereby we provide for the maintenance needs — food, clothing, shelter — and other things that go to make up an appropriate standard of living. Where leisure is considered to be time left over, then, in our time it is thought that one has to earn the right to it. As such, enjoying oneself is suspect and must be explained if not earned. In industry, the boss gets worried if the men seem to be enjoying their work too much.

Our society, therefore, keeps people working by placing a negative value on idleness through requiring that the enjoyment of non-work be accompanied by an explanation. At the same time, increasingly, the only opportunities for working are provided in large organizations. The net result is that the individual finds that in order to earn a living, or to obtain any long-range goal, he must associate himself with some large organization, and usually quite a number of them, for all of his life in order to survive. Hence organizations, though only strategies for the avoidance of stress through routinization, become the only strategies available to the individual. The situation is analogous to the building of large freeways, so that traffic can move much more rapidly, and at the same time forbidding anything other than four-wheeled vehicles to travel on them. The net result is that the person with a motorcycle finds that to participate in this more efficient way of getting from one place to another he must sell his motorcycle and buy a car — there is simply no alternative for him. So, too, the large-scale organization is, indeed, a very efficient way for attaining large-scale goals, but the individual never gets a chance to discover whether any other way of attaining them might not be even better, for there are no other ways provided for him. The magnitude of the problems they solve makes it impossible for the individual (without forming a new organization) to try out some creative alternatives himself. The man who works evenings and Sundays in his garage putting together a car entirely by his own efforts is admired for his craftsmanship. But no one would for a moment call what he is doing "work." It would be assumed that he is doing it for fun. And even here the attempt, if successful, which is unlikely, could hardly be generalized as a way of supplying automobiles even to his neighbors in the same block.

TYPES OF WORK STRESS

The net result of the processes we have described is that the individual finds that the major management technique for handling the potential stress that would come from the deprivation of his standard of living is to go to work for one of the large-scale organizations in which employment is available. A variety of such organizations provide the major means by which the members of the society as a whole are provided with a regularized supply of services that enable them to avoid stresses that persons in other societies without such organizations must face. The organization becomes a major method or set of strategies for managing stress through routinization of the means for handling such stress, and hence for making sure that such stress does not occur to begin with. While, this approach is, in principle, enormously more likely to be successful than any alternative which is available, however, *insisting* that the major method for the management of stress is to go to work for one of the large-scale organizations is a stress in its own right. It is these kinds of stress that we identify here as "work stress," and to which we now turn.

Types of work stress may be categorized under three major headings. First, since security from stress means associating one's self with an organization that then can offer tenure and protection against the vicissitudes of life, the person finds that he now subjects himself to the uncertainties and tensions associated with the organization itself. The major risk is that of losing his job, or organizational failure itself. The person finds that his career is tied up with the organization and dependent on it. He is confronted with the problem of potential unemployment and, to the extent to which the organization offers opportunities for career advancement, with the risks that it may present to his own career ambitions. Since the organization will provide him with his major means of earning a living, and his status, which are then transferrable to the community and which account for his access to the goods and pleasures available in the community, he is confronted with the problem of relating his work status to other statuses that he has. The foregoing we may speak of as the *stress of organizational careers.*

The routinization of work flow to which I referred above results in the conversion of the group goal the organization seeks to attain into a set of *tasks* that individuals perform. A major type of stress, then, is what may be imposed by the difficulties of performing satisfactorily the tasks one is asked to perform. We may call this kind of stress *task stress.*

Third, there are the stresses in organizations that follow from their group character. I refer here to what follows from the demands and needs of working together to obtain any end, such as having to listen to what others have to say, being willing to accept orders, having to enlist the support of and willing cooperation of colleagues, having to work with someone that the worker may not like, having to wait for a person who is late before one can begin, or having to hold up publication of a collection of papers because some authors are late in getting their contributions in. This form of stress we speak of as *organization structural stress.* We proceed next to discuss each of these forms of stress in turn.

Organization career stress. There appear to be three major kinds of career stress in large organizations: risk of unemployment, the career sequence, and the process of disengagement from organizations that must inevitably come at the end of one's career.

Much has been written on the consequences of unemployment and its impact, not only on the reduction of sources of income but also on its impact on the person—his sense of worth and self-esteem, and its effect on family-role relationships. We will not attempt to review such literature, since it has been dealt with in many other sources (Adams, 1939; Bakke, 1939; Caplow, 1955; Eisenberg and Lazarsfeld, 1938; Friedmann, 1961, pp. 126, 128; Watson, 1942). We do wish to call attention to an important change in the manner in which unemployment is being managed in all industrial societies. Increasingly, unemployment has everywhere, and particularly in the United States, become structural; we refer to the fact that economic remedies exhibit high probabilities of being successful in holding unemployment down to extremely low levels through the management of aggregate demand by fiscal and monetary policies of central governments. We (in the United States) appear, however, to be unable to employ economic remedies for reducing unemployment much below a level between 3 and 4 percent. This is because the remaining unemployment is due largely to a refusal to hire a person (the prime example, of course, being American Negroes, but also the Spanish-speaking persons of the Southwest, Puerto Ricans, and Indians), and, secondly, the need for persons to obtain appropriate skills in order to be employable. In the last analysis, the only way of attacking these problems is through large-scale changes in public attitudes and through retraining programs which, however, must proceed in the face of powerful opposition from the very persons whom one seeks to retrain, because of the need to change the self-conception of the individual and to avoid the inevitable affront to his own dignity involved in the need for him to think of himself as unemployable unless he changes in some profound way (Beck, 1967). Until now, programs in the United States have had only very limited success, partly because what was called the War on Poverty in fact has been only a minor skirmish with small rifles when large cannons and missiles are required in great quantity. A second problem has been the inability of those who have designed the programs to develop methods for assisting persons without in the process destroying the individual's dignity and self-respect. The result is what counselors and others who run the programs speak of as "a lack of motivation" on the part of the "clients" (Gross, 1968).

In spite of such problems, there is little question that the major technique now available in modern societies for the management of the stress associated with unemployment is the assumption of responsibility by the government for the full employment of all resources, including human resources. This means that the government recognizes that the need to keep people employed is not only a humanitarian one but also justifiable in economic terms. An employed man is a happier man whose self-esteem is raised; but more, an employed man is a person who is taken off the relief rolls and who pays taxes. Hence, in plain economic terms the whole society benefits by employment, whereas unemployed persons are not only hurt themselves but also create burdens for persons who are employed. An important result of this recognition has been that the value of the stability of employment in large-scale organizations has been even further enhanced.

The second form of organization career stress is that associated with the management of the career itself when the individual is employed. A major stress that can occur here is one in which the individual can find himself placed in jobs or in positions that repre-

sent a lack of full utilization of his ability, payment at levels below
what he requires for the maintenance of the standard of living he
considers desirable or that is essential in the community or by his
other statuses, and other types of demands that the organization may
make of him that he finds unacceptable in light of his private motives
and goals. He may be asked to go out and head the company's branch
in Venezuela, but his wife does not want to leave New York, or he
may be asked to move from the bench he has occupied for twenty
years, and which he now regards as his own, to a new training
program the company is providing which will enable him to start a
new career but which may take two years to complete and require
three more years before he attains a level of skill enabling him to
preserve his present income, or his position as a leader in the work
group.

Since such contingencies are unpredictable (since the company's
own future is seldom clear), the major strategy for managing such
stress is to maintain distance from the organization—that is, to attempt to avoid direct dependence on it for each step of one's career.
(There are international contrasts, however, as illustrated in Abegglen, 1958.) There are two main ways of maintaining such distance.
One is that of having an alternative attachment or another identity as
important as one's work identity and which enables one, therefore, to
avoid the stress of an insult to one's work identity. The other is to
enter with a distinct set of crafts or personal skills that are portable,
so that if one does not like how one is treated, one can get up and
leave.

The major kinds of alternative identities may involve loyalties to a
cause, to an outside group, or to a set of clients. Identification with a
cause is illustrated by Pearl Buck's (1936) description of her father's
behavior as a missionary: he identified with God only. When it came
to disputes between himself and his colleagues in the ministry on
how money should be spent, he would announce that God desired
that the money should be spent in a certain way. The response of his
colleagues who disputed his claim to exclusive contact with God's
will was predictably stormy. She writes:

> They shouted bitter words at him, they threatened him with
> expulsion if he did not cease disobeying rules, over and over they
> called him a heretic, once even called him insane. Yet he seemed
> to hear nothing they said. He was a rock in the midst of all the
> frothing—unmoved, unresentful, serene but so determined, so
> stubborn in his own way, that I know there have been those who,
> seeing that high, obstinate, angelic tranquility, have felt like going

out and groaning and beating their heads against the wall in sheer
excess of helpless rage. But Andrew [her father] did not know that
they were even angry with him. Had he not told them God's will?
He must obey God's will (pp. 68–69).

Persons who are identified with a cause feel they have a higher
allegiance and consequently are not controlled by the dictates of
persons in the organization they work for. This technique for managing organizational stress obviously has its dangers, particularly when
more than one person claims to have direct access to the will of God
and where they get contradictory instructions. Organizations, in turn,
try to protect themselves from such persons by simply not hiring
them to begin with. Such persons, in the less exalted language of
personnel offices "rock the boat," or do not make good cooperating
members of "the team."

A second kind of alternative identity to protect one's self from
organizational pressures may be found in a group outside the organization. Among the most important kinds of groups are ethnic or
racial groups, the sexes, and labor unions. Alternative identifications
of this kind can provide an escape from the controls of the organization or one's occupation. For example, a Negro who is criticized
by his boss or is dealt with in a manner that he considers unfair, can
explain his treatment by attributing it to the color of his skin. He may
seek solace in discussing the matter with fellow Negroes who may
affirm his sense of outrage. So, too, women in industry, when subject
to criticism or to treatment they do not consider they deserve, may
attribute it to discrimination against them because they are women.
Although such may indeed be the case, the point is simply that such
identification provides an escape from legitimate criticism that may
have nothing to do with race or sex. Such a person then has another
identity which enables him to escape the sanctions others cannot
escape because they do not have this alternative identity. At another
level it is always possible, of course, to use the alternative identity to
better one's economic or organization position. The farmer, for instance, may find that a protection against the power of the supermar-
kets and others who pay him whatever they wish, is to use his
alternative identity as a citizen and member of a pressure group to
get price supports enacted in Washington or to get the Secretary of
Agriculture to work out changes in freight rates or other changes that
would benefit him. The widespread tendency for identities to be
associated with separate communities, whether by Negroes, Puerto
Ricans, Jews, or others, or the formation of quasi-communities by
stigmatized persons such as communities of the blind, the deaf, those

who have undergone colostomies, multiple sclerotics, and others, provide ways of avoiding organizational stress through providing protective environments. The community provides not only an escape from stress but also advice and help in the management of work stress when it occurs. A major form that such help takes is in the development of racial or religious monopolies of certain occupations or certain organizations. The management of stress may then take place in the socialization process in the form of urging the person to take up a career in "a field that our people are successful at."

A third type of alternative identity involves identification with one's clients. Hall's (1949) distinction between what he calls the "colleague" type of physician and the "individualistic" type is essentially that between one who is oriented to his colleagues and one who is oriented to his patients (often because he has no alternative). Hall (1949) points out that the former does not have to be aggressive about getting patients, since the referral system keeps him occupied; the latter, however, must depend on attracting patients directly, a much more difficult job. Among college professors, one gets, occasionally, the "student man" — one who spends much time counseling the students, helping them put on dances, and so forth, to the possible neglect of his teaching or research. In social work, one gets the idealistic worker who, in the face of what he feels is an over-bureaucratic approach on the part of his colleagues, is "the only one around here who gives a damn for the client." Such persons may become attached to social movements that seek to improve the position of their clients in society. For example, when the late Nurse Sister Kenny met opposition to her method of treating polio from the medical profession, she took her case to the public. The result was that some worshipped her as the leader in a new social movement, but others regarded her as a quack.

The matter comes to this: if one identifies with one's colleagues, one has to learn to keep certain silences, and one of the most important kinds of silences are about new developments in the occupation or about organizational secrets. The accepted procedure is to let one's colleagues pass judgment on new things. If one takes the new idea or technique to the people, one is rejecting one's colleagues and their opinions. The resulting criticism may be harsh, but it should not be surprising.

The development of alternative identities as a method of maintaining distance from the potential stresses of organizational employment, while itself a technique for the management of such stress, carries its own burden of stress. The most intensively studied has been the possibility that such alternative identities will conflict with one's organizational or occupational identities. Most often this research has taken the form of studies of role conflict. Ethnic or racial identifications often develop with entry of ethnic or racial groups into an occupation previously preempted by another ethnic or racial group. For example, the first Negro physician in an area has often engaged in a fight to secure the right to practice. The question then arises: which identification is uppermost in his mind, that with his medical colleagues or that with his race? His medical colleagues will expect him to behave like a trusted member of the profession; members of his race will hold him up as a model for their children and a symbol of hope, and will expect him to be mindful of the needs of the group. But suppose the Negro doctor learns that a hospital has a racial policy, for example, a quota system on Negro nurses. Shall he notify Negro leaders in the community? If he does not, and it is found out anyway (as it is likely to be), then the Negroes will accuse him of deserting them. On the other hand, if he does inform the group, then it is likely that other doctors will reject him as a man who cannot be trusted to keep his mouth shut on other delicate matters that physicians feel it is necessary to keep secret in a hospital in the best interest not simply of the hospital or themselves, but often of the patients, also.

Hall (1948) has described the dilemma of the doctor of Italian descent. Often he has risen from the slums and wishes to be successful. In order to win the respect of his colleagues he will desire a widespread clientele that will include others besides Italians. He finds, however, that in order to get his clientele he has to refuse to treat some of his poorer Italian patients. This may lead to his being rejected by his own friends and accused of being a renegade, as someone whose success has blinded him to his loyalties to his own group.

The Negro personnel man in industry is not likely to be considered a full member of the department of personnel. He is usually expected and hired to deal with the peculiarly Negro problems in the plant. His position is really that of a straw boss: his job is to interpret management to the Negro workers and vice versa. The question then arises in his mind: what is he—a Negro or a personnel man? A similar problem is faced by the woman in personnel work who is usually hired because there are many women working in the plant and she is to provide "the women's point of view." Shall she be a feminist and fight for the rights of women, or shall she identify with her personnel colleagues? A similar conflict of identification occurs on the part of those who become active in the labor union.

Where do these people belong—to their race, sex, labor union, or organization or occupation? If the number of Negroes in the plant is reduced, will management keep the Negro personnel man as a general personnel man? Probably not. This may push him to identify with Negroes, for what chance does he have anyhow? The situation is similar for the woman. The union man may find a greater personal reward and satisfaction in his union role than in that of worker.

The second kind of technique for the management of stress by maintaining distance from the organization is that of professionalization, or, more broadly, the development of a special set of skills which the person can carry with him from organization to organization. The obvious cases consist of occupations with a strong sense of craft consciousness, such as those in the building trades who have adopted unionization as their major device of protection from the possible stresses of organizational uncertainties. For these persons the union becomes a primary hiring agency and a primary basis of security.

The more interesting case (because less heavily studied) and the more important for the long-range future, however, has been the increasing development of professionalization as a way of organizing work. There is even a tendency at present to regard it as the wave of the future, as the only proper way for work to be organized. The persons called by the U.S. Census "Professional, Technical and Kindred Workers" have increased from a scant one in 25 workers in the year 1900 to the point where they now make up one in seven approximately. This great increase is partly a reflection of the great growth in knowledge since the industrial revolution and the growth of science. Knowledge is not a sufficient explanation, however, and there are some professions that do not even rest on scientific knowledge or research, such as the ministry or law. Social work is partly based on knowledge of human personality, but much of it consists of the systematization of practice.

At least as important as knowledge, as an explanation for professionalization, has been the desire of many occupations to get on the gravy train. Many are found to be fighting not simply to become a profession but for the *right to call* themselves a profession. To get the right to call oneself a professional involves very real advantages. First, one becomes a monopoly in the public interest. One gets the right to call others "incompetent" or "quacks" and this enables the members of the occupation to eliminate competition from outsiders, who are always turning up, and also enables the members of the occupation to validate their claim to be honorable. They can insist on their mandate to do something important that no one else does, such as protect society's health, oversee public safety, take charge of the education of the young, become repositories of great trust, provide protection from enemies, foreign and domestic, counsel people with troubles, or decide who should raise a child. Once that mandate is obtained, then the members of the occupation can get license to do things differently—the lawyer to hear awful secrets, the diplomat to visit hostile countries, the priest to read forbidden books and become an expert in sin in order to do his job, or the social scientist to be objective about society at a time when loyalty is expected to be clear and declared. Of course, the professional does all of the above because his work requires it, but it gives him freedom, nevertheless, that is denied to others and, hence, he becomes a privileged person. Further, since one's work involves an essential service that no one else can perform, that means no one else has the right to tell one how to do it or even how to evaluate it. So the members of the profession get great autonomy and power.

Once one earns the right to call one's occupation a profession, one also can control entry into the profession—that is, decide who gets in, what their qualifications and training must be—and so, one can obtain the rare privilege of deciding who one's colleagues will be. One further gets to control the price of one's services through control of competition and through influence on the state and lawmakers through professional associations. This is done in a variety of ways, either through control of the name (Certified Public Accountant) or through control of the generic work itself (medicine, psychology).

Further, if one earns the right to call one's occupation a profession, then one can control the behavior of the members and hence enforce standards and maintain whatever values the occupation thinks desirable. Most of these standards have to do with work, but many have to do with relations to other professions, to clients, the general public, and politics.

Apart from these formidable advantages, it is in organizations that professionalization shows its greatest uses to its members. And the organizational professional *is* the typical case, for contrary to the picture of the professional in private practice (so frequently used as a model), most professionals are found in organizations, from the law firm, to the university, to the hospital, to the manufacturing organization. In organizations, professional identification provides two major sources of power: validated expertise, and an alternative identity. As a certified member of his profession, the "professional" can lay claim to knowledge and hence can insist that no mere bureaucratic superior has the competence (let alone the right) to evaluate his work or his decisions. His alternative identity makes him into a cosmopolitan (Gouldner, 1957–58): he conceives of himself as a pathologist first, an employee of Zilch Polytechnic second. He therefore reserves for himself the ultimate weapon (and luxury) of rejecting organizational controls by the device of threatening to leave or actually doing so. In fact, such movement may even be expected as part of the career.

In practice, both of these organizational advantages become attenuated. The claimed expertise is subject to severe criticism, not only by bureaucratic superiors but by other professionals in related fields who may know a great deal about the professional's field (Gross, 1967), for the professional increasingly finds himself a part of a team of professionals. As for his ability to move, this is often a purely formal freedom. If he is already at an organization that has the equipment, library, computer, and subprofessionals and technicians he needs to do his work (Weber, 1966), then where can he go that will be any better? The professional needs the organization quite as much as the organization needs him. Hence, the typical organizational professional is a man with a good deal of power who grumbles about how little power he has.

We have so far described the two major kinds of threats that may involve stress on the part of those who seek organizational careers — the risk of unemployment and the problem of maintaining distance from the organization itself, so that one is not directly subject to its vicissitudes, through the maintenance of alternative identities and through professionalization. Insofar as executives in organizations are unable to maintain such distance, they would seem to be peculiarly subject to the stress associated with the progress of a particular organization. If it does poorly, they suffer, and there would seem to be, at the moment, no way that they can avoid a direct connection between their personal good fortune and that of the organization as a whole. However, Galbraith (1967) has suggested that the managers of large corporations themselves have developed a set of strategies for reducing stress by taking advantage of certain important trends that have increased their power in the organization. Increasingly, the owners of large corporations are stockholders who are little interested in the conduct of the corporation as long as it returns them dividends and the price of the stock goes up. The board of directors theoretically selects the management, but increasingly members of management, through proxies, themselves choose the board of directors who, in turn, choose management, that is, themselves. Top management is not likely to be removed by a board of directors unless the firm gets into serious difficulty. Consequently, top management sees that its first task is to assure the security of the organization through continued payment of dividends so that the owners are satisfied. Then, through the same mechanism they pay the creditors. Consequently, they manage the two groups that can give them difficulty. Once the security of the organization is assured, growth becomes a major goal of modern corporations (rather than the traditional goal of profit maximization). Indeed, there is little point in pursuing profit maximization since that may be very risky, and, furthermore, profits do not accrue to the managers but rather to the stockholders. So stockholders are given as little as they will take without complaint. Meanwhile, managers spend their time trying to expand the organization, a goal which interests them since it increases their own power and gives them opportunities for new careers.

The third and last of the techniques for the management of stress associated with organizational careers is that of the threats that are associated with the life cycle, particularly those that occur with aging. Since the association of the individual career with a large organization is so intimate, there occurs for most persons a ·drastic severing of connections at the time of retirement. Increasingly, organizations, in order to make way for those coming up and because of insurance requirements, institute compulsory retirement, so that suddenly one day the individual who has been very busy finds himself severed from the organization and, given the nature of the economy, there is no obvious alternative for him (quite apart from the difficulty old persons find getting a job). Such downward mobility may have begun a number of years before and the firm may well have kept the individual on only out of a sense of loyalty to him, a desire to maintain a reputation for humanitarian concerns in the community, and a feeling that firing persons when they become of less use to a company after 20 years' service may be bad for the morale of the younger persons who see themselves as potentially those who will be thrown on the slagheap when they have worked for the company for 20 years. In general, the problem of downward mobility has been neglected in the study of American organizations, perhaps because of our past experience with economic growth and because of our usual optimism. Inevitably, however, even in a growing economy, everyone will, sooner or later, experience some downward mobility, although for some it may occur only at the end of their work careers. Relatively little research has been done on the social and psychological consequences of demotion, although such evidence as we have indicates that these consequences can be stressful indeed

(More, 1962; Wilensky and Edwards, 1959). Organizations have many ways of managing demotion so as to soften its impact—kicking people upstairs, shifting them to other parts of the company to less demanding jobs, and other ingenious devices (Goldner, 1965; Martin and Strauss, 1956). The sheer size of the large corporation assists in the management of such demotion, since it is often not clear when people are shifted around that they have been demoted.

In addition, the process of resolution of cognitive dissonance operates to assist others to make the adjustment. Thus the historian who becomes a dean finds that his official responsibilities keep him out of touch with research in his own field. For a while he may feel considerable alarm, even panic, as he discovers that he probably cannot return to being a historian in later years (because the kind of department he would like to go to would not accept him because of his lack of contribution over the years). But he eventually discovers that there are satisfactions in being a dean, that it is not such a bad life, and that since *someone* must be dean, who can better do the job than a historian (after all)?

Task stress. The task is, in one sense, the central problem in work situations. It is the reason why the organization has been set up and the overall goal is typically broken up into a set of tasks which are then assigned to individuals to perform. It is obvious that stress would follow from assigning to persons tasks they are unable to perform or threatening to something they value, or that take place in situations where inadequate performance would have punishing consequences. Since work organizations are not mere sports or races designed to pit the individual against others, however, organizational designers clearly have an interest in making sure that individual tasks do *not* result in stress (at least forms of stress that may have negative consequences so that persons withdraw from the situation altogether). Hence, the approach is to try to routinize the process by making sure that stress does *not* occur through making sure that the tasks can be performed by the persons who are hired to do them. The overall approach is to break down the goal(s) of the organization into man-sized roles, select persons who have a high probability of being able to perform each of the tasks, and then to try to insure that conformity to task requirements will be reflected in the behavior of the individual worker. Simon (1959, p. 102) describes five mechanisms of "organization influence" which produce this conformity: the limitation of responsibility for particular tasks, standard practices, the assignment of authority and influence, the limitation of channels of communication, and training or indoctrination of the members.

Only rarely has direct attention been given to the relatively stressful character of different kinds of jobs or tasks. Hence, most of our discussion will be inferential, in that it will be assumed that certain negative consequences associated with certain tasks may have an indirect relationship to the stress that may be produced by those consequences.

The most obvious kind of consequence that has been investigated is job satisfaction, and here there is a general assumption that the more dissatisfaction there is with a particular job (which the individual is unable to escape), then the more stressful is the job. The measurement of job satisfaction is in a parlous state—in spite of the enormous amount of work that has been done in this area—partly because the question of what job satisfaction is is difficult to settle. There appear to be many dimensions of job satisfaction, and there is some question as to whether satisfaction is a subtractive or multiplicative process (the resultant of what the individual wants or needs and what the situation offers him for the satisfaction of those wants and needs). Thus it would seem that two persons might respond very differently to a situation offering equal opportunity for the satisfaction of the particular need because their needs differ. Or, vice versa, persons of similar needs will experience a different kind of satisfaction depending on the opportunities that their respective jobs offer them. Although such a statement seems obvious on the face of it, very few studies of job satisfaction take any account of it; instead, it is assumed that the same variables would explain both the dissatisfaction of the man of very strong ambitions who is high up in a company but does not feel satisfied by the opportunities the company offers and the person whose ambition is very weak and would be happy with a small wage increment but is in a situation in which even a small wage increment but is in a situation in which even a small wage increment is difficult to secure. Other consequences of job difficulties are turnover, absences, accidents, and job performance. These have been studied, too, although not so thoroughly as the determinants of job satisfaction. We shall not try to summarize the literature on this general subject in any detail since good summaries of it are available (Vroom, 1964). We will simply mention some of the major conclusions of this research, selecting those studies we think bear most directly on the relationship between task and stress. We shall make use of the categories for classifying that literature utilized by Vroom (1964).

A large number of studies have dealt with the impact of different styles and types of supervision on job satisfaction. One group of studies has dealt with the effect of consideration by the supervisor of the needs of his subordinates, while a second group has dealt with the impact of the influence that the employee has on making decisions about his own job. Although findings are mixed, we can conclude that consideration of the feelings, needs, and wishes of subordinates on the part of a supervisor tends to increase their level of satisfaction, and results are associated with low turnover rates, grievances, and absences. Although it makes a certain amount of sense to assume that the direction of causation would lie in the suggested way, it could, of course, be the reverse. That is, workers who are satisfied or who show low levels of turnover, grievances, and absences, may report that their supervisor treats them well or may attribute the lack of stress to the treatment of the supervisor, since he is the key representative of management they meet.

Most of the studies on which the above conclusions are based are two-variable correlational studies. A major question would be whether multivariate analysis might alter the conclusion. Such analysis has rarely been carried out, though an indication of the potential significance of it is provided by a study by Pelz (1952; Pelz and Andrews, 1966) in which it was found that the supervisor's consideration for his subordinates made a difference in job satisfaction only in those situations where the supervisor himself was influential with *his* superiors (in being able to *do* something about employee needs). With an effective supervisor, the more consideration he showed for his employees, the more satisfied they were. On the other hand, with an ineffective supervisor, there was no relationship between consideration for employees and their satisfaction.

A great many studies, going back to the classic experiments by Lewin (1956) in attempting to change food habits during World War II, have been concerned with the influence of the opportunity to make decisions about one's work on one's job satisfaction and on other job effects. On the whole, these studies tend to support the claim that the greater opportunity persons have to influence decisions that affect their own work, the more satisfied they will be with their job. The evidence is far from being conclusive, however. Again, it would seem that multivariate analysis would be fruitful, for surely the importance to the individual of his job would be possible influencing variable, as well as the opportunities provided by the job itself for making such decisions. Highly programmed jobs would seem to offer fewer such opportunities and, consequently, the variable under examination would simply have too small a range of variation for any results to be forthcoming.

A second major variable that has been investigated is that of job content. Much interest and controversy revolves about the finding, reported by Herzberg and his colleagues (1959), on sources of job satisfaction and dissatisfaction among a group of accountants and engineers.[4] The study was based on interviews in which subjects were asked to tell the investigators about times when they felt exceptionally good or exceptionally bad about their jobs. They report that the stories dealing with the times when subjects felt good tended to concern the content of the job, including such matters as achievements, recognition, responsibility, and other features of the job. On the other hand, when subjects reported things that they thought were bad, they were likely to mention factors not associated with job content but with job conditions or external conditions associated with the context of the job, rather than the job itself, such as company policies of various kinds, wages, the kind of supervision they had, and working conditions. The first group of factors Herzberg and his colleagues speak of as satisfiers (or "motivating factors"), and the second group as dissatisfiers (or "hygienic factors"). They claim that when the second group is absent, workers will be dissatisfied, but the mere presence of these dissatisfiers will *not* motivate them or lead them to speak of a job as good. Apparently they simply make a job acceptable. Increased motivation or output is associated only with changes in the first kind of variable.

Other studies have not supported this neat distinction between job content and job context, some reporting that changes in working conditions and wages were associated with job satisfaction, others connecting factors associated with the job itself with dissatisfaction. Vroom (1964, p. 129), in a criticism of the Herzberg and others (1959) studies, feels that even if there were no negative findings, it would still be possible that defensive processes are at work. He writes:

> Persons may be more likely to attribute the causes of satisfaction to their own achievements and accomplishments on the job. On the other hand, they may be more likely to attribute their dissatisfaction, not to personal inadequacies or deficiencies, but to factors in the work environment, (i.e., obstacles presented by company policies or supervision).

These questions about job context raise the whole question of what are often spoken of as "conditions of work." The literature on work and stress is curiously deficient in its treatment of these conditions, that is, such matters as noise, dirt, deadlines, isolation, etc.

4. The fact that these were professionals is often forgotten in reports of this study, which simply refer to it as if a good sample of the working force had been employed.

The omission is surprising, since it is precisely such matters that the individual worker himself is likely to bring up when asked directly what he finds stressful about his work. Yet it is a plausible hypothesis that such references constitute proferred explanations or rationalizations offered after the fact, rather than simple causal factors in their own right. This assertion is not to deny that they may not have causal significance, but rather that their being mentioned is not in itself sufficient reason for assuming they are significant in any direct way.

The reasons for believing that working conditions may be more significant as proferred explanations than as causes of stress are: (1) A reference by the individual worker or organizational member to "all this racket," or "the stinking food" is convenient, easy to understand, and likely to provoke ready assent from the would-be-sympathetic listener. It may then be a simple put-off to send the nosy questioner on his way, or a test of whether the questioner is sympathetic or not.[5] (2) Under modern industrial conditions, union and/or governmental controls make the classic conditions described in the horror-works of Marx and Dickens much less likely to occur. (3) Where such conditions do still occur, they are likely to give way to others, simply because such conditions are not efficient. Even the most callous task-master, however Pharoic his temperament, can hardly defend his behavior if the work gets done poorly or late.[6] (4) The hypothesis advanced by Vroom (1964) of the projection of blame outside seems to be applicable in this type of case. That is, when things go well, workers explain it in terms of their own contribution; when they go badly, they blame it on outside conditions or persons. Hence, when

5. In an unpublished study of the "operational problems" of men stationed in isolated radar airsites, my colleagues and I had occasion to travel to a relatively large number of such sites in the United States and Japan. We early encountered the colonel who insisted that he could judge the "combat readiness" or "state of morale" of the men within an hour after arrival at an airsite. As we compared notes with such men, we eventually came to agree on the accuracy of one indicator: statements of the men about the food served in the mess-hall. We stayed at many sites for long periods, so that we were exposed to many kinds and quality of food. Practically always, we, as innocent civilians, thought the food nutritious, attractive, adequate, and often excellent. Yet we noticed a rise and fall in complaints about the food as other things that *were* disturbing occurred elsewhere, the other things having to do with the structure of authority, changes in training or promotion practices, and other social matters. In sum, the food was a convenient thing to complain about, it was always there to complain about, the kitchen staff were fair game as targets of jokes under any conditions (as they usually are), and hence statements about food were good indicators of other troubles.

6. The important deviant cases are presented by the Nazi extermination and the Chinese POW camps, in which extremely adverse conditions were used deliberately to break morale or cause persons to collapse. The evidence is that the desire to exterminate and the desire to function effectively were in continual tension with one

workers are asked what is bad or stressful about the job, they are
likely to refer to outside conditions. (5) It is quite possible that both
Herzberg and others (1959) and Vroom (1964) are correct: working
conditions may be "hygienic" in character but are also useful things
to blame. That is, when some desired condition is *not* present,
persons complain about it and perhaps work more poorly. On the
other hand, when it is provided, persons take the view that it was
"necessary" to do the job at all, and hence feel that it was simply due
them. For example, when female employees complain about a "filthy
toilet," the provision of a good one is likely to be met with the
comment: "It's about time. I would have quit if I'd had to go into
that filthy place once more." Possibly, then, working conditions are
just that—the conditions required for working. They must indeed be
provided, but are in the same category as having material to work on,
having a machine that functions, and the like. Hence, if they remain
deficient for any length of time, they can only be regarded as evi-
dences of poor management which must be corrected. Their absence
is a rarity that is usually temporary. They do not explain much of
worker discontent most of the time, but they are always available as
"explanations."

My claim that the references to working conditions are usually
rationalizations is, of course, difficult to prove, just as any claim that a
statement is a rationalization is difficult to prove. But two suggestive
works may be cited. The first is a study of Whyte (1961, chap. 12) of a
petroleum operator at an aviation gasoline plant who walked off his
job. The operator, called Joe Sloan, walked off at a time when the
plant was shifting over from production of one kind of gasoline to
another. To make the shift, the pipes had to be emptied of the old
gasoline, requiring venting of the vapors and liquids onto the floor of
the control room. Apparently, for a few minutes until the liquid
evaporated, it was all over the floor, with its fumes filling the air. A
companion said of Joe Sloan:

> It was really a hazard, but I didn't know what Joe was going to
> do until he just tapped me on the back and says, "Johnny, I am

another. If the camp had a production job (as some did), then the able-bodied and
unencumbered were selected for at least temporary life and minimal survival conditions. Even if the camp was purely for extermination, that grisly activity was also a
"job," requiring a minimum of reasonably healthy inmates as helpers. Since most
investigators (including myself) do not have the stomach to seek amid the records for
such kinds of data, the remarks in this footnote are hardly more than a hint from such
work as Abel (1951); Adler (1958); Bettelheim (1960); Biderman (1963); Cohen (1954);
Kogon (1946); Leighton (1945); Lifton (1961); and Schein, Schneier and Barker (1961).

leaving you with it." I sure was sorry to see him go (Whyte, 1961, p. 199).

Sloan had previously called the foreman down to see the situation, and demanded that it be improved, saying: "A man ought not to have to work in conditions like this." The foreman did not take him seriously since this had occurred "fifty times before." According to the foreman, Sloan repeated the statement about "not having to work under such conditions," then shortly afterwards said, "I don't think I will work under such conditions." He then left.

Here, then, was clearly a case where working conditions were highly unsatisfactory (the foreman conceded that Sloan's complaint was entirely justified; the condition has since been corrected). Yet it is the whole point of Whyte's discussion of the case that that particular condition hardly begins to account for Joe Sloan's walking off the job. Even his co-workers (who did not like the condition any more than Joe Sloan) were the first to discount it as a "cause." As a fellow operator said: "They say the man blowed up. But why does a man blow up like that? They ought to try to find that out."

Whyte, as the sociological analyst, does seek to find that out and ends with a highly complex set of social factors, including loss in status, marked reductions in opportunities to initiate activities for others, instabilities and fluctuations in the interactions experienced, age and promotions, and other broader generalizations about relationships among activities, interactions, and sentiments. The incident preceding Sloan's walking off the job is seen to have functioned as an occasion for doing so, or a proper moment to do so.

The second case is drawn from the writings of Che Guevara (1968) on guerrilla warfare. He writes much of the difficult conditions under which such warfare must be carried:

[The guerrilla fighter's] normal life is the long hike. Let us take as an example a mountain guerrilla fighter located in wooded regions under constant harassment by the enemy. In these conditions the guerrilla band moves during daylight hours, without eating, in order to change its position; when night arrives, camp is set up in a clearing near a water supply according to a routine, each group assembling in order to eat in common; at dusk the fires are lighted with whatever is at hand.

The guerrilla fighter eats when he can and everything he can. Sometimes fabulous feasts disappear in the gullet of the combatant; at other times he fasts for two or three days without suffering any diminution in his capacity for work.

His house will be the open sky; between it and his hammock he places a sheet of waterproof nylon and beneath the cloth and hammock he places his knapsack, gun and ammunition, which are the treasures of the guerrilla fighter. At times it is not wise for shoes to be removed, because of the possibility of a surprise attack by the enemy. Shoes are another of his precious treasures. Whoever has a pair of them has the security of a happy existence within the limits of the prevailing circumstances.

Thus the guerrilla fighter will live for days without approaching any inhabited place, avoiding all contact that has not been previously arranged, staying in the wildest zones, knowing hunger, at times thirst, cold, heat; sweating during the continuous marches, letting the sweat dry on his body and adding to it new sweat without any possibility of cleanliness. . . . During the recent war, upon entering the village of El Uvero following a march of sixteen kilometers and a fight of two hours and forty-five minutes in a hot sun (all added to several days passed in very adverse conditions along the sea with intense heat from a boiling sun) our bodies gave off a peculiar and offensive odor that repelled anyone who came near. Our noses were completely habituated to this type of life; the hammocks of guerrilla fighters are known for their characteristic, individual odor (pp. 40–41).

Here, then, we have a set of working conditions obviously and patently unpleasant and stressful. Guevara describes them mainly to show that such is the case. His point is to emphasize that only certain kinds of persons can possibly survive such arduous conditions. After describing a number of desirable personal and moral requirements (adaptiveness, inventiveness, courage, asceticism), he goes on to add:

He must be indefatigable. He must be able to produce another effort at the moment when weariness seems intolerable. Profound conviction, expressed in every line of his face, forces him to take another step, and this not the last one, since it will be followed by another and another and another until he arrives at the place designated by his chiefs.

He ought to be able to endure extremities, to withstand not only the privations of food, water, clothing, and shelter to which he is subjected frequently, but also the sickness and wounds that often must be cured by nature without much help from the surgeon. This is all the more necessary because usually the individual who leaves the guerrilla zone to recover from sickness or wounds will be assassinated by the enemy.

To meet these conditions he needs an iron constitution that will enable him to resist all these adversities without falling ill and to make of his hunted animal's life one more factor of strength. With the help of his natural adaptability, he becomes a part of the land itself where he fights (pp. 37–38).

The inference I draw from Guevara's discussion is that *of course* physical conditions can and are likely to be stressful. But if a man believes in a cause and has the capabilities, he triumphs over them, and in the process of triumphing, becomes even stronger. Group solidarity itself owes much to the experience of facing such conditions as a band.

My general conclusion, then, is that (whatever people say about them) physical and other working conditions are stressful only insofar as they affect the individual through their impact on the social structure and group values. Poorly organized men of low group attachment will not simply complain about poor working conditions: they will collapse under them. But well-organized men, who fight in the muck for a noble cause, will revel in it, considering bruises and filth as marks of glory. Such conditions are variably present in organizations. They are probably at their minimum in coercive organizations such as prisons and the back wards of mental hospitals, and at their maximum in organizations with powerful ideological components (universities, some political parties, some armies in battle). They are probably present to a moderate extent in business organizations, becoming more important near the top. Stated in plainer language, I conclude that arduous working conditions will become more and more closely related to stress as the identification of the member with the organization declines. In reverse, as identification increases, persons become increasingly tolerant of working conditions until, at an extreme, they may even take pride in their own toughness in handling such conditions.

The previous discussion has dealt with "conditions," that is, context variables. We turn now to studies of job content. Among the job content variables that have been examined are specialization, work pace, use of skills and abilities, success or failure in work performance, interruption of work on tasks, and job level. The major findings on these variables may be summarized as follows: Where specialization leads to repetitiveness, in general, the more repetitive the job, the less satisfying it is. Attempts to deal with repetitiveness have included both job enlargement (giving the person more operations to perform) and job rotation (in which the person may have a relatively small number of operations to perform but shifts from one to another with a greater degree of frequency). Both measures have been found to reduce feelings of frustration and boredom and to increase satisfaction and, often, quality of work. A famous study was that performed by Trist and Bamforth (1951) of a change in the technique of mining coal from one in which individuals had control over all operations and a later specialized situation in which each task was limited. A marked drop in job satisfaction occurred in the specialized situation, and both absenteeism and psychosomatic illnesses increased. A variety of other factors besides the task organization changed, however, including group size and the functional basis of group organization.

Repetitiveness has also been shown to be associated with turnover. As we have already indicated, that relationship too may be affected by a third variable. For example, a number of experiments have shown that the intelligence of the individual affects the impact of repetitive work on him, with studies of more intelligent persons showing a closer relationship between repetitiveness of the job and their dissatisfaction with it.

On the matter of control over work pace, the overall findings tend to support the assertion that inability to control one's pace of work is associated with low worker satisfaction. The work of Maslow (1943, 1954) on self-actualization has led to many studies of the extent to which jobs permit individuals to make use of their potentialities, particularly with reference to their skills and ability. Maslow's hypothesis can be modified (as suggested by Vroom, 1964, p. 142) to read: "Greater job satisfaction may be expected on the part of people who believe that their jobs require abilities which they believe they possess," and a number of studies support this claim. For example, Brophy (1959) asked a group of nurses to estimate the extent to which they believe they possessed a number of traits, and then asked them also which traits they thought their jobs offered opportunity to express. The discrepancy between these two sets of ratings was found to correlate negatively with job satisfaction. The less the nurse saw her job as demanding the qualities she possessed, the lower her job satisfaction. Similarly, Kornhauser (1965) also found a strong relationship between mental health (conceived of as the relative efficiency of the person in handling the problems he faced) and the extent to which the job enabled workers to use their abilities.

Although success or failure in work performance would seem to be an obvious subject to study in its impact on work satisfaction, most studies are confined to the laboratory, and they do indeed show the obvious predicted relationship. Studies in industry, however, do not show any relationship, perhaps because there is not an adequate feedback mechanism to the worker; that is, because there is no unequivocal indication to him as to whether he has succeeded or failed. Even in situations where the evidence is negative, the worker seeks solace from some positive feature of the situation. The interruption of work on tasks is associated with dissatisfaction, although there is some evidence that when the task is a long one, then interruptions may be welcomed as breaks.

Finally, it has been found that job satisfaction correlates positively with the job level. Why this is the case is not clear and has not been investigated. One can speculate that the higher the job the better paid it will be; that it often involves less repetitiveness, allows more freedom for the worker to determine how the job shall be done, and may be a more pleasant job. Kornhauser (1965) raises the possibility that persons low in the hierarchy may be those who gripe about their jobs, since those who are able to do something about it will have left the job and expressed their abilities somewhere else. When Kornhauser compared long-term and short-term workers, however, he found no difference in this variable.

The relation of wages or payment to job satisfaction has not been clearly shown, even though a relatively large number of studies have dealt with this subject. An important distinction appears to be between the absolute level of income (which enables the individual to make purchases in the community in which he lives) and the relationship of the person's payment to what he thinks he deserves, that is, to some conception of equity. Whether investigators pay attention to one or the other of these variables often depends on ideology, with the economists tending to emphasize the level of wages, and human relations theorists, considerations of equity. The evidence seems to support the claim that both are associated with job satisfaction, but any attempts to evaluate their relative importance have not been successful. For example, the simpleminded use of rankings of lists of factors have a built-in bias that guarantees the success of the investigator's attempt to prove his hypothesis. They are typically used by those who seek to show the importance of equity. A list of factors is given to the worker or he is asked to make a list; and it is usually found that level of wages is not at the top of the list, other factors such as fairness, and "opportunity to use my ability," and so forth, often being placed above wages. Such studies are typically made among workers who are relatively well paid to begin with, however, or who are at least employed. Consequently, it may be assumed that wages would not be salient in comparison to other factors. If one were to make such a study among the unemployed or among severely deprived workers such as Negroes working at low-level jobs, however, the results might be very different indeed.

Hours of work have received some attention from researchers. The study of number of hours worked, the length of the work week, work year, and the work life will yield different conclusions depending on which of these is in fact employed as the measure. Although most persons assume that the average number of hours worked in a week has declined, Wilensky (1961) offers historical data to the effect that most of these conclusions have been too much affected by the situation immediately after the coming of the Industrial Revolution, when the hours of daily work increased enormously. At present the average hours of daily and weekly work seem to be about those that were employed by peasants in the thirteenth and fourteenth centuries in Europe. Average hours of work have declined since the Industrial Revolution in Western countries, although the impact differs among workers; farmers and higher executives and professionals have not reduced their hours of work appreciably, whereas blue-collar workers, particularly those in unionized industries, have. On the other hand, the evidence seems to be that in the last 25 years the average hours of work per week in the United States have increased slightly. Even when given the opportunity for increased leisure, workers are likely to choose a second job or to work overtime, preferring the income and the opportunities it provides to leisure. As Galbraith (1967) points out, there would seem to be no reason why men will prefer leisure over work if the work is pleasant. In the period immediately after the Industrial Revolution, and in jobs offering very unpleasant working conditions or other features that the worker finds unpleasant, he will prefer leisure, but even more likely he will seek a different job in which unpleasant features are not present.

Results more relevant to our concern with stress have been produced by studies of the consequences of shift work (Dankert and others, 1965). With increasing mechanization and automation, it becomes economically desirable to run equipment 24 hours a day. As a consequence, workers find themselves working deviant hours: late afternoon, early evening, late at night, or being required to change from one shift to another one. The question is how stressful either working a deviant shift or changing shift is. The literature suggests that many night and rotating shift workers report trouble with basic rhythms of sleeping, eating, and eliminating. They have trouble getting to sleep and staying asleep and complain about the quality of their sleep. When more serious health problems are examined, however, the relationship of shift work to such results is not so clear. Thiies-Evansen (1958) found that 30 percent of a group of workers who had transferred from shift work to day work reported gastritis to a greater extent than was expected. On the other hand, Bjerner, and others (1948) found little difference between shift workers and nonshift workers on either the frequency of consulting a physician or on the rate of hospitalization for stomach disorders. When they divided their day workers into those who had previously worked shifts and those who had not, however, significantly higher rates were found for the day workers who had formerly been shift workers. Pierarch (1955) reported that German workers showed an ulcer rate eight times as high for rotating than for fixed shift workers, and several others have confirmed this finding. Thiies-Evansen (1958), however, suggests that before one can make any direct inferences from such studies it is essential to know when the ulcers were contracted. Shift workers may aggravate ulcers that are already present, or speed their reactivation.

The most intensive study of the effects of shift work has been carried out by Mott and his colleagues (1965). The groups they compared worked for different companies but were comparable within those companies in that, within the same company plants, persons worked fixed and rotating shifts, and the plants manufactured approximately the same product. Data were collected in 1960 by comprehensive paper-and-pencil questionnaires and interviews from 1,045 blue-collar workers and 661 of their wives. Workers were questioned on how different shift patterns affected their family and social life. The results generally reported the greatest difficulty in role behaviors associated with early evening. Workers had the greatest difficulty spending time with their children and doing things with them, in teaching their children skills and socializing them, and in providing their wives with companionship, diversion and relaxation from their household duties. Rotating shift workers scored about the same on these roles, since they experienced difficulties with them one-third of the time. Night-shift workers reported much more difficulty than the afternoon workers in meeting aspects of family roles associated with the late evening hours, such as sex relations and the protection of the wife from harm. While these findings would seem to be what one would expect, it was also found that working shifts was inversely related to the adequacy of coordination and problem-solving in the family and that the amount of strain and tension was greater. There was, however, no relationship to amount of marital happiness that persons reported.

Shift work did not interfere with informal social life, although rotating shift workers reported far fewer friends than either day workers or other shift workers. It is not clear what the direction of causation is here. Shift workers also belonged to fewer organizations than did day workers, and when they did they were less likely to be an officer or to hold a committee assignment. Self-esteem, anxiety, and conflict pressure were also measured and none of them was found to be directly related to the worker's shift. A measure of total interference felt by the worker across all of his role behaviors was constructed; this measure of perceived interference was, however, found to be related negatively to the person's self-esteem and positively to his level of anxiety and conflict pressure. On the other hand, difficulties in performance of roles as members of voluntary associations was not found to be related to psychological health. As reported in other studies, workers on the steady night and rotating shift reported difficulty in adjusting body functions to the needs of their shift. The more serious health complaints, however—for example, ulcers—were found to be highest among day and afternoon shift workers. One reason may be that the shift worker who had experienced the most serious physical problems had often been able to obtain a transfer to the day shift. (This inference was somewhat speculative in the absence of data about the onset of illness.) In sum, the authors conclude that, all things considered, the fixed afternoon shift creates the most difficulty for the worker's family and social roles, but the rotating shift is a close second. However, body functions are more severely interfered with in the rotating shift than they are in steady night work.

Whatever the determinants of job satisfaction may be, and our brief review of the literature suggests that they are by no means simple, their impact on job *behavior* requires a separate analysis. Only a small number of studies have, in fact, been made of the relationship between job satisfaction and turnover, but all support the expected negative relationship. March and Simon (1958), as well as others, have pointed out that whether job satisfaction results in turnover depends not only on the person's feelings about the job but also on the kind of alternatives available to him. Thus it has been shown by many that voluntary turnover increases markedly in periods of full employment as compared to periods of less than full employment (Behrend, 1953; Woytinsky, 1942).

Job dissatisfaction might be predicted to be associated with an increase in absences, but the evidence is far from clear; some studies show a relationship, others show none, some show negative relationships. Even those that do show a relationship show very low correlations. The relationship is improved when one uses not total number of days lost as the measure of absences but frequency of absences. There is some evidence that job dissatisfaction is associated with accidents as well. However, Stagner and others (1952), who report a correlation of −.42 between mean job satisfaction scores and accident rates on a railroad, suggest that the direction of causation is in fact the reverse of what the psychoanalytically inclined might infer. They suggest that it is not that persons who are unhappy have more accidents as a defense against unpleasant work situations, but rather that those that have accidents are likely very soon to become unhappy about their jobs.

Lastly, we come to the enormous literature on the relationship between job satisfaction and job performance. That literature can be summarized roughly in one sentence: no clear relationship has been shown between job satisfaction and job performance. The major reviews of this literature (Brayfield and Crockett, 1955; Herzberg and others, 1957) lead one to the conclusion that these clearly are multivariate phenomena. When workers are satisfied with their jobs they may increase productivity (for example, if they feel that they have a common interest with management or are otherwise positively disposed to support the goals of management). On the other hand, if there is satisfaction, then, precisely for that reason, workers will not feel that they ought to increase their productivity. Some studies also suggest that a moderate amount of dissatisfaction is necessary as a motivator to increase effort. On the other hand, there may not be any obvious relationship to size of effort but merely that the effort will be different. For example, creative solutions of problems may or may not involve less effort, or more productivity.

Looking back over the findings on the relationship between task and stress as reflected in those factors that seem to be associated with job satisfaction, turnover, absenteeism, accidents, and performance, no clear findings emerge and it would be hazardous to attempt to single out any relationship as being supported by any large amount of evidence. Rather, one is impressed with the fact that most studies are overly simple in design and that there is no particular reason to expect findings when variables are being examined two at a time as is true in practically all of these studies. A second major problem about such studies is that a very high proportion are carried out in the laboratory in the interests of controlling variables, but that corresponding attempts to study the phenomena in industry are far less successful. Consequently, one is left with grave uncertainty about the stressful effect of work in real situations when it is not clear at all that the variables examined in the laboratory are present. Third, the findings, even when they occur, are overwhelmingly of a very small degree. It is very rare for any correlation to exceed .5. Some researchers defend this general result by asserting that there are "many factors" involved in task stress. With this claim there can hardly be any argument, but it leads one to ask why, if this is the case, researchers go on examining only one factor at a time. On the whole, one is not greatly impressed with the relationship between task and stress as a fruitful area of inquiry. The findings seem much less impressive, in spite of the enormous amount of research, than those in which the work is related to unemployment of the career.

Organization structure stress. When we turn to look at the structure of relationships among persons within organizations, we may conveniently divide the available research materials relating to stress into two major groups: studies of microrelationships, or those in-the-small, and studies concerned with the organization as a whole.

Micro studies may be grouped into two kinds: those dealing with interaction, and those dealing with role conflict. Studies of work interaction received their major impetus from the classic experiments of Elton Mayo and his colleagues at the Western Electric Corporation in the 1920's. Their work led to a great emphasis on the importance of the informal group and interpersonal relationships, and also to the development of management training programs, in which it was assumed that a basic reason for difficulties and stresses was that persons in organizations did not understand each other and needed to communicate with each other more effectively. That assumption has been severely disputed in recent years. For example, one careful study (Kerr and Siegel, 1954) of time lost due to strikes in a large number of industries in eleven Western countries concluded by casting severe doubt on the role of interpersonal communication skills in explaining these interindustry differences. Rather, certain characteristics of the structure of the industry, particularly the position of the worker in society, explained far more than did any interpersonal differences in communication skills.

The interest in the small group has continued, however, and there have been a number of studies of the impact of interactional variables. A major hypothesis was advanced by Homans (1950): "If the frequency of interaction between two or more persons increases, the degree of their liking for one another will increase, and vice versa." In work situations this would mean that the greater the extent to which the work groups that people found themselves in permitted interaction, then the more the workers would like each other or be attracted to each other. Further, if they found one another's company pleasing, they would also find cooperation and other of the pains associated with working together to be less stressful. There is some evidence to support Homans. Worker satisfaction with jobs is found to be related to the opportunity for interaction with others on the job. For example, Walker and Guest (1952, p. 76) state that "Isolated workers disliked their jobs and gave social isolation as the principle reason." Similarly Richards and Dobryns (1957) report that the morale of a group of workers in an insurance company was greatly lowered by a change which restricted their opportunity for social interaction. Large work groups have been shown to have lower cohesiveness or morale than have smaller ones. Some have inferred from these results that smaller groups offer greater opportunities for intimate interaction than do large groups, which are often likely to be more formalized.

On the whole, the evidence hence seems to support Homans, and the criticisms of the hypothesis have represented misunderstanding of it. For example, Vroom, Cartwright, and Zander maintain "There is no convincing evidence, however, that interaction which is unpleasant will make persons better like one another (Vroom, 1964, p. 120)." This, in turn, has led to a number of inquiries into the conditions of interaction that do in fact lead to interpersonal liking. We shall turn to that literature presently, but here we note that it is entirely irrelevant to the question, for Homans pointed out that increase in frequency of interaction would be associated with liking for one another, *provided the increase was voluntary*. The explanation is simply that if persons discover that they dislike each other, they will stop interacting with each other, and thus frequency of interaction does reflect feelings towards one another. It has nothing to do with the question of whether they find one another pleasant or not. This effect can only occur where the interaction is voluntary. Where it is involuntary, as, for example, in the relationship between a supervisor and a subordinate, then no relationship between frequency of interaction and liking for one another is shown.

In attempting to explain what it is about interaction that persons may find pleasant or unpleasant, some investigators have suggested that persons with similar attitudes will find one another's company pleasant. The findings are mixed on this subject and there is no clear conclusion. On the other hand, those studies that have sought a relationship between personal satisfaction with group membership and being liked by other group members have been much more successful. It has also been shown that where persons have a job that requires that they cooperate in order to attain a common end, they are more likely to like one another and to have other positive feelings toward one another (Deutsch, 1949).

Studies of role conflict in work situations are not extensive, although there is a good deal of anecdotal literature on this subject. The classic case that has been referred to by many is that of the foreman who is conceived of as the man in the middle, subject to conflicting pulls from his subordinates, who expect him to look after them and take care of their needs, and his superiors, who expect him to interpret company policy and act as a member of management. One would expect such conflict to be stressful, and there is some slight evidence that foremen so experience it. Strauss and Sayles, (1967), however, suggest that a more serious problem for the foreman has been the attrition of his power due to the increase in the power of the personnel department, the coming of labor unions, and other causes. These do not result in role conflict, but simply in a reduction in power that may, in turn, have stressful consequences.

The most intensive and careful study of what the authors call "role conflict" has been carried out by Kahn and his associates (1964). They conducted a national survey to determine the amount of role conflict in the population, and did an intensive study in seven industrial locations in the oil, automobile, electronics, and machine parts industries. The latter involved the selection of fifty-three "focal offices." These consisted of male occupants of positions of foreman or higher. The investigators examined the relationship of each focal person to those with whom he had regularized job relationships (who are known as "role senders"). The national survey showed that the experience of role conflict is common. Almost half of the respondents reported being caught "in the middle" between two conflicting persons or factions. Most of these conflicts are hierarchal, involving someone above them in the organization. Less than half report conflicts in which one of the parties is outside the organization altogether.

The intensive study of the fifty-three focal persons resulted in the conclusion that role conflict had definite emotional costs and resulted in low job satisfaction, low confidence in the organization, and a high degree of job-related tension. Persons who experience such conflict withdraw or avoid those who are seen as aiding the conflict. The conflicted person will reduce communication with his co-workers, and perhaps assert that they lack power over him. This mechanism, however, does not solve the problem but often makes things worse, since interaction is required with the role senders to produce results.

The authors also examined the impact of role ambiguity and found results that were essentially comparable. Role ambiguity includes uncertainty about the way in which one's supervisor evaluates one's work, opportunities for advancement, scope of responsibility, and the expectations of others regarding one's performance (each of these areas of ambiguity being mentioned by approximately one-third of the respondents). Consequences of ambiguity for the individual were also low job satisfaction, low self-confidence, a high sense of futility, and a high level of tension. These results are not uniform, however, and appear to depend on the source of ambiguity. For example, ambiguity regarding the evaluations of others does not decrease the intrinsic satisfaction of the employee with the job, although it does decrease self-confidence and weaken his positive affect for co-workers. The authors also examine organizational determinants of conflict and ambiguity, finding them to be the requirement for crossing organizational boundaries, the requirements for producing innovative solutions to nonroutine problems, and the requirements for being responsible for the work of others. For example, the frequency and importance of making contacts outside of one's company are associated with experience of role conflict. The authors conclude with the recommendation that because of the widespread occurrence of role conflict and its association with interactive opportunities, a firm should do what it can to reduce the sheer amount of interaction as a way of reducing the possibility of occurrence of role conflict, which appears to be endemic to organized effort as such.

Although the Kahn study is unique in its coverage and in the care with which it was carried out, and although it provides data in an area in which such data are relatively scarce, it is marred by certain methodological difficulties as well as theoretical ones. In the treatment of role conflict (pp. 19–21), a number of types of role conflict are distinguished: intrasender, intersender, inter-role, person-role, and role overload. In the national survey, questions were asked that got directly at these types, and thus the authors are able to present the survey information they offer (pp. 55–60): 48 percent report inter-sender conflict, 45 percent feel they have too heavy a workload (though why this is necessarily a kind of conflict is hard to say; it could be self-imposed, it could be due to machine breakdown or peaks which are no one's fault or intention, etc.), 45 percent report feeling they have to do things against their better judgment (presumably person-role), and a third are disturbed by the extent to which their jobs interfere with their family life (inter-role).

It should be noted, however, that all of these data are not forms of "objective" role conflict, as the authors define such conflict, but of experienced conflict. When they come to the analysis of role conflict (pp. 65 ff.), they now use only objective role conflict data, and that kind of data is quite difficult to interpret. After a discussion of the types of role conflict (pp. 19–21), the authors conclude that all types have in common this characteristic: "members of a role set exert role pressures to change the behavior of a focal person (p. 21)." Having so concluded, they then use, as a measure, a set of questions that yield a single "role conflict index" (Appendix C, pp. 411 ff.).[7] In sum, the "role conflict" faced by a focal person is an average of the extent to which his role senders wish him to act differently. It is difficult to say just what this corresponds to, in conceptual terms, but it is certainly not the same as "role conflict" as that concept is used in sociology. They seem to be measuring something that could be called, simply, "pressure to change behavior," which seems to be close to "influence attempts."

However, even if we substitute for "role conflict" the phrase "pressure to change" the case that the authors seek to make for the harmful effects of pressure to change is not proven, for two main reasons. First, pressure to change ("role conflict") is not found to be closely related to "intensity of experienced conflict." The p value is less than .07. Unless one argues that persons do not experience conflict even when they are in the middle of it, this result raises the question of the validity of their measure. Second, the authors assume the following direction of causality: pressure to change produces tension, low trust, low respect, dislike, low communication frequency, and low power attributed to others (such are the findings). Actually, the reverse is quite as plausible, or there may be a third variable at work. Tension between subordinates and a focal person, low trust, low respect, etc., may result in pressure on him to change. The study of Kahn and others, hence, does not establish a case for the "negative costs" of conflict.

7. This measure is in four parts and consists essentially of (1) extent to which a role sender would like a focal person to do his job differently; (2) extent to which a role sender would like the focal person to allot his time among his job activities differently; (3) extent to which the role sender would like the focal person "to be different from the way he is now" (open-ended); and (4) extent to which focal person fits a 22-trait list in terms of sender's conception of the ideal trait list for the focal person's job (traits included "shy," "self-confident," "excitable," "cheerful," "ambitious," "carefree," "easygoing," etc.).

Stress impacts of the organization as a whole. We turn, last, to the widespread attempt to show that there is something about organizations as such which have serious and harmful effects on individuals in organizations. Within recent years a growing number of critics of modern organization have called attention to what they feel are the great costs of organization in the form of pressures on the individual and restrictions on his creativity (Argyris, 1957; Herzberg, 1960; Maier, 1955; Maslow, 1954; McGregor, 1960; Whyte, 1956). The claim that organizations have harmful effects on the individual has been called by Strauss (1963) the "personality-versus-organization theory."

The basic principles of this theory can be stated as follows: It is assumed that humans have certain needs they carry into all situations that confront them. There are many schemes of needs but the most popular is that put forth by Maslow (1943), to whom I alluded earlier. He claims that there are five needs arranged in a hierarchy as follows:

5. self-actualization
4. esteem
3. social satisfaction
2. safety
1. physical well-being

It is maintained that a higher need does not motivate unless all of the lower needs below it are satisfied. Further, once a need is satisfied it no longer motivates the individual. Physical needs must be satisfied first. Once these are satisfied, in our society, usually through gainful employment, the person will become more concerned with his other needs. He will be concerned with safety by seeking security through seniority and other fringe benefits. Once these needs are realized he can turn to his needs for friendship and group support. It is assumed, then, that hungry men have little interest in whether or not their working companions are satisfactory. One must be relatively well-off before one even begins to worry about such things. When all of the lower needs are satisfied, the person can turn to the highest one of all: self-actualization. This need is not described with clarity but it is the need that occupies the greatest attention of these thinkers. Maslow himself describes self-actualization as "the desire to become more and more what one is, to become everything one is capable of becoming . . . a musician must make music, an artist must paint, a poet must write, if he is to be ultimately happy. What a man *can* be he *must* be (1943, p. 372)."

It is maintained that healthy persons desire to mature. Maturing means moving up the hierarchy of needs; that is, not being satisfied to take care only of the needs for physical well-being or safety. Being completely mature means taking care of the need to actualize one's self through creativeness, autonomy, the use of discretion, independence, and thus to express one's unique personality with freedom.

The attempt on the part of a person to express his unique personality runs into severe opposition from organizations, particularly large-scale organizations. By definition, organizations seek to reduce discretion and creativity, to control and direct behavior. In opposition to a person's needs, organizations demand conformity, obedience, and dependence, and hence keep the person at an immature level. The favorite citations are studies of assembly-line workers, engineers, and the business executive and manager. The latter has, perhaps, been most celebrated because of the popularity of the work by Whyte (1956) which gave birth to the phrase the "organization man." Whyte maintains that the emphasis on conformity and obedience is found not only in organizations but infects the entire society, child-rearing techniques, literature, residential practices, and government and political ideologies as well.

Since these needs continue to press for satisfaction, the attempt to frustrate them will produce various pathological reactions. Some persons will fight back. They will exhibit sabotage, output restriction, union activity, and other forms of rational as well as aggressive behavior. Others will withdraw, regress, engage in childish behavior, or try to do as little work as they can. Management therefore finds that even to bring workers up to minimum standards it must impose still more restrictions. It will install a rule which says "Obey all rules" and attempt to secure obedience to that rule. This produces even more disobedience, and so on, in a vicious circle. For some, the pressure may become so great that they break down and exhibit various forms of mental disturbance or psychosomatic disorders. The result is a great battle between the organization and the individual to get the latter to alter his personality; of course, since the needs are unalterable, the person must fight back or collapse.

Those who present the picture that we have just given suggest various alternatives. In the main, since they lay the blame for this presumed state of affairs at the door of the organization, they insist that it is the organization that must do the changing, on the assumption that individual needs are invariable. An example of the approach suggested is that offered by Herzberg and his colleagues (1960), discussed above. It will be recalled that they distinguish between dissatisfiers (also called "hygienic factors") and satisfiers (also called "motivating factors"). Hygienic factors refer to harmonious interpersonal relations, good working conditions, good wage and salary, enlightened company policies, and administrative practices, various benefits, and job security. Motivating factors consist of challenging work, autonomy, and interesting work (these come close to self-actualization in work). Herzberg maintains that if the hygienic factors are provided, all that will happen will be that the employees will not be unhappy; they will not, however, be motivated to produce at a high level. If deprived of these factors, they will complain and feel dissatisfied. On the other hand, if these are provided they will simply feel that this is no more than their due; hygienic factors take care of only the lower needs and do not touch the need for self-actualization. Herzberg maintains that one must provide the motivating factors if one wishes high production.

The way in which one can solve the organization individual dilemma is therefore to promote intrinsic job satisfaction, individual development, and work creativity. Employees thus will willingly work toward organization objectives because they enjoy their work and it enables them to develop. Specifically this calls for job enlargement, general supervision, decentralization, and participation by employees in decision-making.

This position is becoming increasingly popular. It is essential, therefore, to attempt to balance the picture by pointing out that in their attempts to criticize the impact of organizations on the individual, theorists present as unbalanced a picture as do the enthusiasts for organization who pay no attention to its unhappy effects. Strauss (1963) presents a critique of the position that helps to balance the picture. First, Strauss points out, the personality-versus-organization theorists are guilty of overemphasis on the uniqueness of the problem in large organizations. There is an inevitable conflict between the individual and the group, the individual and environment, between desire and reality. This is not to be laid at the door of large-scale organization, but is rather the consequence of the discipline required by *any* form of organized activity. Insofar as one desires the goals of such organized activity, one must agree to submit to whatever discipline is necessary to reach those goals.

The best place to observe the tyranny of organization over the individual is *not* in the large organization, but in the small group, as exemplified by the family, the small town, a group of friends, a fraternity, the clique. These are the groups that do not tolerate any variation, any deviation from the values or from the party line. In a very real sense, then, organizations offer a major protection from this tyranny through the very rules to which the personality-versus-organization theorists object. Rules, after all, are the considered solutions for recurring problems. Rules do restrict the individual but they also protect him from arbitrary action and the invasion of privacy. Knowing what the rules are he must obey them, but once having obeyed them he knows that his obligations to the group are fulfilled. On the other hand, in situations where rules do not exist, the person is placed in the position of dependence on other persons. He never knows when he has satisfied them and consequently can enjoy no sense of relief at knowing he has done his job. His job will be done when others say it is done and not any sooner. Such a tyranny is equivalent to slavery.

A second criticism of the personality-versus-organization position is its tendency to exaggerate the limitations of large organizations on personal freedom and on the sense of autonomy. There is a considerable literature on alienation dealing with the sense of powerlessness of the worker in the face of large-scale standardized industry and organization. Often a comparison is made between the old-time craftsmen who did the whole job and the mass production worker today. This is an unfair comparison. Actually only a very small proportion of the workers in the middle ages were craftsmen, so that what one is doing is comparing the best conditions of the middle ages to the worst conditions of modern times. During the middle ages the typical worker was a peasant who was little better than a working beast. It is certainly doubtful that the medieval serf or the Egyptian slave enjoyed much of a sense of autonomy or creativity.

We do not have data on historical shifts in job satisfaction, but there have been a large number of studies in recent years. The average percentage expressing dissatisfaction with their jobs is only 13 percent. Further, this median has fluctuated between 12 and 13 percent for over a decade. Of course, these studies differ in degree of sophistication and controls, but when one has a large number of studies they begin to assume considerable validity. One can, of course, quarrel with the general conclusion of such studies, which is that most workers are satisfied with their jobs. It is difficult to get reliable data on job satisfaction. In addition, in our society there is a strong tendency for persons to express satisfaction with their jobs. Because of the importance of work to the individual, to express dissatisfaction with one's job simply raises the question of why one does not change it. In spite of the questions that could be raised, however, if the worker is supposed to be such a miserable, alienated, unhappy wretch, then the evidence certainly does not support it. The evidence is overwhelmingly the other way. The supporters of alienation theory, therefore, will have to offer evidence; the burden of proof is on them.

A third criticism has to do with how universal, in fact, is the need for self-actualization. It is difficult to separate the objective elements from the biases and value judgments of those holding the position. They make use of terms such as "individual dignity," "creative freedom," "self-development," and the like, which often are items in a set of beliefs rather than objective findings. Strauss suggests that the emphasis on such values betrays the academic origin of this theory, for such matters as creativity are particularly dear to academicians. The majority of the population probably does not share these values, and probably would not be happy at all in academic positions. From this point of view the theory starts where it ought to finish. The claim is made that self-actualization is universal. Actually it should be offered as a *conclusion* from many empirical studies rather than as a flat assertion. The claim could certainly be made that for most persons security and predictability, especially in their work, are more important than self-actualization. That does not mean they do not desire self-actualization, but that they may secure it in their families, their recreation, or in other areas, and not necessarily in their work.

Even if self-actualization were essential, there would be little one could do to provide it for a high proportion of the population. If persons possess feelings of dependence, these surely have been internalized and become part of their reaction patterns. Intensive psychotherapy would be required to produce any change. To throw such a person into challenging situations would be terrifying to him and might very well increase his dependence. Furthermore, the findings of the impact of organization on mental health do not give much comfort to the personality-versus-organization theorist. Actually, disturbances of mental health and psychosomatic disorders are found throughout industry and in all positions; they are found in some of their most intense forms among scientists and other professionals, and among managers who have more opportunity than most to realize their creative needs. A major study by Hinkle (1963) and his associates of the lifetime health patterns of 3,000 persons suggests that those persons who are changing jobs, who are moving up the ladder, and who are presented with the most challenging opportunities are *most* likely to suffer from various mental disorders and other disturbances, rather than those who are dependent and conformist.

A fourth criticism is the tendency of the theory to overemphasize the importance of work to the individual. Clearly, if the organization has such a great impact on needs, it would have to be an important part of the individual's life. A person would permit these horrors to be perpetrated on him only if his work were very important to him. This does happen in some professions or occupations where the sense of vocation or mission is very strong, but in most organizations nothing like any great change of one's personality is really demanded and the job is not nearly so important to the individual. The central focus of a man's life may be not his job but his home or community (Dubin, 1956; Orzack, 1959).

The theory tends to underemphasize economic rewards. In the attempt to offset the traditional overemphasis on money as the major motivator, the theory goes to the other extreme. In Herzberg's work, money is listed as one of the hygienic factors rather than as one of the motivators, yet certainly money is a means for the satisfaction of all of the needs, whatever they are. Furthermore, it is not unimportant even in the professions; it is necessary to pay professionals a great deal of money in order to be sure that their work will not be influenced by money. There is little evidence that money ever ceases to be a motivator, no matter what one's needs may be.

Finally, the supporters of this position argue on the relative costliness of the organization's impact on the individual. They argue that failing to satisfy needs is costly both to the individual and to the organization. Presumably then, self-actualization or autonomy, if provided, would cost less. The cost claim is most interesting. The values of the personality-versus-organization analysts revolve around autonomy, freedom, self-actualization, challenge, and achievement. These all have a strongly democratic ring. To make it even more obvious, they devalue autocratic, authoritarian structures. If these theorists, therefore, simply said that one *should* provide workers with more challenge or autonomy, because that is consistent with democratic values, then one could not argue with them. They do not say that, however, nor can they. If they were to rest their case on such an assertion, then this would not be a scientific theory but a program for the organization. Instead, they say that one should provide more challenge and autonomy because it is *more efficient* to do so. One can examine the truth of that claim.

They claim that traditional organization methods lead to dissatisfaction, anxiety, and aggression, or to dependency, conformity, and doing only a minimum of work. The implication is that these are costly or harmful to the individual and the organization. How costly are they, in fact? There is no question that, if carried to excess, anxiety, dissatisfaction, and aggression are costly, but a certain amount of them are not only unavoidable but necessary and helpful. Anxiety is the means whereby the individual is mobilized for action. Aggression is normal and healthy when the individual is confronted with threat. Dissatisfaction occurs when one begins in making changes, including those that are absolutely essential.

It is harder to make a positive case for dependency and conformity, but even there it is easy to exaggerate the possible cost gains from independence and creativity. On many jobs creative and original persons are a positive liability. The outstanding illustration would be assembly-line work. Here one does not want the worker to demonstrate initiative. One does not want him to work faster, nor does one want him to work slower. One wants him simply to work according to an established pace. Creativity, then, is not always desirable. In fact, most organizations, by their very nature, involve a set of prescriptions for role behavior and these involve expectations as to what each person is supposed to do. He may exercise some initiative but only within certain limits. So it is in the conduct of an orchestra. If each person attempted to exercise his own initiative in the playing of a symphony, wholesale chaos would result. Nor would persons necessarily feel better for having satisfied personal needs.

If one looks more closely at organizations, one discovers that there is creativity, originality, and self-development being exhibited continually. For example, the worker who restricts output, who attempts to hide original contributions he might make to management, who works very hard to save a half hour which he can then spend loafing, is in fact demonstrating originality. Similarly, those who spend their time in industry battling for a better power position and playing politics are also demonstrating originality and expressing their creativity, although it may be expressed in such a form as reducing someone else's chance for promotion or getting an undesirable person pushed out of the way or even fired. When this is pointed out, many supporters of the personality-versus-organization theory claim that that is not the *kind* of originality of which they are speaking. To insist that one is only talking of *desirable* originality is to beg the whole question, however, for then one will have conceded that the organization does *not* squash the individual. The problem then becomes: How does one get persons to behave in the way in which one wishes?—and that is essentially a problem in social control and not one in creativity or in the frustration of personal needs.

In sum, the personality-versus-organization theory errs insofar as it

overstates its case. It is indeed true that organizations have an impact
on the persons in them and that they do not attain their remarkable
goals free of any cost. Some of these costs are undesirable and should
certainly be eliminated or reduced as far as possible. They will not
be eliminated completely, however, unless one is willing to give up
the organizations themselves and the goals that they enable us to
attain.

CONCLUSION

Work in Western society and perhaps everywhere presents the individual with a dilemma. By definition, it is disciplining insofar as
the rational pursuit of desired goals involves restraining impulses
and controlling emotions so that they are payed out at desired times
and in desired places. The dilemma, therefore, is that the very
disciplining will inevitably be stressful. This will be true whether
the stress takes the form of risks to the individual's career, difficulties
he experiences in performing a task as desired, or problems he
encounters in relationships with other persons because of the need
to coordinate effort in organization. But organizations are the dominant means Western industrialized societies have adopted to attain
almost all of their larger ends, and consequently they are the major
means of avoiding the serious stresses to which persons in other
cultures (or those that attempt to stay outside of organizations) are
subject to. Thus organizations are the major means of protecting us
from enemies, for healing the sick, for insuring continued high standards of living, for insuring the production of goods and services we
desire, for mass education in democratic society. Without organizations, providing our level of wants and expectations remains what it
is, clearly the amount of stress would be far greater than it is, insofar
as stress is conceived as the condition associated with the anticipated
deprivations associated with threat. Work in its organized form, then,
is stressful, and yet is the major means that modern society offers for
preventing or avoiding even greater stress.

Perhaps the most general conclusion we can draw is that since
organizations appear to be inevitable as ways for insuring the attainment of most of our larger desires, and since no alternative way of
attaining them appears to be available, a major type of socialization
of the young ought to include methods for dealing with the organizations that they will spend most of their lives in. This subject is
usually neglected in formal education and tends also to be neglected
by youth counselors. For example, life in an organization means a
position in a hierarchy of authority. An important consideration in

the preparation of individuals for work should include training for the handling of or adjustment to authority. Authority can be different kinds – charismatic (based on personal devotion to a leader of remarkable qualities), traditional, legal-bureaucratic (based on rules or what may be thought to be the rights that inhere in a particular position), or expert (based upon the reputation of the person who wields authority). Different types of background and different types of values will mean that the individual who has difficulty with one kind of authority may be quite at home with a different kind. There is certainly no simple relation between personality and authority although, of course, certain persons have difficulty with authority of any kind. Organizations may be analyzed in terms of the kind of structure they provide, but no organization is devoid of some kind of assumptions of authority. Organizations are always coordinated structures and this means that some persons must make critical decisions on work flow and on the manner in which the various parts of the organization will be articulated.

Another major feature of organization for which persons can be trained is working by routine. Organizations are typically places that assume they know how to attain their goals, and consequently much of the work will inevitably go by routine. Persons can be trained in the handling of routine. On the other hand, organizations always have unsolved problems and have need for creative original solutions. At the same time, precisely because organizations assume they have solved most of the problems, they will not necessarily respond to creative and original solutions. Thus, the scientist or researcher can expect opposition, but that should not lead him to believe that such opposition is malicious or that conditions are necessarily better anywhere else. Organizations offer too much in the way of facilities, fellow professionals, and other kinds of help for the researcher to think that he can retire to some laboratory of the type preferred by the mad scientists on the late show on television.

The training of the young should include training in job shifting and handling demotion when it occurs. Other important changes are necessary to enable persons to make those shifts, such as aid to persons in changing jobs, the provision of subsidies for migration, and other forms of assistance.

There seems no alternative to organizations. They inevitably have built-in stress, and future research as well as the efforts of public authority should deal with attempts to keep such stress at a minimal level. What that minimum is is not known. It is certainly greater than zero.

REFERENCES

ABEGGLEN, J.C. 1958. *The Japanese Factory: Aspects of Its Social Organization.* New York: Free Press.

ABEL, T. 1951. "The Sociology of Concentration Camps." *Social Forces,* 30: 150–155.

ADAMS, G. 1939. *Workers on Relief.* New Haven: Yale University Press.

ADLER, H. G. 1958. "Ideas toward a Sociology of the Concentration Camp." *American Journal of Sociology,* 63: 513–22.

ARGYRIS, C. 1957. *Personality and Organization.* New York: Harper.

BAKKE, E. W., 1939. *Citizens Without Work.* New Haven: Yale University Press.

BASOWITZ, H., PERSKY, H., KORCHIN, S. J., and GRINKER, R. R. 1955. *Anxiety and Stress.* New York: McGraw-Hill.

BECK, B. 1967. "Bedbugs, Stench, Dampness, and Immorality: A Review Essay on Recent Literature about Poverty." *Social Problems,* 15 (Summer): 101–14.

BECKER, H.S. 1967. "History, Culture, and Subjective Experience: An Exploration of the Social Bases on Drug-Induced Experiences." *Journal of Health and Social Behavior,* 8:163–76.

BEHREND, H. 1953. "Absence and Labour Turnover in a Changing Economic Climate." *Occupational Psychology,* 27:69-79.

BENDIX, R., and LIPSET, S. M. 1952. "Social Mobility and Occupational Career Plans: II, Social Mobility." *American Journal of Sociology,* 57: 494–504.

BENEDICT, R. 1934. *Patterns of Culture.* Boston: Houghton Mifflin.

BETTELHEIM, B. 1960. *The Informed Heart.* Glencoe, Ill.: Free Press.

BIDERMAN, A.D. 1963. *March to Calumny: The Story of American POW's in the Korean War.* New York: Macmillan.

BJERNER, V., HOLM, A., AND SWENSSEN, A. 1948. "Om Nott – Och Shiftavhete, Stockholm, Statnes Offenttiga Utredningar 51, 1948," cited in C. E. Dankert and others, eds., *Hours of Work.* New York: Harper, p. 117.

BRAYFIELD, A. H., AND CROCKETT, W.H. 1955. "Employee Attitudes and Employee Performance." *Psychological Bulletin,* 52:396–424.

BROPHY, A.L. 1959. "Self, Role, and Satisfaction." *Genetic Psychology Monographs,* 59:263–308.

BUCK, P.S. 1936. *Fighting Angel.* New York: Reynal and Hitchcock.

CAPLOW, T. 1955. "L'adaptation a la retraite chez les travailleurs de l'industries," communication to the Industry Sociology Group (Centre d'Etudes Sociologiques), 4, March 1955, cited in G. Friedmann, *The Anatomy of Work.* New York: Free Press, 1961, p. 130.

COHEN, E. A., 1954. *Human Behavior in the Concentration Camp.* New York: Norton.

DANKERT, C.E., MANN, F.C., AND NORTHRUP, H.R. eds. 1965. *Hours of Work.* New York: Harper.

DEUTSCH, M. 1949. "An Experimental Study of the Effects of Co-operation and Competition upon Group Process." *Human Relations*, 2:199–231.

DUBIN, R. 1956. "Industrial Workers' Worlds: A Study of the Central Life Interests of Industrial Workers." *Social Problems*, 3:131–42.

EISENBERG, P., and LAZARSFELD, P. F. 1938. "The Psychological Effects of Unemployment." *Psychological Bulletin*, 35:358–90.

FREUD, S. 1930. *Civilization and Its Discontents*. London: Hogarth Press.

FRIEDMANN, G. 1961. *The Anatomy of Work*. New York: Free Press.

GALBRAITH, J. K. 1967. *The New Industrial State*. Boston: Houghton Mifflin.

GARFINKEL, H. 1959. "Common Sense Knowledge of Social Structures." *Transactions of the Fourth World Congress of Sociology*, vol. 4, pp. 51–65. Milan.
    1964. "Studies in the Routine Grounds of Everyday Activities." *Social Problems*, 11 (Winter): 235–50.
    1967. *Studies in Ethnomethodology*. Englewood Cliffs, N.J.: Prentice-Hall.

GLASER, B. G., and STRAUSS, A. L. 1968. *Time for Dying*. Chicago: Aldine Publishing Company.

GLAZER, N., and MOYNIHAN, D. P. 1963. *Beyond the Melting Pot*. Cambridge, Mass.: M.I.T. Press and Harvard University Press.

GOLDNER, F. H. 1965. "Demotion in Industrial Management." *American Sociological Review*, 30:714–24.

GOULDNER, A.W. 1957–58. "Cosmopolitans and Locals: Toward an Analysis of Latent Social Roles." *Administrative Science Quarterly*, 2:281–306. 444–80.

GROSS, E. 1964. "Sources of Lateral Authority in Personnel Departments." *Industrial Relations*, 3 (May):121–33.
    1967. "When Occupations Meet: Professions in Trouble." *Hospital Administration*, 12 (Summer):40–59.
    1968. "Counseling Special Populations." *Employment Service Review*, 5 (Jan.-Feb.):14–19, 29.

GUEVARA, CHE. 1968. *Guerrilla Warfare*. New York: Vintage.

HALL, O. 1948. "The Stages of a Medical Career." *American Journal of Sociology*, 53:327–36.
    1949. "Types of Medical Careers." *American Journal of Sociology*, 55:243–53.

HERZBERG, F., MAUSNER, B., PETERSON, R. O., and CAPWELL, D. F. 1957. *Job Attitudes: Review of Research and Opinion*. Pittsburgh: Psychological Services of Pittsburgh.

HERZBERG, F., MAUSNER, B., and SNYDERMAN, B. 1959. *The Motivation to Work*. New York: John Wiley.

HINKLE, L. E., JR. 1963. "Physical Health, Mental Health and the Corporate Environment," ch. 11 in L. R. Salyes, ed., *Individualism and Big Business*. New York: McGraw-Hill.

HOMANS, G. C. 1950. *The Human Group.* New York: Harcourt Brace.

HORNEY, K. 1937. *The Neurotic Personality of Our Time.* New York: Norton.

HOWARD, A., and SCOTT, R. A. 1965. "A Proposed Framework for the Analysis of Stress in the Human Organism." *Behavioral Science,* 10:141–60.

KAHN, R.L., WOLFE, D.M., QUINN, R.P., and SNOEK, J.D. 1964. *Organizational Stress.* New York: John Wiley.

KERR, C., and SIEGEL, A. 1954. "The Interindustry Propensity to Strike — An International Comparison," ch. 14 in A. Kornhauser, R. Dubin, and A. M. Ross, eds., *Industrial Conflict.* New York: McGraw-Hill.

KOGON, E. 1946. *The Theory and Practice of Hell: The German Concentration Camps and the System behind Them.* New York: Berkeley.

KORNHAUSER, A. 1965. *Mental Health of the Industrial Worker.* New York: John Wiley.

LAZARUS, R.S. 1966. *Psychological Stress and the Coping Process.* New York: McGraw-Hill.

LEIGHTON, A.H. 1945. *The Governing of Men.* New York: Octagon.

LEWIN, K. 1956. "Studies in Group Decision," ch. 21 in D. Cartwright and A. Zander, eds., *Group Dynamics.* Evanston, Ill.: Row, Peterson.

LIFTON, R. J. 1961. *Thought Reform and the Psychology of Totalism: A Study of "Brainwashing" in China.* New York: Norton.

MARCH, J. G., and SIMON, H. 1958. *Organizations.* New York: John Wiley.

MARTIN, N. H., and STRAUSS, A. L. 1956. "Patterns of Mobility within Industrial Organizations." *Journal of Business of the University of Chicago,* 20:101–10.

MCGREGOR, D. 1960. *The Human Side of Enterprise.* New York: McGraw-Hill.

MAIER, N.R.F. 1955. *Psychology in Industry.* Boston: Houghton Mifflin.

MASLOW, A.H. 1943. "A Theory of Human Motivation," *Psychological Review,* 50:370–96.

——— 1954. *Motivation and Personality.* New York: Harper.

MECHANIC, D. 1962. *Students under Stress.* New York: Free Press.

——— 1968. *Medical Sociology.* New York: Free Press.

MERTON, R. K. 1949. "Social Structure and Anomie," in Ruth N. Anshen, ed., *The Family: Its Function and Destiny.* New York: Harper. Reprinted, with a supplementary essay, ch. 4 and 5, in R. K. Merton, *Social Theory and Social Structure.* Glencoe, Ill.: Free Press, 1957.

MORE, D.M. 1962. "Demotion." *Social Problems,* 9:213–21.

MOTT, P.E., MANN, F.C., MCLOUGHLIN, Q., and WARWICK, D.P. 1965. *Shift Work.* Ann Arbor: University of Michigan Press.

MURPHY, L. B., and Collaborators, 1962. *The Widening World of Childhood: Paths Toward Mastery.* New York: Basic Books.

ORZACK, L.H. 1959. "Work as a Central Life Interest of Professionals." *Social Problems*, 7:125–32.

PELZ, D.C. 1952. "Influence: A Key to Effective Leadership in the First-Line Supervisor." *Personnel*, 29:209–17.

PELZ, D.C., and ANDREWS, F.M. 1966. *Scientists in Organizations*. New York: John Wiley.

PIERARCH, A. 1955. "'Nachtarbeit and Schichtwechsel Beim Gesunden und Kranken Menschen." *Acta Medica Scandinavia*, supp. 307, pp. 159–66.

RICHARDS, C. B., and DOBRYNS, H. F. 1957. "Topography and Culture: The Case of the Changing Cage." *Human Organization*, 16 (Spring):16–20.

SCHEIN, E.H., SCHNEIER, I., and BARKER, C.H. 1961. *Coercive Persuasion*. New York: Norton.

SIMON, H. 1959. *Administrative Behavior*. New York: Macmillan.

SMELSER, N.J. 1963. *Theory of Collective Behavior*. New York: Free Press.

STAGNER, R., FLEBBE, D.R., and WOOD, E.F. 1952. "Working on the Railroad." *Personnel Psychology*, 5:293–306.

STRAUSS, G. 1963. "The Personality vs. Organization Theory," ch. 8 in L.R. Sayles, ed., *Individualism and Big Business*. New York: McGraw-Hill.

STRAUSS G., and SAYLES, L.R. 1967. *Personnel*, p. 391 ff. Englewood Cliffs, N.J.: Prentice-Hall.

SUDNOW, D. 1967. *Passing On*. Englewood Cliffs, N.J.: Prentice-Hall.

THIIES-EVENSEN, E. 1958. "Shift Work and Health." *Industrial Medicine*, 27:493–97.

TRIST, E.L., and BAMFORTH, K.W. 1951. "Some Social Psychological Consequences of the Longwall Method of Coal-Getting." *Human Relations*, 4:3–38.

VROOM, V.H. 1964. *Work and Motivation*. New York: John Wiley.

WALKER, C.R., and GUEST, R.H. 1952. *The Man on the Assembly Line*. Cambridge: Harvard University Press.

WATSON, G. 1942. "Morale during Unemployment," in G. Watson, ed., *Civilian Morale*. Boston: Houghton Mifflin.

WEBER, G.H. 1966. "Conflicts Between Professional and Nonprofessional Personnel in Institutional Delinquency Treatment," reprinted from a 1957 publication in H. M. Vollmer and D. L. Mills, eds., *Professionalization*. Englewood Cliffs, N.J.: Prentice-Hall.

WHYTE, W.F. 1961. *Men At Work*. Homewood, Ill.: Dorsey and Irwin.
1956. *The Organization Man*. New York: Simon and Schuster.

WILENSKY, H. L., and EDWARDS, H. 1959. "The Skidder: Ideological Adjustments of Downwardly Mobile Workers." *American Sociological Review*, 24:215–31.

WILENSKY, H.L. 1961. "The Uneven Distribution of Leisure: The Impact of Economic Growth on 'Free Time'." *Social Problems*, 9:32–56.

WOYTINSKY, W.S. 1942. *Three Aspects of Labor Dynamics*. Washington, D.C.: Social Science Research Council.

4. Class and Race as Status-Related Sources of Stress[1]

BARBARA SNELL DOHRENWEND AND BRUCE P. DOHRENWEND

DESPITE anecdotes about harried business executives and unhappy suburban housewives, most people would probably agree that conditions are more stressful for those at the bottom of our society than for those nearer the top. With least share in the available resources of society, persons of low status seem virtually guaranteed more than their share of misfortune.

Although an inverse relationship between social status and amount of stress seems obvious, the relationship is not easy to test—largely because of the complexity of the two major constructs

Barbara Snell Dohrenwend is associate professor of psychology at The City College of the City University of New York, and Bruce P. Dohrenwend is associate professor of social sciences in the Department of Psychiatry at the College of Physicians and Surgeons, Columbia University, New York.

1. This chapter has been adapted from pp. 3–5 and pp. 131–150 of Bruce P. Dohrenwend and Barbara Snell Dohrenwend, *Social Status and Psychological Disorder: A Causal Inquiry*, New York: Wiley, 1969. Grateful acknowledgment is made to John Wiley and Sons, Inc. for permission to use this material here.

involved. Before attempting to assess the evidence concerning this relationship, therefore, let us make explicit our conceptions of status and of stress.

RACE AND CLASS AS BASES FOR SOCIAL STATUS

In their description of social stratification in a major city in the Deep South before the second World War, Davis, Gardner, and Gardner (1958) wrote of the distinction between the white and Negro castes:

> The "caste line" defines a social gulf across which Negroes may not pass either through marriage or those other intimacies which Old City calls "social equality." A ritual reminder is omnipresent in all relationships that there are two separate castes — a superordinate white group and a subordinate Negro group (p. 371).

Within each of these two castes, the investigators point out, there were further distinctions:

> As one becomes acquainted with the white people of Old City, he soon realizes that they are continually classifying themselves and others. There are "Negroes" and "whites" — the caste groups — a relatively simple dichotomy. There are also "leading families," "fine old families," "the four hundred," "the society crowd," "plain people," "nice respectable people," "good people, but nobody," "po' whites," "red necks," etc. (pp. 371-72).

The importance of these distinctions, both within and between the two main castes, the investigators made clear, is that they described conceptions people had of their "place" in society and that, moreover, people tended to act in terms of these conceptions. These conceptions of place are important aspects of what we have referred to as social status.

In our analysis of social status as a source of stress, we shall limit our problem to the two most important bases for status in our own relatively open-class society. Class is one of these; the other is ethnicity. With regard to the latter, our focus will be on race because — given the history of racial prejudice in this country — it is the sharpest of the current ethnically based distinctions in our society. Aside from its importance as a basis for status, emphasis on race as well as class gives us a distinct methodological advantage. As a characteristic ascribed at birth, race anchors our analysis to a factor clearly antecedent to stress.

Let us distinguish more formally between the conception of class and status as we will be using them. Max Weber used the term "class situation" to describe the individual's "typical chance for a supply of goods, external living conditions, and personal life experiences, insofar as this chance is determined by the amount and kind of power or lack of such, to dispose of goods or skills for the sake of income in a given economic order (Gerth and Mills, 1946, p. 181.)."

In addition to his formulation of the concepts of class and class situation, Weber developed the ideas of "status situation" and "status group." He wrote: "In contrast to the purely economically determined 'class situation' we wish to designate as 'status situation' every typical component of the life fate of men that is determined by a specific positive or negative estimation of *honor*" (Gerth and Mills, 1946, pp. 186–187). As he pointed out, this honor or prestige may be connected with any quality shared by a plurality. Class is one such quality; ethnicity, especially as it is based on race, probably the only other in our own society that rivals class in importance.

The difference in such factors as class and race that determine differences in social prestige are accompanied by differences in what Weber terms "styles of life" (Gerth and Mills, 1946, pp. 187–188) — including place and type of residence, formal and informal associations, reading habits, leisure time activities, and, in some degree, beliefs and values. Note, then, what Weber means by "status groups" is quite similar to what some other students of social stratification such as Warner and others (1963, pp. 36–37) have meant by social class. Following Weber, we will keep conceptually distinct the notions of social class and social status, with the latter the more inclusive term. In this way, we shall be able to analyze both class and race as they contribute to status differences and hence to possible differences in the intensity of stress experienced by indivduals.

With race, we shall be concerned with differences between Negroes and whites. In the case of class, we shall be concerned with differences associated with indicators such as occupation, education, and income. We will, for the most part, make only the gross distinction between middle and lower class. While it may be that there are important intraclass differences, particularly between upper-lower and lower-lower (e.g., Cohen and Hodges, 1963), the available data do not permit a consistent breakdown at this more refined level. This is particularly true when we distinguish, as we shall, between classes within races. Moreover, the contrasts between middle and lower classes are sufficiently complex and extensive to justify the grosser analysis, even if some intraclass differences are lost.

THE CONCEPT OF STRESS

Stress is a term that has been used in different ways by different investigators (Janis, 1958, pp. 11–13; Lazarus, 1966, pp. 1–28.) Since there is no one accepted definition, let us say what we shall mean by stress for purposes of the present analysis. The framework that we propose is Selye's (1955) paradigm of the stress response, translated into social and psychological terms (Dohrenwend, 1961).

Selye views stress as a state of the organism that underlies both its adaptive and maladaptive reactions. His paradigm of the stress response contains four main elements: antecedent *stressor*, defined as any agent that produces stress—frequently a poison or electric shock in his physiological research with animals; antecedent *mediating factors* that increase or decrease the impact of the stressor—such as climate or diet; the *adaptation syndrome*, indicating an intervening state of stress in the organism—for example, nonspecific chemical changes; and consequent *adaptive* or, when there has been "derailment" of the mechanisms underlying the adaptation syndrome, *maladaptive* responses—such as, in Selye's examples, high blood pressure, or diseases of the heart and kidneys. This paradigm, as we have translated its main elements, is diagrammed in Figure 4.1. Within this framework, we view the intervening state of stress as essentially a condition of emotional arousal.

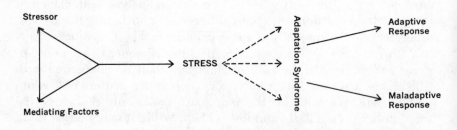

Fig. 4.1 – General paradigm of the stress response

Our concern in this chapter is with status-related sources of stress. Our focus, therefore, will be on the antecedent elements shown in Figure 4.1, the stressors and mediating factors as these are associated with the social status of the individual. We make only one assumption about the outcome variables shown in Figure 4.1; namely, that the greater the intensity *and* the duration of stress, the greater its severity and the likelihood of "derailment" of the mechanisms of adaptation. We will, therefore, attempt to evaluate sources of stress stemming from the individual's social status in terms of the likelihood that these antecedent factors will increase or decrease the intensity and the duration of the stress he experiences.

Major social stressors. Koos (1946), on the basis of his analysis of what "trouble" meant to respondents from a small sample of low-income families in New York City, made a distinction that partially anticipates our translation of Selye's formulation into social and psychological terms. "Troubles" are "situations outside the normal pattern of life . . . situations which block the usual patterns of activity and call for new ones (p. 9)." Such situations were distinguished from "exigencies" of life such as a month-to-month struggle to pay the rent.

We agree with much of Koos' formulation, since we define major social stressors as objective events that disrupt or threaten to disrupt the individual's usual activities. Unlike Koos' formulation, however, ours contains no necessary negative implication. Nor does the notion of stressors, as we use it, necessarily imply the subjective upset of "crisis" as used by such theorists as Lindemann (1944), Caplan (1964, esp. pp. 39–40,) and the Cummings (1962, esp. pp. 54–55). For example, an event that would be a small problem for most people may be a "crisis" for a psychiatric patient, if it arouses subjective distress. For present purposes, whether a stressor induces a "crisis" is an empirical question. We limit the term stressor to objective events. Moreover, we concentrate on *major* social stressors; that is, on those stressors that are likely to disrupt the customary activities of all or most normal individuals exposed to them.

Some stressors are relatively rare and restricted to limited populations—for example, natural disasters such as floods and tornadoes. Such events occur without reference to social status. They will, therefore, not concern us here.

In contrast, stressors such as marriage and birth of a first child are experienced by most people. Much has been written about the role of such stressors in "developmental crises" (e.g., Erikson, 1959), and we would expect their impact to be strongly affected by mediating factors associated with social status.

Another class of stressors is related to the fact that in our society upward mobility is the norm. The progression of ethnic groups over succeeding generations is from positions of lower to positions of higher social status. Within the life span of any given individual, however, the obstacles to such mobility are greater or lesser depending on such characteristics as race and class. Given our interest in status-linked sources of stress, therefore, it seems meaningful to distinguish between stressors that exert pressure on the individual to change from his customary activities to a new set of higher status activities, in contrast to events that exert pressure on him to change his customary activities to a new set of lower status activities. The former we shall term "achievement-related" events, for example, promotion. The latter, we shall call "security-related" events, for example, losing a job.

Since the same event can be classified both in terms of whether it is developmental or non-developmental, and in terms of whether it is achievement-related or security-related, we can start with the typology of major stressors shown in Table 4.1.

There are no a priori grounds for attributing greater intrinsic severity to one rather than another of the four types of major social

Table 4.1. Examples of four types of social stressors

	Developmental	*Non-developmental*
Achievement	Finish regular schooling	Training for new skills
	Obtain first adult job	Job promotion or business expansion
	Leave parental home	Assignment of non-job leadership responsibilities
	Marriage	Move to more prestigeful neighborhood
	Birth of first child	Nonroutine vacation
	Birth of later child	
	Marriage of child	
	Birth of grandchild	
Security	Unable to finish regular schooling	Failure in training course
	Unable to obtain first adult job	Job demotion or business failure
	Loss of job	Deprivation of non-job leadership responsibilities
	Jilted	Move to less prestigeful neighborhood
	Divorce	
	Death, illness or injury of breadwinner	
	Miscarriage	
	Illness, injury of death of child	
	Divorce of child	
	Illness, injury or death of grandchild	

stressors set forth in Table 4.1. Moreover, it seems certain that any given stressor can be more or less severe depending upon the context in which it occurs. Such context we referred to earlier as being supplied by the antecedent mediating factors associated with a particular stressor.

Antecedent mediating factors. To avoid confusion with the conditioning concepts of learning theory, we have substituted the term "mediating factors" for Selye's "conditioning factors" in our translation of the paradigm of the stress response shown in Figure 4.1. Selye discussed two different types of such factors — "internal," that is, those that have become part of the body through heredity, past experience, etc., and "external," that is, those factors acting from without, such as climate, which influence the response to a physical stressor such as a poison or electric shock that is simultaneously acting on the organism. In changing from Selye's focus on physical and chemical aspects of stress responses to their social and psychological aspects, we have maintained his basic distinction between *internal mediating factors* and *external mediating factors.*

Under internal mediating factors we include such characteristics of the individual as his abilities, drives, values and beliefs. External mediating factors consist of more or less adequate material resources, such as savings, and health facilities, as well as social support or opposition from primary groups consisting of family and friends (Hamburg and Adams, 1967).

We shall be concerned with mediating factors both as they increase or decrease the impact of stressors, and as they increase or decrease the duration of the effects of this impact on different status groups. Thus, among external mediating factors we shall be concerned, for example, not only with level of savings and other factors that define the person's situation at the time, say, of the impact of unemployment, but also with factors such as social support or rejection, which could mediate the duration of the emotional effects of unemployment. Similarly, among internal mediating factors we will be concerned not only with the individual's values that determine the severity of the loss suffered from the stressor, but also with his abilities, and his beliefs concerning his own abilities, which may determine the effectiveness of his response and hence the duration of the effects of a stressor.

STRESSORS

Social class. The hypothesis that there is an inverse relation between the amount of stress an individual experiences and his social class position implies that stressors are more common in the lower class. Evidence from census data concerning developmental security stressors seems to support this suggestion. The shorter life expectancy in the lower class (Mayer and Hauser, 1950; Moriyama and Guralnick, 1956, Tuckman and others, 1965) implies that families in this group are more likely to be disrupted by premature death of a parent (e.g., Langner and Michael, 1963, p. 161). The inverse relation between social class and rate of marital breakdown by divorce or separation (Bernard, 1966; Hollingshead, 1953; Udry, 1967) indicates that even when both parents survive, the lower-class family is less likely to remain intact.

Lower-class members are also likely to experience more developmental achievement stressors, because of their relatively high birth rate. Although higher birth rates in higher income groups have been reported, this finding may not be generalizable, for example, beyond the special conditions found in the university town that was the setting for one such study (Dice and others, 1964). The more general finding is that the highest birth rate is in the lowest social class (e.g., Duncan, 1964; Notestein, 1953). Furthermore, this stressor is more likely in the lower class to take the form of premature birth (Menchaca, 1964; World Health Organization, 1961).

Nondevelopmental stressors do not present an equally clear picture of relatively high rates in the lower class. For nondevelopmental security stressors, the evidence is mixed. Job loss or layoff is more likely to be the lot of the lower-class hourly wage worker than the middle-class salaried worker. Moreover, physical health is more often disrupted in lower-class persons by some diseases, such as cervical cancer (e.g., Paloucek and Graham, 1966), and by accidents and injuries to both adults (Haddon and others, 1964; Sanders, 1964) and children (Deutsch, 1961). On the other hand, many types of cancer (e.g., Paloucek and Graham, 1966), as well as disorders of the circulatory system (Marks, 1967), are no more common in the lower than in the middle class.

Furthermore, most nondevelopmental achievement stressors are probably almost entirely outside the experience of most lower-class members. Job promotions and business expansions are by their very nature almost exclusively middle-class stressors. In addition, it is characteristically the middle-class member who seeks or has thrust on him responsibilities for community organizations and activities. Even vacations, particularly when they involve extensive travel or other radical changes from usual living patterns, are more likely to impose stressors on the middle than the lower class.

On balance, the evidence concerning the relationship between social class and rates of stressors of all types is equivocal. While some types of stressors are more common in the lower class, others are equally common in all classes, and still others appear to be more frequently experienced by persons in higher class positions. To determine precisely how to weight these different patterns, it would be necessary to have data on the actual rates of the various types of stressors. One would, for instance, have to determine the frequency of layoffs in the lower class as against promotions and business expansions in the middle class. In the absence of such figures, the most reasonable conclusion seems to be that there is no firm evidence that the overall rate of stressors varies with social class.

Race. Previous writers have pointed out that many comparisons between whites and Negroes are misleading because they fail to control social class (e.g., Dreger and Miller, 1968; Pettigrew, 1964, p. 70). Since Negroes are on the whole poorer than whites, such uncontrolled comparisons may reveal differences that are entirely due to the class difference between the races. Although we found no clear evidence of class differences in overall rates of stressors, the fact that certain types of stressors are more frequent in one class or another means that we should ask whether the rates of stressors experienced by Negroes and whites differ when social class is controlled.

In his review of the literature on race differences, Pettigrew presented evidence that the higher rate of physical illness and shorter life expectancy among Negroes, while due primarily to the difference in average class status of Negroes and whites, cannot be explained entirely in these terms (1964, pp. 97–99). In particular, when the physical health of Negroes and whites in the lowest occupational groups is compared, Negro laborers are found to have relatively high rates of illness.

Lower class Negroes also experience higher rates of several other stressors, when compared to lower-class whites. Security is more often threatened not only by ill health but also, according to U.S. government statistics, by loss of employment (Shanahan, 1966), which is likely to be prolonged (Aiken and Ferman, 1966), and by disruption of marriage through divorce or separation (Bernard, 1966; Udry, 1966; Udry, 1967). Moreover, lower class Negroes more often suffer the developmental achievement stressors of premature or abnormal birth (Pasamanick and others, 1956). On the other hand, there appears to be no major category of stressor in which the rate for lower-class whites is higher than for lower-class Negroes.

The same generalization appears to be true for middle-class Negroes with respect to their white class counterparts. While there is no evidence of areas in which middle-class Negroes experience fewer stressors, they have higher rates of divorce and separation than their white class counterparts (Udry, 1966), and higher rates of premature and abnormal births (Pasamanick, and others, 1956). The evidence suggests that both lower-class and middle-class Negroes experience stressors more frequently than their white class counterparts.

EXTERNAL MEDIATING FACTORS

Social class. Insofar as the lower-class person attempts to deal with stressors by manipulation of objective conditions, he is disadvantaged with respect to external mediating factors, since his relatively small income makes him less able than a member of the middle class to command needed goods and services. For example, medical services available to the lower-class person are likely to be less adequate than those available to the middle-class person (e.g., Langer, 1966; Marden, 1966). Faced with the stressor of forced residential relocation, the lower-class person is likely to be offered less satisfactory alternative living quarters (Dohrenwend, 1961). Similarly, in almost any stressor situation, the lower-class person is likely to find that his leverage on agencies that might provide help is relatively weak.

Whether the lower-class person is also disadvantaged with respect to external factors that directly mediate his ability to adjust emotionally to a stressor is not so obvious. The question here is, first, whether there is any evidence of a class difference in the availability of social support to mediate the impact of a stressor. The data on shorter life expectancy (Mayer and Hauser, 1950) and relatively high rates of broken marriages in the lower class (Bernard, 1966; Hollingshead, 1953; Udry, 1966), cited earlier in discussing stressors, are also relevant here. Not only is the family disruption itself a stressor, but the lower-class person is more likely to face other stressors in the setting of a family in which one parent is missing. Even when the marriage is not broken, it appears that lower-class husbands and wives tend to behave toward each other in such a way as to provide relatively little mutual psychological support (e.g., Komarovsky, 1962, pp. 144–147, 156–159, 170–171; Rainwater, 1965). Furthermore, the lower-class person is less likely to be involved in voluntary organizations that might provide extrafamilial supportive relationships (Cohen and Hodges, 1963; Wright and Hyman, 1958).

The ability of an individual to adjust emotionally to a stressor depends not only on whether social support is available, but also on the extent to which others are tolerant of signs of emotional disturbance that deviate from everyday behavior. Studies of tolerance of deviance have presented contradictory conclusions with respect to class differences, suggesting that on some issues the lower class is more tolerant (e.g., Hollingshead and Redlich, 1958) and on others that it is less so (e.g., Stouffer, 1955). Some of these conclusions, however, have relied on questionable inferences (e.g., Hollingshead and Redlich, 1958). A recent study based on more direct evidence indicates that the lower-class person, while tending to define deviance in relation to emotional disturbance more narrowly, includes within his definition the types of deviant behavior most commonly observed among lower-class persons who are emotionally disturbed (Dohrenwend and Chin-Shong, 1967; Dohrenwend and Dohrenwend, 1969). Moreover, the lower-class person shows less tolerance than more educated persons toward behavior that both define as seriously deviant (Dohrenwend and Chin-Shong, 1967). Thus, it appears that the lower-class person faced with a stressor is both less likely to receive emotional support from his family, and, in addition, faces intolerant attitudes toward deviance from behavioral norms.

Race. The overriding issue here is the extent to which the disadvantaged group status of Negroes mediates the impact of stressors. Does racial prejudice, for instance, tend to alter the relations among the various components of class? For example, do Negroes who are at comparable levels with whites with respect to indicators of class other than income, also have the same income levels? In general, the occupations in which there are relatively high proportions of Negroes tend to yield low income (Hodge and Hodge, 1965; Taeuber and others, 1966[2]). Furthermore, there is evidence that at any level of education below college, Negroes' incomes are markedly lower than whites (Blau and Duncan, 1967; Dohrenwend, 1966; Hare, 1965; Levenson and McDill, 1966).

A second question concerning the external factors that mediate the impact of stressors on Negroes is whether, given a comparable income, a Negro can buy as much in goods and services as a white. With respect to many types of goods and services, the middle-class Negro is probably not particularly handicapped in most sections of the United States. A study of nine Negro families who moved into white middle class suburbs of Boston, however, indicates that this cannot be said of housing (Hughes and Watts, 1964). Although all were able to make the move, even a strong Massachusetts law

---

2. Although these two articles disagree on the cause of the relation between low income and high proportions of Negroes in certain occupations, the relationship itself is not in doubt.

against discrimination did not prevent some families from experiencing long delays, a factor which could prove a severe handicap
if the move were a nonvoluntary consequence of a stressor such as
forced relocation for slum clearance. Moreover, middle-class Negroes have been found to live in more crowded conditions than their
white class counterparts (Tulkin, 1968), and the general trend in the
United States seems to be toward a heightening of the barriers
excluding Negroes from nonghetto residential areas (Schnore and
Evenson, 1966; Farley and Taeuber, 1968; Taeuber and Taeuber,
1965). Thus, it appears unreasonable to assume that even
middle-class Negroes, if faced with a stressor that required a change
of residence, would not be more handicapped than their white class
counterparts.

The middle-class Negro is also relatively handicapped with respect to availability of social support to ameliorate the impact of
stressors. The finding, based on 1960 U.S. census data, of a relatively
high rate of family instability among middle-class Negroes (Bernard,
1966; Udry, 1966) implies that the Negro is more likely to face a
stressor in the context of a family from which one spouse is absent.

Lower-class Negroes also appear to be relatively handicapped,
compared to their white class counterparts, by external factors that
mediate the impact of stressors, except in one respect. Relative disadvantage for the Negro is implied, for example, by lower levels of
income at comparable levels of education below graduation from
college (e.g., Dohrenwend, 1966), by severe and increasing
restrictions on residential choice (Schnore and Evenson, 1966; Farley and Taeuber, 1968), and by relatively high rates of marital breakdown (Bernard, 1966; Udry, 1966). On the other hand, there is evidence from both local and nationwide studies that lower class Negroes have more extrafamilial sources of social support than lower
class whites. They are more likely to belong to organizations, and to
participate more actively in the organizations to which they belong
than their class counterparts among whites (Orum, 1966; Rainwater,
1965, p. 232). Furthermore, some of these organizations characterizing the Negro lower class are specifically designed to deal with the
stressor of death in the family (e.g., Davis and Dollard, 1940,
pp. 53-54). However, this one area of advantage does not seem
sufficient to counterbalance the lower-class Negro's relative disadvantage with respect to material conditions and familial stability.
Therefore, lower-class Negroes are probably more handicapped
overall than lower-class whites by external factors that mediate the
impact of stressors.

INTERNAL MEDIATING FACTORS

To investigate the question of whether class and racial groups differ with respect to internal mediating factors, we will draw on the extensive literature on group differences in abilities, motives, and values, with two restrictions. First, because we cannot assume long-term stability in either class differences (Bronfenbrenner, 1958), or race differences, we will emphasize recent work.

The second restriction arises from the fact that many studies comparing social class and racial groups use school children as subjects. If we were to extrapolate the results of these studies to adults, our conclusions would probably be in error for one of two reasons. In order to use studies whose subjects were young enough so that the entire population was in school, we would have to assume stability of both social class and personality from childhood to adulthood. At least for recent years in the United States, this does not appear to be a reasonable assumption (e.g., Haan, 1964, p. 598). If, on the other hand, we were to try to minimize the amount of extrapolation by choosing studies whose subjects were students close to adulthood, we would have a selected population that excluded school dropouts (e.g., Empey, 1956, p. 705). For these reasons, we will rely as much as possible, and except where otherwise noted, on studies using adult subjects.

Social class. Let us consider first the internal mediating factors that influence the likelihood of the individual being effective in manipulating objective conditions. One factor of this type is intellectual ability. Because of the difficulty of obtaining reliable and representative measures of adult intelligence, studies of school children have to be relied on for information on this question.

In recent years a number of questions have been raised about the well-known finding of lower average measured intelligence in lower-class children. The first question is whether the tests used to measure intelligence yield a spuriously low estimate of the intelligence of lower-class children because the test content is more familiar to middle-class children. Studies designed to investigate the effect of this bias showed that a relatively unbiased test still yielded results favoring middle-class children (Eells and others, 1951; Haggard, 1954) and that the scores on this type of test were not as closely related to success in school work as other intelligence scores (Eells and others, 1951). Therefore, it is not possible to dismiss the observed class difference on this count when one is concerned with predicting level of intellectual performance.

Another question about the class difference in intelligence scores is whether it is an artifact produced by the nature of the incentives offered to children in the test situation. It has been argued from experimental evidence that lower-class children respond more favorably to personal reinforcement than to task-oriented reinforcement (Zigler and Kanzer, 1962), and that they require more tangible rewards than middle-class children (Haggard, 1954; Zigler and de Labry, 1962). Since the intelligence tester typically offers nontangible, verbal rewards that are frequently task-oriented, the implication is that the intelligence scores of lower-class children are invalid. The findings of a difference in response to personal as against task-oriented reinforcement, however, has failed to replicate (Rosenhan and Greenwald, 1965). Furthermore, direct evidence showing that class differences remain significant even when money is offered challenges the argument concerning tangible rewards (Klugman, 1944). In addition, the finding that some performance scores differ little among social classes (Cropley, 1964) suggests that ineffective incentives cannot explain the discrepancies that are found.

The class difference in verbal intelligence scores appears to be substantial (Cropley, 1964; Haywood and Dobbs, 1964; Karp and Silberman, 1966) even when performance scores are matched (Jahoda, 1964). Moreover, this difference between classes increases with age from 10 to 14 (Jahoda, 1964), indicating that it is reasonable to extrapolate to adults the class difference observed in children. Since problems as diverse as getting a good job and getting good psychiatric care (e.g., Hollingshead and Redlich, 1958, chap. 9) are related to verbal skill, the implication of this difference is that lower-class individuals are handicapped in trying to deal with stressors by manipulation of objective conditions.

Another factor that could affect the likelihood of success in manipulating objective conditions is an individual's confidence in his ability to do so. The relevant finding is that members of the lower class are more likely than members of the middle class to see themselves as powerless to manipulate their environment in their own interest (e.g., Archibald, 1953; Bell, 1957; Dean, 1961; Lefcourt, 1966; Mechanic, 1965, p. 449; Simpson and Miller, 1963). Consistent with this class difference is the finding that lower class persons tend to devalue mastery over nature (Schneiderman, 1964).

Whether this tendency of lower-class persons toward resigned acceptance of their lot is, on balance, disadvantageous or not is, however, a matter of controversy. One view emphasizes ". . . the vitally important survival value of this life-style under the actual conditions of life for the impoverished" (Schneiderman, 1964, p. 17), with the implication of a situation so hopeless that the impoverished person, like an animal in a trap, will only injure himself by struggling. Recognizing that some external as well as internal mediating factors tend to make it difficult for the lower-class person to manipulate his environment effectively, we nevertheless question whether the contribution made by resignation toward psychic adjustment to the disadvantaged situation outweighs the fact that this attitude of helplessness further impedes dealing with stressors by manipulation of objective conditions. The answer seems to lie in historical as well as current cases suggesting that resignation has never proved more than a temporary palliative for the individual, since it has serious consequences in ordinary situations (e.g., Deasy, 1956; Koos, 1954) and disastrous results in the face of severe stressors (e.g., Lukas, 1966). Therefore, recognizing that we are, in the view of some social commentators, adopting a class-tied value position, we interpret the attitude of resignation on balance as aggravating rather than ameliorating the impact of stressors on the lower class.

It is important to distinguish between the attitude of hopelessness about being able to get what one wants and an internalized value that defines certain goals as more desirable than others. The latter may indeed serve to protect lower-class individuals from the impact of certain stressors. In particular, the lower-class emphasis on economic security rather than achievement, insofar as the two are opposed (Centers and Bugental, 1966; Gunderson and Mahan, 1966; Hyman, 1953; Larson and Sutker, 1966; Rosen, 1959), appears to be such a protective value. Evidence that it is not simply a rationalization for lack of ability is found in studies showing that the lower-class preference for security holds in junior high school (Wylie, 1963) and high school students (Sewell and others, 1957) even when intelligence is controlled, and that it is found among the parents of gifted children in their aspirations for their children (Frierson, 1965).

There is, however, another question — should this valuation of security be interpreted as a rationalization based on veridical perception of the *limited opportunities* open to the lower-class person rather than as an internalized value (e.g., Merton, 1957; Miller, 1958)? We could find no evidence that permits a clear choice between these much debated alternatives. Pearlin and Kohn (1966) have argued plausibly, however, that related differences in the valuation of self-direction versus obedience to external authority can be traced to differences in the structural requirements of middle-class as opposed to working-class occupations. On these grounds, it would also seem plausible to interpret the lower-class adult's expressed preference for economic security as a learned value rather than to assume that it represents a rationalization of unresolved chronic conflict about frustrated achievement needs. This interpretation is also indirectly supported by evidence that aspirations for achievement are in some cases directed toward the children of lower-class persons (Chinoy, 1952), indicating one way in which potential conflicts concerning own achievement may have been avoided.

An experiment comparing reactions of unemployed males of higher and lower status is suggestive of the way in which the security value may mediate the impact of the unemployment stressor (Goodchilds and Smith, 1963). The results showed that, whereas higher-status subjects tended to perform worse in group problem-solving and to give lower self-ratings with longer periods of unemployment, lower-status subjects were likely to improve in both performance and self-ratings with longer unemployment. A difference in values between low- and high-status subjects could explain these results. That is, since the subjects were receiving unemployment insurance, economic security was, at least for the time, not threatened, whereas achievement was threatened by the very fact of unemployment. Thus, the psychological loss from unemployment for the security-oriented lower-status subjects would have been less than for the achievement-oriented higher-status subjects. This interpretation of these results must be considered highly speculative, however, particularly since the index of status was composed of four elements, two of which—age and marital status—are not indicators of social class.

Although the available evidence is far from decisive, we suggest, on the basis of the observed class difference in valuation of economic achievement and security, that nondevelopmental achievement stressors would have more severe impact on members of the middle class, and nondevelopmental security stressors on members of the lower class. In a fully developed welfare state in which a firm floor has been constructed to provide basic security for the lowest social class, this class difference in aspirations would leave the middle class more vulnerable to stressors insofar as their impact is mediated by values. Where such a floor has not been established, however, neither class would seem to be clearly advantaged by the way in which their values mediate the impact of stressors.

Race. Let us first compare lower-class Negroes and lower-class whites. With respect to intelligence, the general finding is that, on the average, Negroes score lower than whites (e.g., de Neufville and Conner, 1966; Dreger and Miller, 1968; Pettigrew, 1964, p. 131; Shuey, 1966; Tulkin, 1968). However, the Negro deficit is not necessarily uniform for all intellectual abilities (e.g. Dreger and Miller, 1968) or for all age and sex groups. A recent study showed, for example, that by age 14, as Negro girls improved and white boys declined somewhat in verbal skill relative to their age norms, these two subgroups approached the same level (Baughman and Dahlstrom, 1968, p. 52).

A further difficulty in generalizing about race differences is that many studies do not control for class. Furthermore, even when controls are attempted, the lower-class Negro is frequently found to be more disadvantaged than the lower-class white with respect to some factors associated with class position (e.g., Dreger and Miller, 1968, p. 9). This fact, together with the finding that the difference between Negro and white average intelligence scores is sharply reduced when the two groups are approximately equally deprived (Pettigrew, 1964, pp. 118–20) has been used to argue against drawing any conclusions about the comparative intelligence of lower-class whites and Negroes. However, this argument holds only if one is interested in determining why Negroes score lower. Our question, in contrast, is whether lower-class Negroes are disadvantaged, for whatever reason, by poorer development of intellectual abilities. Their lower average intelligence scores suggest that this is the case.

Before drawing a conclusion, however, we must consider the argument that the lower Negro scores are an artifact of the testing situation. In particular, it has been shown that Negro subjects respond better to Negro testers (e.g., Klugman, 1944; Pettigrew, 1964, p. 117). Nevertheless, the evidence to date does not suggest that this factor can explain fully the race difference in scores (e.g., Dreger and Miller, 1968, pp. 18–19).

Although it appears that lower-class Negroes probably do score lower on general intelligence tests even when possible artifacts are allowed for, some recent studies indicate that this finding cannot be generalized to all types of intellectual performance. For example, one study of creativity showed that, particularly in the older student group compared, ranging from five to nine years old, Negroes scored as high as whites or higher on the Unusual Uses Test (Iscoe and Pierce-Jones, 1964), and another study revealed that creativity scores of Negro and white first and sixth graders generally did not differ (Singh, 1968). Second, an investigation of the effects of impulsivity among fifth-grade students on errors on the Matching Familiar Figures Test found the Negro students were significantly less impulsive and made significantly fewer errors than white students (Coyle, 1967).

Thus, there is no decisive evidence that, overall, either Negro or white lower-class members are handicapped by intellectual abilities, relative to each other, in manipulating objective conditions in response to stressors. To the extent that intelligence test scores themselves are a factor in manipulating these conditions, however, as, for example, in obtaining certain types of jobs, the fact that lower-class Negroes probably score lower than their white class counterparts on the more conventional measures of intellectual ability puts them at a disadvantage (e.g., de Neufville and Connor, 1966).

Lower-class Negroes also appear to be handicapped relative to their white class counterparts by less confidence in their ability to manipulate their environment in their own interests (e.g., Hammonds, 1964; Lefcourt, 1966; Lefcourt and Ladwig, 1965; Pettigrew, 1964, p. 19). The nature of this handicap is indicated by evidence that Negroes' lack of self-confidence is particularly acute when they are interacting with whites (e.g., Pettigrew, 1964, p. 50). What we may be seeing here are negative effects on self-confidence stemming from relative deprivation felt by the Negroes when called upon to compare themselves with whites (Stouffer and others, 1949). This inference is supported by the finding that Negroes gained when competing with whites if their status in the situation was defined with reference to a group having high prestige among Negroes (Lefcourt and Ladwig, 1965).

Thus, it appears that lower-class Negroes are more handicapped by internal factors than lower-class whites in dealing with stressors by manipulation of objective conditions. Although this handicap stems partly from lack of self-confidence in situations involving whites, this specificity has little practical significance since, despite efforts of Negro separatists, the numerical minority status and economic weakness of the Negro community probably mean that there are few stressors with which a lower-class Negro can deal effectively without any involvement with whites.

We face two problems in comparing lower-class Negroes and lower-class whites with respect to values that mediate the impact of stressors by affecting the severity of subjective loss from the stressor. The first problem is that almost all of the relevant studies use school children as subjects. Since the school dropout rate is particularly large among lower-class students, conclusions drawn from such studies may be limited to a subgroup of upwardly mobile lower-class youth.

The second problem is how to interpret complex results. Studies have reported that lower-class Negro mothers (Bloom and others, 1965; Rosen, 1959) and lower-class Negro students have higher educational aspirations (Gottlieb, 1964; Wylie, 1963) and higher occupational aspirations (Brown, 1965) than comparable whites, as well as higher levels of aspiration in a test of skill (Boyd, 1952). Two studies contradict these results, however, by showing that Negro high school students are less likely to aspire to occupations requiring graduate or professional training (Gottlieb, 1964), and that Negro mothers' occupational aspirations for their sons are lower than whites' (Rosen, 1959). At the same time, it has been reported that Negro and white students' realistic educational and occupational expectations do not differ (Gist and Bennett, 1963), and that the discrepancy between aspirations and realistic expectations is greater for Negroes than for whites (Gottlieb, 1964). The problem is to determine what these findings indicate about the value placed on achievement by lower-class Negroes.

A lead is found in studies showing that in game situations subjects with relatively low levels of need achievement tend to choose plays with either a very high or a very low probability of success (McClelland, 1961, p. 212). Such a relationship between extreme goal setting and relatively low need achievement was predicted by Atkinson from his theory of risk-taking behavior, on the assumption, supported by independent evidence, that low-need achievers are concerned more with fear of failure than with hope for success (Atkinson, 1966). Atkinson argued that low-need achievers "are setting their aspiration level either *defensively* high or *defensively* low" (p. 20). If this interpretation is correct, it suggests that the high levels of aspiration assessed as unrealistic by lower-class Negroes indicate a high degree of ego involvement and anxiety with respect to failure, and hence vulnerability to achievement stressors. It appears, therefore, that there may be a subgroup of lower-class Negroes, represented by students who do not drop out of school, who are more vulnerable than their white class counterparts to achievement stressors.

With regard to middle-class Negroes, the evidence is that they do not differ from their white class counterparts in average intelligence (Pettigrew, 1964, p. 119; Tulkin, 1968). In this respect, therefore, they suffer no handicap in ability to manipulate objective conditions in reaction to stressors. The evidence is less clear, however, about their confidence in their ability to manipulate their environment. The relevant data come both from studies comparing middle-class with lower-class Negroes, and from experimental studies comparing middle-class Negro college students with their white class counterparts.

The most extensive study comparing Negro middle and lower-class subjects surveyed 1,119 respondents in cities in the North and the South (Marx, 1967). This investigation found that Negroes who held more militant attitudes on civil rights were more self-confident (p. 90), and that attitudes were more militant among middle-class than among lower-class Negroes (p. 63). This direct relationship between social class and militant attitudes is consistent with two studies of civil rights activity that showed that activism was associated with middle-class status in both the South (Weinstein and Geisel, 1962) and the North (Hughes and Watts, 1964). One study, possibly because of a relatively narrow range on the socioeconomic variable, however, reported no such relationship among a group of southern subjects (Gore and Rotter, 1963), while another study showed that lower-class Negroes were more active than middle-class Negroes in school desegregation, possibly as the result of a "prolonged and intense desegregation movement" (Luchterhand and Weller, 1965, p. 88). Inconsistency is also found in studies of the relation between social status and self-hate, a characteristic that appears to be particularly incapacitating in Negroes (Roen, 1960). A study of Philadelphia Negroes showed that self-hate is greater in higher socioeconomic groups (Parker and Kleiner, 1964), and a study of Negroes in Georgia and California cities revealed a negative association between self-hate and social class (Noel, 1964).

Experimental evidence suggests, however, that, like lower-class Negroes, middle-class Negro students suffer particularly from lack of self-confidnce in situations that require interaction with their white class counterparts (Katz and Benjamin, 1960; Katz, Goldston, and Benjamin, 1958). The dynamics of this reaction appears to be that the white person represents a threat so that his presence leads to emotional arousal, and that level of arousal in turn influences performance as predicted from the inverted U function (Katz and Greenbaum, 1963). Thus, in a situation that is otherwise not arousing, the Negro subject will probably perform better in the presence of a white person, but in a situation that is otherwise threatening, the heightening of arousal by the presence of a white leads to poorer performance. If this model of the reaction is correct, it suggests that the middle-class Negro would be most likely to be disadvantaged by interaction with whites when the severity of the stressor and the

nature of other mediating factors highlighted the Negroes' perception of relative deprivation and hence made the situation a particularly threatening one.

The extent to which a stressor is threatening depends on external
mediating factors and on the relation of the consequences of the
stressor to the individual's values. In regard to levels of aspiration,
insofar as student subjects can be taken as representative, the picture
for middle-class Negroes does not differ from that for lower-class
Negroes. That is, levels of aspiration are higher than those of white
class counterparts in tests of skill (Boyd, 1952), and for education
(Gottlieb, 1964) and occupation (Brown, 1965), with the possible
exception that whites are more likely to aspire to highly prestigious
professional occupations (Gottlieb, 1964). Furthermore, the finding
of greater discrepancy between aspirations and realistic expectations
among Negroes than among whites seems to apply to the middle
class (Gist and Bennett, 1963). These findings, together with the
argument presented earlier with respect to lower-class Negroes, imply that middle-class Negroes also have relatively low levels of need
achievement and the associated high levels of fear of failure.

Direct comparisons of Negro and white students' levels of need
achievement suggest, however, that this generalization may apply
only to certain subgroups among middle-class Negroes. Specifically,
these comparisons reveal both regional and sex differences, with
Negroes showing higher levels of need achievement than whites in
the north (Rosen, 1959) but not in the south (Brazziel, 1964; Grossack, 1957), and Negro females displaying higher levels than white
females at the same time that either Negro and white males do not
differ (Grossack, 1957) or Negro males show lower levels than whites
(Brazziel, 1964). Thus, it appears that middle-class Negro students
vary considerably in their levels of need achievement relative to
whites.

THE SEVERITY OF STRESS

The severity of stress experienced depends, according to our model,
on its duration and intensity. These, in turn, are consequences of the
amount of exposure to stressors, together with the nature of the
external and internal factors that mediate the impact of stressors. The
issue with which we are concerned is how the severity of stress
varies with social status. Our central problem has been to find empirical evidence confirming or disconfirming the common-sense notion
that the severity of stress varies inversely with status.

The data available on stressors, external mediating factors, and internal mediating factors in different class and ethnic groups have proved far from definitive. With the aid of some simplifying assumptions, however, they do provide a basis for the construction of hypotheses that can be tested against a wide range of outcomes. Accordingly, Table 4.2 presents our hypotheses about the relative severity of stress likely to be experienced by persons in each of four status groups.

Table 4.2. Relative severity of stress in four status groups

Severity predicted from:	Order of groups from low to high severity*			
Frequency of exposure to stressors	Middle-class white ?	Lower-class white <	Middle-class Negro ?	Lower-class Negro
External mediating factors	Middle-class white <	Lower-class white ?	Middle-class Negro <	Lower-class Negro
Internal mediating factors	Middle-class white ?	Middle-class Negro <	Lower-class white <	Lower-class Negro
Combination of above	Middle-class white <	Lower-class white ?	Middle-class Negro <	Lower-class Negro

* Question marks indicate that the evidence does not clearly suggest a differential severity between adjacent groups.

The first line of Table 4.2 shows that, with respect to stressors: (1) The evidence is inconsistent and does not indicate, overall, that the rate of exposure to stressors varies with class; (2) Negroes appear to be exposed to higher rate of stressors than their class counterparts among whites.

Concerning external mediating factors, the second line of Table 4.2 indicates that: (1) Lower-class persons are disadvantaged in comparison to middle-class persons; (2) Negroes are disadvantaged in comparison to whites of comparable class.

The third line of Table 4.2 indicates that, taking together all types of internal mediating factors, the most reasonable generalizations appear to be that: (1) Lower-class persons are disadvantaged in comparison to middle-class persons; (2) The evidence is inconsistent and does not indicate, overall, that middle-class Negroes are disadvantaged in comparison to middle-class whites; (3) Lower-class Negroes are disadvantaged in comparison to lower-class whites.

The most speculative comparison in this table is between middle-class Negroes and lower-class whites, where direct evidence is almost totally unavailable. The hypothesis that stressors impinge more frequently on middle-class Negroes than on lower-class whites rests on the finding that they suffer more than their white class counterparts from developmental stressors, as do lower-class whites, without the compensating relative freedom of the lower-class whites from nondevelopmental achievement stressors such as job promotions and other types of increases in assigned responsibility.

Our inference that the lower-class white and middle-class Negro cannot be assigned different severities of stress on the basis of the part played by external mediating factors rests on the assumption that the middle-class Negro's advantages due to his class—for example, relatively high income—are approximately balanced by disadvantages due to his race, such as exclusion from most desirable housing. A firmer conclusion could only be drawn if we had an empirical basis for assessing the relative importance of different types of external factors in mediating the impact of various stressors.

The relatively lower severity of stress predicted from assessment of the contribution of internal mediating factors for middle-class Negroes compared to lower-class whites is based on the complex picture of advantage and disadvantage for the middle-class Negro. The equality of the average intelligence scores of middle-class Negroes and middle-class whites implies that lower-class whites are disadvantaged relative to middle-class Negroes on this count. Both lower-class whites and middle-class Negroes appear to have less confidence than middle-class whites in their ability to manipulate their environment in their own interest, but this picture of disadvantage appears to be less consistent for the Negro middle class than for the white lower class.

Finally, the fact that some subgroups of middle-class Negroes score higher than their white class counterparts on need achievement while some score lower suggests that, overall, they are similar to the white middle class with respect to vulnerability to nondevelopmental achievement stressors. Hence, as with the white middle class, we infer that when both achievement and security stressors are taken into account, middle-class Negroes are neither clearly advantaged nor disadvantaged relative to lower-class whites by the way in which their values mediate the impact of stressors.

In combining degree of exposure to stressors, external mediating factors and internal mediating factors for a summary prediction of relative severity of stress, we have weighted each of the three components equally. On this basis we predict, not surprisingly, that the severity of stress is lowest for middle-class whites and highest for lower-class Negroes. There is, however, no basis for distinguishing between middle-class Negroes and lower-class whites, since the severity for these two groups appears, on balance, not to be clearly different.

Our predictions, based as they are on simplifying assumptions, ignore qualitative differences in both the sources and consequences of stress that are likely to show important variations according to status (e.g., Henry and Short, 1954). Rather than further stretch our limited data with still more assumptions about the role of such qualitative differences, let us suggest that the best corrective would be investigation of the power of the present hypotheses to predict some of the problems of health, illness, and social pathology considered in this book as possible outcomes of stress.

REFERENCES

AIKEN, M., and FERMAN, L. A. 1966. "The Social and Political Reactions of Older Negroes to Unemployment." *Phylon*, 27:333–346.

ARCHIBALD, K. 1953. "Status Orientations among Shipyard Workers," in R. Bendix and S. M. Lipset, eds., *Class, Status and Power*. New York: Free Press.

ATKINSON, J. W. 1955. "The Achievement Motive and Recall of Interrupted and Completed Tasks," in D. C. McClelland, ed., *Studies in Motivation*. New York: Appleton-Century-Crofts.

ATKINSON, J. W. 1966. "Motivational Determinants of Risk-taking Behavior," in J. W. Atkinson and N. T. Feather, eds., *A Theory of Achievement Motivation*, New York: John Wiley and Sons.

BACK, K., and SIMPSON I. H. 1964. "The Dilemma of the Negro Professional." *Journal of Social Issues*, 20, no. 2:60–70.

BAUGHMAN, E. E., and DAHLSTROM, W. G. 1968. *Negro and White Children: A Psychological Study of the Rural South*. New York: Academic Press.

BELL, W. 1957. "Anomie, Social Isolation, and the Class Structure." *Sociometry*, 20:105–16.

BERNARD, J. 1966. "Marital Stability and Patterns of Status Variables." *Journal of Marriage and the Family*, 28:421–39.

BLAU, P. M., and DUNCAN, O. D. 1967. *The American Occupational Structure*. New York: John Wiley and Sons.

BLOOM, R., WHITEMAN, M., and DEUTSCH, M. 1965. "Race and Social Class as Separate Factors Related to Social Environment." *American Journal of Sociology*, 70:471–76.

BOYD, G. F. 1952. "The Levels of Aspiration of White and Negro Children in a Non-segregated Elementary School." *Journal of Social Psychology*, 36:191–96.

BRAZZIEL, W. F. 1964. "Correlates of Southern Negro Personality." *Journal of Social Issues*, 20, no. 2:46–53.

BRONFENBRENNER, U. 1958. "Socialization and Social Class through Time and Space," in Eleanor E. Maccoby, Theodore M. Newcomb, and Eugene L. Hartley, eds., *Readings in Social Psychology*, 3rd ed. New York: Henry Holt.

BROWN, R. G. 1965. "A Comparison of the Vocational Aspirations of Paired Sixth-grade White and Negro Children Who Attend Segregated Schools." *Journal of Educational Research*, 58:402–4.

CAPLAN, G. 1964. *Principles of Preventive Psychiatry.* New York: Basic Books.

CENTERS, R., and BUGENTAL, D. E. 1966. "Intrinsic and Extrinsic Job Motivations among Different Segments of the Working Population." *Journal of Applied Psychology*, 50:193–97.

CHINOY, E. 1952. "The Tradition of Opportunity and the Aspirations of Automobile Workers." *American Journal of Sociology*, 57:453–59.

COHEN, A. K., and HODGES, H. M., JR. 1963. "Characteristics of the Lower-blue-collar Class." *Social Problems*, 10:303–34.

COYLE, P. J. 1967. "Differences in Reflection-impulsivity as a Function of Race, Sex, and Socio-economic Class." *Dissertation Abstracts*, 27 (12-B): 4549.

CROPLEY, A. J. 1964 "Differentiation of Abilities, Socioeconomic Status, and the WISC." *Journal of Consulting Psychology*, 28:512–17.

CUMMING, J., and CUMMING, E. 1962. *Ego and Milieu.* New York: Atherton Press.

DAVIS, A., and DOLLARD, J. 1940. *Children of Bondage: The Personality Development of Negro Youth in the Urban South.* Washington, D. C.: American Council on Education.

DAVIS, A., GARDNER, B. B., and GARDNER, M. R. 1958. "The Class System of the White Caste," in E. E. Maccoby, T. M. Newcomb, and E. L. Hartley, eds., *Readings in Social Psychology*, 3rd ed. New York: Henry Holt.

DEAN, D. G. 1961. "Alienation: Its Meaning and Measurement." *American Sociological Review*, 26:753–58.

DEASY, L. C. 1956. "Socio-economic Status and Participation in the Poliomyelitis Vaccine Trial." *American Sociological Review*, 21:185–91.

DE NEUFVILLE, R., and CONNER, C. 1966. "How Good Are Our Schools?" *American Education*, 2:1–7.

DEUTSCH, M. 1961. "Socio-developmental Considerations in Childrens' Accidents," in *Behavioral Approaches to Accident Research.* New York: Association for the Aid of Crippled Children.

DICE, L. R., CLARK, P. J., and GILBERT, R. I. 1964. "Relation of Fertility to Occupation and to Income in the Male Population of Ann Arbor, Michigan, 1951–54." *Eugenics Quarterly*, 11:154–67.

DOHRENWEND, B. P. 1961. "The Social Psychological Nature of Stress: A Framework for Causal Inquiry." *Journal of Abnormal and Social Psychology*, 62:294–302.

1966. "Social Status and Psychological Disorder: An Issue of Substance and an Issue of Method." *Americal Sociological Review,* 31:14–34.

DOHRENWEND, B. P., and CHIN-SHONG, E. 1967. "Social Status and Attitudes toward Psychological Disorder: The Problem of Tolerance of Deviance." *American Sociological Review,* 32:417–33.

DOHRENWEND, B. P., and DOHRENWEND, B. S. 1969. *Social Status and Psychological Disorder: A Causal Inquiry.* New York: John Wiley and Sons.

DREGER, R., and MILLER, S. 1968. "Comparative Psychological Studies of Negroes and Whites in the United States: 1958–1965." *Psychological Bulletin Monograph Supplement,* 70: No. 3, Part 2.

DUNCAN, O. D. 1964. "Residential Areas and Differential Fertility." *Euginics Quarterly,* 11:82–89.

EELLS, K., DAVIS, A., HAVIGHURST, R. J., HERRICK, V. E., and TYLER, R. W. 1951. *Intelligence and Cultural Differences.* Chicago: University of Chicago Press.

EMPEY, L. T. 1956. "Social Class and Occupational Aspiration: A Comparison of Absolute and Relative Measurement." *American Sociological Review,* 21:703–9.

ERIKSON, E. H. 1959. "Identity and the Life Cycle." *Psychological Issues Monograph,* no. 1. New York: International Universities Press.

FARLEY, R., and TAEUBER, K. E. 1968. "Population Trends and Residential Segregation since 1960." *Science,* 159:953–56.

FRIERSON, E. C. 1965. "Upper and Lower Status Gifted Children: A Study of Differences." *Exceptional Children,* 32:83–90.

GERTH, H. H., and MILLS, C. W., eds. 1946. *From Max Weber: Essays in Sociology.* New York: Oxford University Press.

GIST, N. P., and BENNETT, W. S., JR. 1963. "Aspirations of Negro and White Students." *Social Forces,* 42:40–48.

GOODCHILDS, J. D., and SMITH, E. E. 1963. "The Effects of Unemployment as Mediated by Social Status." *Sociometry,* 26:287–93.

GORE, P. M., and ROTTER, J. B. 1963. "A Personality Correlate of Social Attention." *Journal of Personality,* 31:58–64.

GOTTLIEB, D. 1964. "Goal Aspriations and Goal Fulfillments: Differences between Deprived and Affluent American Adolescents." *American Journal of Orthopsychiatry,* 34:934–41.

GROSSACK, M. 1957. "Some Personality Characteristics of Negro College Students." *Journal of Social Psychology,* 46:125–31.

GUNDERSON, E. K., and MAHAN J. L. 1966. "Cultural and Psychological Differences among Occupational Groups." *Journal of Psychology,* 62:287–304.

HAAN, N. 1964. "The Relationship of Ego Functioning and Intelligence to Social Status and Social Mobility." *Journal of Abnormal and Social Psychology,* 69:594–605.

HADDON, W., JR., VALIEN, P., MCCARROLL, J. R., and UMBERGER, C. J. 1964. "A Controlled Investigation of the Characteristics of Adult Pedestrians Fatally Injured by Motor Vehicles in Manhattan," in W. Haddon, Jr., E. A. Suchman, and D. Klein, eds., *Accident Research: Methods and Approaches.* New York: Harper and Row.

HAGGARD, E. A. 1954. "Social Status and Intelligence: An Experimental Study of Certain Cultural Determinants of Measured Intelligence." *Genetic Psychology Monographs,* 49:141–86.

HAMBURG, D. A., and ADAMS, J. E. 1967. "A Perspective on Coping Behavior." *Archives of General Psychiatry,* 17:277–84.

HAMMONDS, A. D. 1964. "Socio-economic Status and Anomia: An Interpretation and Specification of the Relationship." *Dissertation Abstracts,* 24:4833.

HARE, N. 1965. "Recent Trends in the Occupational Mobility of Negroes, 1930–1960: An Intracohort Analysis." *Social Forces,* 44:166–73.

HAYWOOD, H. C., and DOBBS, V. 1964. "Motivation Anxiety in High School Boys." *Journal of Personality,* 32:371–79.

HENRY, A. F., and SHORT, J. F., JR. 1954. *Suicide and Homocide.* New York: Free Press.

HODGE, R. W., and HODGE, P. 1965. "Occupational Assimilation as a Competitive Process." *American Journal of Sociology,* 71:249–64.

HOLLINGSHEAD, A. B. 1953. "Class Differences in Family Stability," in R. Bendix and S. M. Lipset, eds., *Class, Status and Power.* New York: Free Press.

HOLLINGSHEAD, A. B., and REDLICH, F. C. 1958. *Social Class and Mental Illness.* New York: John Wiley.

HUGHES, H. M., and WATTS, L. G. 1964. "Portrait of the Self-Integrater." *Journal of Social Issues,* 20, no. 2:103–14.

HYMAN, H. H. 1953. "The Value Systems of Different Classes: A Social Psychological Contribution to the Analysis of Stratification," in R. Bendix and S. M. Lipset, eds., *Class, Status and Power,* New York: Free Press.

ISCOE, I., and PIERCE-JONES, J. 1964. "Divergent Thinking, Age, and Intelligence in White and Negro Children." *Child Development,* 35:785–97.

JAHODA, G. 1964. "Social Class Differentials in Vocabulary Expansion." *British Journal of Educational Psychology,* 34:321–23.

JANIS, I. L. 1958. *Psychological Stress.* New York: John Wiley.

KARP, S. A., and SILBERMAN, L. 1966. "Field Dependence, Body Sophistication, and Socioeconomic Status." *Research Reports, Sinai Hospital of Baltimore,* 1:17–25.

KATZ, I., and BENJAMIN, L. 1960. "Effects of White Authoritarianism in Biracial Work Groups." *Journal of Abnormal and Social Psychology,* 61:448–56.

KATZ, I., GOLDSTON, J., and BENJAMIN, L. 1958. "Behavior and Productivity in Bi-racial Work Groups." *Human Relations,* 11:123–41.

138   PART TWO   :   *Sources of Stress*

KATZ, I., and GREENBAUM, G. 1963. "Effects of Anxiety, Threat, and Racial Environment on Task Performance of Negro College Students." *Journal of Abnormal and Social Psychology*, 66:562–67.

KLUGMAN, S. F. 1944. "The Effect of Money Incentives versus Promise upon the Reliability and Obtained Scores of the Revised Stanford-Binet Test." *Journal of General Psychology*, 30:255–69.

KOMAROVSKY, M. 1962. *Blue-Collar Marriage*. New York: Random House.

KOOS, E. L. 1946. *Families in Trouble*. New York: Kings Crown.

———. 1954. *The Health of Regionville*. New York: Columbia University Press.

LANGER, E. 1966. "Medicine for the Poor: A New Deal in Denver." *Science*, 153:508–12.

LANGNER, T. S., and MICHAEL, S. T. 1963. *Life Stress and Mental Health*. New York: Free Press.

LARSON, R. F., and SUTKER, S. S. 1966. "Value Differences and Value Consensus by Socioeconomic Levels." *Social Forces*, 44:563–69.

LAZARUS, R. S. 1966. *Psychological Stress and the Coping Process*. New York: McGraw-Hill.

LEFCOURT, H. M. 1966. "Internal versus External Control of Reinforcement: A Review." *Psychological Bulletin*, 65:206–20.

LEFCOURT, H. M., and LADWIG, G. W. 1965. "The Effect of Reference Group upon Negroes (*sic*) Task Persistence in a Biracial Competitive Game." *Journal of Personality and Social Psychology*, 1:668–71.

LEVENSON, B., and McDILL, M. S. 1966. "Vocational Graduates in Auto Mechanics: A Follow-up Study of Negro and White Youth." *Phylon*, 27:347–57.

LINDEMANN, E. 1944. "Symptomatology and the Management of Acute Grief." *American Journal of Psychiatry*, 101:141–48.

LUCHTERHAND E., and WELLER, L. 1965. "Social Class and the Desegregation Movement: A Study of Parents' Decisions in a Negro Ghetto." *Social Problems*, 13:83–88.

LUKAS, J. A. 1966. "Village of Hunger and Lethargy." *N. Y. Times Magazine*, 2 (October): 30–31, 88–109.

MARDEN, P. G. 1966. "A Demographic and Ecological Analysis of the Distribution of Physicians in Metropolitan America, 1960." *American Journal of Sociology*, 72:290–300.

MARKS, R. 1967. "A Review of Empirical Findings," in S. L. Syme and L. G. Reeder, eds., *Social Stress and Cardiovascular Disease*. New York: Milbank Memorial Fund.

MARX, G. T. 1967. *Protest and Prejudice: A Study of Belief in the Black Community*. New York: Harper and Row.

MAYER, A. J., and HAUSER, P. 1950. "Class Differentials in Expectation of Life at Birth." *La Revue de L'Institut International de Statistique* 18:197–200.

McCLELLAND, D. C. 1961. *The Achieving Society*. New York: Van Nostrand.

MECHANIC, D. 1965. "The Influence of Mothers on Their Children's Health Attitudes and Behavior." *Pediatrics*, 33:444–53.

MENCHACA, F. J. 1964. "Facteurs Sociaux de la Prématurité." *Courrier*, 14:76–81.

MERTON, R. K. 1957. "Social Structure and Anomie," in R. K. Merton, *Social Theory and Social Structure*. Glencoe, Ill.: Free Press.

MILLER, W. B. 1958. "Lower Class Culture as a Generating Milieu of Gang Delinquency." *Journal of Social Issues*, 14, no. 3:5–19.

MORIYAMA, I. M., and GURALNICK, L. 1956. "Occupational and Social Class Differences in Mortality." *Trends and Differentials in Morality: Papers Presented at the 1955 Annual Conference of the Milbank Memorial Fund.* New York: Milbank Memorial Fund, pps. 61–73.

NOEL, D. L. 1964. "Group Identification among Negroes: An Empirical Analysis." *Journal of Social Issues*, 20, no. 2:71–84.

NOTESTEIN, F. W. 1953. "Class Differences in Fertility," in R. Bendix and S. M. Lipset, eds., *Class, Status and Power*, New York: Free Press.

ORUM, A. M. 1966. "A Reappraisal of the Social and Political Participation of Negroes." *American Journal of Sociology*, 74:32–46.

PALOUCEK, F. P., and GRAHAM, J. B. 1966. "The Influence of Psychosocial Factors in the Prognosis of Cancer of the Cervix." *Annals of the New York Academy of Sciences*, 125:814–16.

PARKER, S., and KLEINER, R. 1964. "Status Position, Mobility, and Ethnic Identification of the Negro." *Journal of Social Issues*, 20, no. 2:85–102.

PASAMANICK, B., KNOBLOCH, H., and LILIENFELD, A. 1956. "Socio-economic Status and Some Precursors of Neuropsychiatric Disorder." *American Journal of Orthopsychiatry*, 26:594–601.

PEARLIN, L. I., and KOHN, M. L. 1966, "Social Class, Occupation, and Parental Values: A Cross-national Study." *American Sociological Review*, 31:466–79.

PETTIGREW, T. F. 1964. *A Profile of the Negro American.* Princeton, N.J.: Van Nostrand.

RAINWATER, L. 1965. *Family Design: Marital Sexuality, Family Size, and Contraception.* Chicago: Aldine Publishing Company.

ROEN, S. R. 1960. "Personality and Negro-white Intelligence." *Journal of Abnormal and Social Psychology*, 61:148–50.

ROSEN, B. C. 1959. "Race, Ethnicity, and the Achievement Syndrome." *American Sociological Review*, 24:47–60.

ROSENHAN, D., and GREENWALD, J. A. 1965. "The Effects of Age, Sex, and Socio-economic Class on Responsiveness to Two Classes of Verbal Reinforcement." *Journal of Personality*, 33:108–21.

SANDERS, E. P. 1964. "Relation between Accident Incidence and Types and Level of Job." *Psychological Reports*, 14:670.

SCHNEIDERMAN, L. 1964. "Value Orientation Preferences of Chronic Relief Recipients." *Journal of Social Work*, 9:13–19.

SCHNORE, L. F., and EVENSON, P. C. 1966. "Segregation in Southern Cities." *American Journal of Sociology*, 72:58–67.

SEARLES, R., and WILLIAMS, J. A., JR. 1962. "Negro College Students' Participation in Sit-ins." *Social Forces*, 40:215-20.

SELYE, H. 1955. "Stress and Disease." *Science*, 122:625–631.

SEWELL, W., HALLER, A., and STRAUS, M. 1957. "Social Status and Educational and Occupational Aspirations." *American Sociological Review*, 22:67–73.

SHANAHAN, E. 1966. "Negro Jobless Up—Why?" *N.Y. Times*, 11 September:6E.

SHUEY, A. M. 1966. *The Testing of Negro Intelligence*, 2nd. ed. New York: Social Science Press.

SIMPSON, R. L., and MILLER, M. 1963. "Social Status and Anomia." *Social Problems*, 10:256–64.

SINGH, S. P. 1968. "A Comparison between Privileged Negroes and Underprivileged Negroes, Privileged Whites, and Underprivileged White Children on a Test of Creativity." *Dissertation Abstracts*, 28 (7-A): 2569–2570.

STOUFFER, S. A. 1955. *Communism, Conformity and Civil Liberties*. New York: Doubleday.

STOUFFER, S. A., SUCHMAN, E. A., DEVINNEY, L. C., STAR, S. A., and WILLIAMS, R. M., JR. 1949. *The American Soldier Vol. I: Adjustment during Army Life*. Princeton, N.J.: Princeton University Press.

TAEUBER, A. F., TAEUBER, K. E., and CAIN, G. G. 1966. "Occupational Assimilation and the Competitive Process: A Reanalysis." *American Journal of Sociology*, 72:273–85.

TAEUBER, K. E., and TAEUBER, A. F. 1965. *Negroes in Cities*. Chicago: Aldine Publishing Company.

TUCKMAN, J., YOUNGMAN, W. F., and KREIZMAN, G. B., 1965. "Occupational Level and Mortality." *Social Forces*, 43:575–77.

TULKIN, S. R. 1968. "Race, Class, Family, and School Achievement." *Journal of Personality and Social Psychology*, 9:31–37.

UDRY, J. R. 1966. "Marital Instability by Race, Sex, Education, and Occupation Using 1960 Census Data." *American Journal of Sociology*, 72:203–209.

——— 1967. "Marital Instability by Race and Income." *American Journal of Sociology*, 72:673–74.

WARNER, W. L., LOW, J. O., LUNT, P. S., and SROLE, L. 1963. *Yankee City*, 1-vol. abridged ed. New Haven: Yale University Press.

WEINSTEIN, E. A., and GEISEL, P. A. 1962. "Family Decision Making over Desegration." *Sociometry*, 25:21–29.

WORLD HEALTH ORGANIZATION. 1961. "Public Health Aspects of Low Birth Weight. Third Report of the Expert Committee on Maternal and Child Health." *Technical Report Series*, no. 217, Geneva.

WRIGHT, C. R., and HYMAN, H. H. 1958. "Voluntary Association Memberships of American Adults: Evidence from National Sample Surveys." *American Sociological Review*, 23:284–94.

WYLIE, R. C. 1963. "Children's Estimates of their Schoolwork Ability, as a Function of Sex, Race, and Socioeconomic Level." *Journal of Personality*, 31:203–24.

ZIGLER, E., and DE LABRY, J. 1962. "Concept-switching in Middle-class, Lower-class, and Retarded Children." *Journal of Abnormal and Social Psychology*, 65:267–73.

ZIGLER, E., and KANZER, P. 1962. "The Effectiveness of Two Classes of Verbal Reinforcers on the Performance of Middle- and Lower-class Children." *Journal of Personality*, 30:157–63.

PART THREE
Consequences of Stress

5. Cognitive and Personality Factors Underlying Threat and Coping

RICHARD S. LAZARUS

IT HAS BEEN traditional, especially in causal analysis, to view the emotions as causes of cognitive and behavioral reactions, especially when these reactions appear to the observer as "irrational" or maladaptive. When the emotions involved are negatively toned ones like fear, anger, or depression, we then speak of psychological stress. Stress reactions are said to organize our thinking and our actions, making an individual do things that he would not otherwise do.

I would like to propose that this conceptualization, which blames emotion or stress for irrational thought or maladaptive behavior, is misleading in that it covers up some conceptual confusions and directs our attention to the wrong problems. My purpose here is to support an alternative way of thinking about psychological stress and emotions which reflects increasing concern with cognitive processes (Lazarus, 1966).

From *Psychological Stress*, edited by Mortimer H. Appley and Richard Trumbull. Copyright © 1967, Meredith Corporation. Reprinted by permission of Appleton-Century-Crofts.

Richard S. Lazarus is professor of psychology at the University of California, Berkeley.

SOME CONFUSIONS IN THE TRADITIONAL CONCEPTIONS OF STRESS AND EMOTION

There are three sources of confusion in the traditional conception that emotion organizes behavior. One of these concerns the hedonistic implication that it is the pain of negatively toned emotions that motivates coping behavior. It is commonly stated, for example, that the individual is reacting against anxiety when he engages in some defensive process. Although Freud introduced the alternative conception that anxiety produces defense by serving as a signal of danger, it is still implied in much literature that it is the pain of anxiety against which the individual is defending.

The notion of the cue value of anxiety tends to turn our attention toward the cognitive processes underlying the anxiety and defense reaction, and as such it is a step forward in our thinking. Anxiety is said to provide information to the individual about his fate should defensive activity not be called into play. It is not the anxiety, *per se,* that activates the defense but the signal of danger. There remains an unstated difficulty about this formulation, however, a confusion which I wish to note here. To what agency does the anxiety serve as a signal? The Freudian answer would appear to be, "to the ego." But why does the ego, whose function it is to cognize the danger in the first place, have to be informed about what it has already done, that is, appraise danger. Why can't any stimulus be interpreted as a sign of danger if it has previously been followed by harm in the experience of the individual? Why should anxiety be necessary? It appears odd that the agency or structure which engages in a function must be informed that this function has indeed been engaged in.

The third confusion arises because, in psychological stress analysis and in conflict theory, anxiety alone is made the intervening variable. Yet, in practice, clinicians speak of reaction formation as a defense against anger and of manic euphoria as a defense against depression. In the latter instances, there appear to be many emotional intervening variables rather than just one. Thus, the emphasis on anxiety is far too simple in stress analysis. Stress theory speaks of anxiety alone as the culprit, while in practice, any emotional state is presumed to have behavior-organizing properties.

THE OVERRIDING IMPORTANCE OF COGNITIVE PROCESSES IN PSYCHOLOGICAL STRESS AND EMOTION

By making emotion the cause rather than the effect, I believe that we turn our attention away from the critical problem in psychological stress analysis—namely, identifying the processes and conditions that produce different stress reactions. We must explain not only the presence of a defense mechanism but also why one mechanism occurs and not another. I want to support the notion that the whole equation should be turned around (that emotional reactions should be regarded as effects rather than causes, and that these effects, in turn, depend heavily on cognitive processes.) It is the cognitive processes leading to emotion that organize behavior, not the emotions themselves. Our theoretical and research problem then becomes, "What are these cognitive processes, and what are the conditions that determine them?" Such a view is compatible, of course, with the treatment of anxiety as at least one hypothetical construct, since it then becomes necessary to identify the antecedent and consequent conditions that result in anxiety and the coping processes that arise from it. However, traditional associative-learning conflict theory tends to be oversimple in the number of intervening constructs, in its identification of such variables, in the classes of coping processes dealt with, and in the patterns of reactions that are studied in consequence.

For some years now, there has been an increasing tendency for psychologists interested in psychological stress and emotion to emphasize the cognitions producing these reactions. For example, Magda Arnold (1960, 1967) has emphasized the process of appraisal in the production of emotion. An influential study by Schachter and Singer (1962) not only attacks the unidimensional concept of arousal in defining emotion but also points up the crucial role played by cognitive activity in the production of emotion. In his review on emotion, Peters (1963) again and again underscores the "tendency to ignore the cognitive . . . elements . . . in emotion." I, too, regard appraisal as the intervening process in psychological stress analysis, as the precursor of stress reaction. Research from my laboratory has shown that a stressful film will produce less stress reaction if the appraisal of the harmful significance of the events portrayed is altered.

In the full analysis of psychological stress, it is necessary to separate processes involved in threat production from those concerned with coping. The mere fact that the individual anticipates harm and is therefore threatened or anxious does not, by itself, permit us to predict the nature of the reaction. Knowing that he is threatened does not allow us to specify, for example, why anger occurs instead of fear, or why anxiety, depression, or guilt are experienced rather than some other affect. It does not enable us to understand the variable behavioral and physiological pattern of reaction within the same individual across occasions, and between individuals, and the apparent contradictions that appear between levels of measurement. For example, when the individual shows physiological signs of threat but gives verbal reports denying that anything is wrong, the intervening psychological processes are evidently different than when his reported affect agrees with the physiological measures.

THE IMPORTANCE OF DISCREPANCIES BETWEEN STRESS IN-DICATORS — AN EMPIRICAL EXAMPLE

Before proceeding with the remainder of my thesis, I want to digress by describing some data that provide a concrete, empirical example of one commonly observed discrepancy between the response indicators of psychological stress. This example illustrates how the nature of the inferences we make about the intervening psychological process varies with the type of patterning of these indicators. Elsewhere (Lazarus, 1965), I have tried more systematically to make the general point that, without exception, all indicators of psychological stress are subject to individual response and stimulus specificity. Different intervening mechanisms are often reflected by each indicator and by the pattern of these indicators. The example comes from a recent attempt by my colleagues and me to study Japanese stress reactions. The material I will present here is part of a larger study (Lazarus and others, 1966).

In our original planning, we wanted to answer a number of cross-cultural questions, for example, whether Japanese reactions to a silent film entitled *Subincision* would be similar to those of Americans. Earlier studies (Lazarus and others, 1962) had shown that this film which depicts a puberty ceremony in an Australian stone age culture involving partial dissection of the penises of adolescent boys by means of a stone knife, was highly disturbing to watch. In addition, further research had demonstrated that the magnitude of the reaction could be reduced by the introduction of experimentally-created sound tracks based on the ego-defensive concepts of denial and intellectualization (Speisman and others, 1964). Moreover, self-reported affective disturbance to the film, as well as autonomic indicators of threat, such as heart rate and skin conductance, could be "short-circuited" by playing the denial and intellectualization passages to the individual before he viewed the *Subincision* film (Lazarus and Alfert, 1964). In effect, the defense-oriented passages served prophylactically to reduce the stress reaction normally produced by watching the film, presumably by altering the subjects' appraisal of the disturbing events that were depicted. We wanted to see whether these passages had the same effect on people living in a different culture. As it turned out, none of the original questions posed in this research could be properly answered because of an unexpected difference between Japanese and Americans in the way in which the experience of being an experimental subject was handled.

In brief, two populations were sampled, a college group of eighty young men from Waseda University in Tokyo and an older sample of sixty men between the ages of 36 and 58, roughly matched socioeconomically and educationally. On entering the laboratory individually, (GSR) electrodes were attached to the subject. After a baseline period, a control movie was shown on the subject of rice-farming in Japan. Subsequently, one of four orientation conditions was administered to the subjects. There were twenty subjects in each of these conditions. Following this set of conditions, another baseline reading was obtained, and then the *Subincision* film was shown. During both film presentations, skin conductance was measured continuously, and a series of self-reported estimates of degree of distress was obtained at numerous intervals during both films. This latter was done by inserting five-second blank leaders into the film and requesting the subject to rate on a seven-point scale his degree of distress during the preceding film segment whenever a blank leader appeared on the screen. In this way, a near-continuous picture of self-reported distress could be obtained as well as a continuous record of skin conductance. There were other procedures in the experiment that I shall not mention here because they are not germane to the findings I want to present.

The graphs in Figure 5.1 represent the self-reported distress of the subjects in the Japanese groups as they watched the control and stressful movie. Because we are not interested here in the effects of the experimental treatments, these conditions are combined into one curve. For comparison purposes, a curve of reported affective disturbance obtained by Mordkoff (1964), using a similar procedure with American subjects, is presented also. One notes that ratings of distress are rather low during the control film but show a consistent pattern of disturbances during the *Subincision* film. Rises to the highest levels of distress are reported during the operation scenes of the film, with sharp drops occurring during the benign scenes in-between operations and during a long ceremonial period just past the middle of the film. This pattern of reported distress shown by the

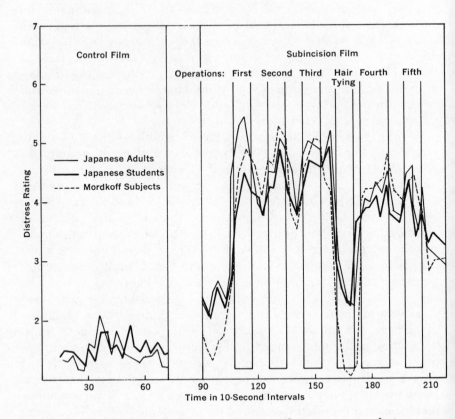

Fig. 5.1. Self-reported distress ratings of Japanese and American groups (see text).

Japanese subjects is identical to that observed by Mordkoff among American students.

The picture changes dramatically when we examine the variable of skin conductance, as is seen in Figure 5.2. Here are shown the Japanese population's curve of skin conductance during the rice-farming and *Subincision* films and, for comparative purposes, data from Mordkoff showing control and *Subincision* film levels among American students. We have used this film many times in the United States, and the pattern is always roughly the same: low levels of autonomic reactivity during the control film, high levels during the *Subincision* film. Moreover, these levels nicely reflect the contents of the film, going up sharply during operation sequences, down during the non-operation scenes. Actually, Mordkoff's curves are not

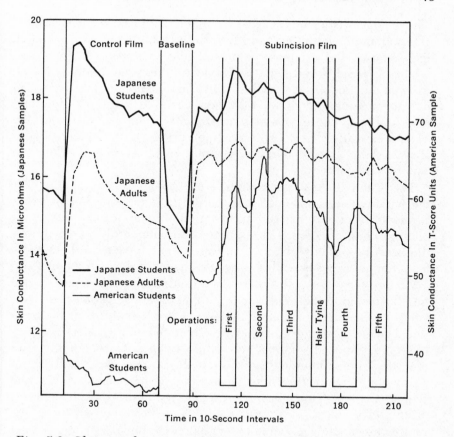

Fig. 5.2. Skin conductance of Japanese and American groups (see text). From Psychological Stress and the Coping Process by Richard S. Lazarus. Copyright 1966. McGraw-Hill Book Company. Used by permission.

the clearest or best with which to make this point, but they were selected because they were most readily available for this comparison. Both the Japanese students and older subjects show essentially the same picture.

There is little change in skin conductance between the control film level and that for the *Subincision* film in the Japanese subjects. Moreover, the correspondence between reactivity level and the content of the scenes is very poor, fluctuations in level appearing almost random. There is clearly something different occurring as between the Japanese and American samples. What are some of the possible explanations?

One possibility is that racial differences in sweat gland activity or skin characteristics might exist between Orientals and Caucasians. Johnson and Corah (1963) and Bernstein (1965) have demonstrated, for example, the existence of racial differences (for Negroes and whites) in basal skin resistance. However, this is not likely to be the explanation for our data. Close examination of the Japanese skin conductance curves shows that their baseline levels are low and comparable to those observed in our other studies of Americans. Moreover, during the second baseline period, the Japanese subjects show a sharp drop in skin conductance, rising again only when the experiment resumes.

The best hypothesis seems to be a psychological one, namely, that the Japanese are unusually sensitive to the total experimental situation and react with marked and continued apprehension during all phases of that situation. The apprehension temporarily wanes during the baseline periods because the experiment appears to the subject to be temporarily suspended in accordance with the instructions.

As our Japanese colleagues have pointed out, the Japanese are unaccustomed to the impersonal probing and observation characteristic of a laboratory situation. Moreover, most analyses of their national character suggest that Japanese tend to be threatened by being observed, especially from outside the group with whom they are identified, being more easily threatened with ridicule or criticism in a situation in which they must measure up to some standard (e.g., see Benedict, 1946). Thus, they are reacting, not to the specific contents of the experiment or to the distinctions between what the experimenter regards as benign or threatening, but rather to the total evaluative situation. This general apprehension overshadows any specific variation there might be in the impact of the different film contents.

Close analogies to this can be found in certain experiments within the American literature on psychological stress. For example, using heart rate as their index of stress reaction, Glickstein and others (1957) have shown that subjects with high levels of independently assessed anxiety showed uniformly high levels of heart rate during both benign and stressful procedures of an experiment, while those low in anxiety exhibited low heart rates for the benign portions but reacted sharply to the stressful aspects as defined by the experimenters. Similar findings with serum hydrocortisone as the stress measure are reported by Persky and others (1959), and by other groups of researchers as well. Recently, for example, a finding similar to this has also been reported by White (1965), who divided subjects on the basis of a questionnaire measure of anxiety. In discussing their findings, Glickstein and others have written:

The more disturbed subject, we might suppose, starts each experimental day with a distinctly greater amount of anticipatory anxiety. Taken from familiar surroundings and people with whom he has worked out some mode of adjustment, he is acutely aware of the potential threats in a strange laboratory, with its imposing wires and machinery and the business-like, but somewhat cold experiments.. ... *To be in an experiment in the first place is the stress ... With somewhat less anxiety, a patient becomes less sensitive to the more implicit threats of the situation in general and, simultaneously, is more capable of distinguishing and reacting to the more explicitly disturbing events* (1957, p. 106; emphasis added).

But we still must explain why the self-report picture displayed by the Japanese subjects conforms so closely to that of the American subjects in exquisitely reflecting the disturbing and nondisturbing sequences of the *Subincision* film and distinguishing so nicely between the benign control and stressful movie. Here, too, there are alternative interpretations. One is that the Japanese were simply dutifully expressing verbally what appeared to them as appropriate reactions without, indeed, experiencing comparable states of disturbance. In effect, they might be giving the experimenter what they thought he expected, as communicated by the "demand characteristics" of the situation.

A more probable guess is that the report did, indeed, reflect genuinely experienced ups and downs of distress, but that these were comparatively small in magnitude against the larger impact of the apprehension over being in the experimental situation itself. When asked to attend to the distress experienced in relation to the specific movie scenes, or to the differential impact of the control and stressful movie, they could indeed make clear discriminations. But with respect to the autonomic reaction, the larger and more continuous apprehension created by being a subject overshadowed the more minor variations resulting from specific stimuli.

This latter explanation has both methodological and theoretical implications. Methodologically, it implies the possibility that individual sources of stress reaction are not additive with respect to such autonomic indicators of arousal as skin conductance. Any simple, unidimensional indicator (as exclusive of multidimensional response patterns) reflects the largest source of disturbance, regardless of what it is. Alternatively, but not exclusive of the above, when the level of disturbance is high for any reason, a single measure (such as skin conductance) is less sensitive to small sources of variation than it is when the level of disturbance is low.

With respect to the intervening psychological mechanisms, we see

here an instance of failure of agreement between different indicators of psychological stress processes. Either the disagreement is
the result of different ways in which the Japanese cope with situations, or it derives from different sources of threat in the two populations. If the latter, we would say the Japanese subjects are more
threatened by being in an experiment than the Americans. If the
former, we might say that the Japanese are more sensitive than the
Americans to what is expected in social situations and therefore
comply more readily with the demand characteristics of the situation.
They thus report distress accordingly. In either case, the pattern of
response indicators provides the basis for different inferences about
the underlying psychological processes. It is clear that we must learn
more about the psychological rules which explain agreements and
disagreements between behavioral and physiological indicators of
stress reaction.

In the remainder of this chapter, I shall focus on one phase of this
problem, namely that dealing with the importance of individual
differences in coping processes that arise in response to threat and
which influence the observable reaction pattern. I want to underscore two main themes: (1) that *stress reactions are reflections or
consequences of coping processes* intended to reduce threat, and (2)
that *these coping processes (and the observable reactions themselves) depend, in part, on cognitive activity* very similar in kind to
the process of threat appraisal.

STRESS REACTIONS ARE REFLECTIONS OF COPING PROCESSES

With respect to the first point, when the individual is threatened,
activities are aroused to ward off the anticipated harm. Unless something is done to protect the psychological system, a damaging state of
affairs will occur (by the definition of threat). The individual may
attempt to avoid the danger, overcome it by attack on the harmful
agent, or engage in autoplastic defense activity, reappraising the
danger even in defiance of reality. It follows that the observable
reactions to threat will depend on the nature of the coping process
that is activated. For example, anger accompanied by behavioral
attack on the threatening agent will appear to be quite different in
response characteristics than anger in which the behavioral expression of aggression is inhibited, and even more different from the
reaction of fear associated with behavioral flight to avoid the impending harm. The motor-behavioral correlates of different forms of coping will obviously differ, as will the affects experienced and physi-

ological stress reaction observed. While there may be physiological features in common (for example, as postulated in the concept of arousal and in Selye's adaptation syndrome), the patterns of reaction will also diverge in important details as a function of different types of coping processes.

This point is more obvious when it involves patterns of behavior and affect rather than physiological response patterns, but its significance is the same. There is evidence that even the pattern of autonomic nervous system activity, as revealed by end-organ reactions, such as heart-rate, skin conductance, and respiration, is determined by the nature of the coping process. The research of Lacey and others (1963) suggests, for example, that when the individual is oriented to take in environmental input, there will be cardiac deceleration; contrariwise, an orientation to reject the environment would be associated with heart-rate acceleration. In an earlier study by Weiner and others (1962), processes of coping in a threatening situation were shown to insulate hypertensive patients from the relationship with the experimenter in such a way as to prevent the heightened blood pressure that might have been expected on the basis of their characteristic symptom pattern.

What do these findings mean? I think they say that the type of coping process (or as Lacey and others put it, the orientation with respect to the stimulus) influences the physiological pattern of reaction. If we take this seriously, it means that to understand and predict the physiological pattern of stress reaction we must know the nature of coping; conversely, the coping processes can be inferred from the pattern of reaction.

It is necessary now to raise the question of how different coping mechanisms are capable of producing different kinds of response patterns, including discrepancies between behavioral and physiological indicators. The fullest statement of the principle is that all categories of the observed threat reaction reflect the nature of the process of coping with threat.

I think the same position has been taken by Arnold (1960) in her analysis of emotions. Arnold suggests that the quality of an emotion (fear as opposed to anger) is explained by the motoric impulse that is generated by the stimulus whose value to the individual is appraised as positive or negative. In fact, says Arnold, this impulse with its psychological and physiological correlates *is* the emotion. She writes:

> As soon as we appraise something as worth having, in an immediate and intuitive way we feel an attraction toward it. As soon as we intuitively judge that something is threatening, we feel re-

pelled from it, we feel urged to avoid it. The intuitive appraisal of the situation initiates an *action tendency that is felt as emotion,* expressed in various bodily changes, and that eventually may lead to overt action (1960), vol. *1*, p. 177).

The action tendency, which in Arnold's view is the emotional reaction, should be interpreted functionally in psychological stress analysis as the process of coping with threat when the emotions involved are activated by the anticipation of harm. Since the action tendency is considered to be motivated by threat, its goal is the reduction or elimination of the anticipated harm. In effect, the action tendency resulting from the appraisal of threat is an effort on the part of the individual to cope with the harmful condition.

If an individual attempts to cope with a defense such as denial, then his self-report concerning affective distress will reflect this denial. But unless the denial is successful in eliminating the threat, the physiological stress reaction will remain, producing a pattern of discrepancy between the observed reaction at each level. As Lazarus and Alfert (1964) have shown, subjects prone to denial defenses do indeed report less anxiety but show larger autonomic disturbance than nondeniers who exhibit less autonomic evidence of stress reaction and report considerable anxiety. Such discrepancies between self-report and physiological indicators of stress reaction are usually accounted for by coping processes that intervene between threat and the observed stress reaction. It is perhaps a little more unusual to maintain, as is done by Lacey and his associates (1963), that even the physiological response pattern reflects the orientation toward, or as I would say, the form of coping with, the demands or threats of the situation.

COPING PROCESSES ARE, IN TURN, DEPENDENT ON THE COGNITIVE PROCESS OF APPRAISAL

Now I come to my second major theme—that the coping process itself depends, in part, on cognitive activity that is loosely called appraisal. When Arnold states that "The intuitive appraisal of the situation initiates an action tendency that is felt as emotion . . . ," she manages ingeniously to link cognitive activity with the characteristics of the emotional reaction. Arnold, too, treats emotion as an effect of cognitive processes. But she does not tell us how the appraisal leads to the particular action tendency, and so we are unable to take the next step of specifying the conditions under which one or another action tendency or emotion will occur. Remember that in psychological stress analysis, Arnold's action tendency is regarded as a process of coping with threat. We need ultimately to describe the kinds of appraisal that lead to each action tendency or coping impulse and the conditions that determine each kind of appraisal.

What is the significance of making this assertion that cognitive processes underlie not only threat but the form of coping with threat selected by the individual? Partly it adds the crucial dimension to our analysis of interaction between stimulus factors and the personality or dispositional factors characteristic of the individual. Up to now we have tended to emphasize either of these alone in predicting the reaction. For example, if we speak of stimulus specificity in physiological analysis, we mean that some portion of the variance of the reaction is normatively predicated on variations in the stimulus. If we speak of response or individual specificity, then we are saying that characteristics of the individual determine the reaction in a wide range of stimulus conditions. We have our stimulus and response specificities at the behavioral level, too. For example, most social psychological research involves systematic variation in the social structure and the measurement of the main effects of this variation. Most personality research, in contrast, involves systematic variation in the traits or dispositions in which individuals vary and the measurement of the main effects of these traits on the observed behavior.

But we are somehow reasonably sure that it is the combination of interaction of stimulus and dispositional properties that determines much of the reaction. And when we say that an individual appraises a situation in choosing a form of coping process, we are opening the way to seeing the effects as caused by a transaction with a particular environment by an individual with a particular psychological structure. We are implying in this way that if we knew the factors in the stimulus configuration and those within the psychological structure that jointly influence this appraisal, we could then predict the coping process and the observed reaction. In my mind, appraisal signifies such a transaction, and, as such, offers an advance over purely stimulus- and trait-centered analysis of psychological stress. How is this so?

The concept of appraisal makes us ask about the information concerning the environment that is relevant to the decision about how the individual will cope with threat. In effect, we are asking what the individual needs to know or believe about the situation for him to react in one way or another.

You will notice that I have repeatedly said that cognitive processes *in part* determine coping activities. I mean by this qualification to recognize that not all personality characteristics influence coping by the mediating cognitive process of appraisal, but that many do. For example, social constraints may not have much force in inhibiting the expression of a coping impulse if the individual lacks what is often called the capacity to control impulse expression. We even speak of this kind of individual as not "looking before he leaps," as being impulsive and often regretting actions after they have been made rather than evaluating their consequences beforehand and inhibiting the course of action which may be damaging. Thus, the capacity to control impulse expression, as studied by Block and Block (1952), is an example of a personality trait that influences coping directly, without the mediation of an appraisal process.

INTERACTIONS BETWEEN SITUATIONAL AND PERSONALITY DETERMINANTS OF APPRAISAL AND COPING

I said earlier that the concept of appraisal makes us ask what information is relevant to the decision about coping, information which comprises the external and internal conditions of appraisal. What are some of the factors in the stimulus configuration that research has indicated are important? Degree of threat is one. Greater sacrifices of other goals will be made, for example, if the goal that is endangered is important than if it is not. Another is the location of the agent of harm. For example, attack cannot be mounted, or flight mobilized, if a harmful agent is not identified, that is, if there is nothing to attack or flee. The viability of alternative actions is a third. As Berkowitz (1962) has said in paraphrasing Janis (1958), "the extent to which this emotion [fear] is stronger than anger may be a function of the individual's perceived power to control or hurt his frustrator relative to the frustrator's power to control or harm him" (1962, p. 45). An interesting example of this principle is the observation that in situations of extreme helplessness, such as the concentration camp, people show surprisingly little anger against the agents of their distress but are very quick to show anger against their fellow prisoners, or outsiders, who are less able to retaliate. A fourth factor is the social or situational constraints that catapult the individual into further harm were he to cope with threat in a particular way.

As I have said, the role of these situational variables in coping depends on factors within the psychological structure, some of which are important in influencing appraisal. One example would be the motivational structure of the individual which determines whether any given result of coping will be appraised as harmful and to what degree. Another comprises the general beliefs of the individual about the environment and his resources for coping with it. Highly generalized attitudes, such as trust or distrust, as described by Erikson (1950), should be very important in determining what reliance the individual will place on environmental resources for mastering dangers.

Qualities of the psychological or personality structure will determine how this information is to be utilized or modified. For example, if the individual believes that attack on the threatening agent cannot possibly overcome the threat, then attack as the coping impulse is not likely to be activated. Or if attack might overcome the threat, but the individual believes it is wrong or will be severely punished, then even if it arises as the coping impulse or action tendency, it is likely to be inhibited.

The role of appraisal in coping is nicely illustrated in some of the research reviewed by Berkowitz (1962), which shows that aggression is not an automatic or inevitable accompaniment of frustrating or threatening conditions. Its evocation depends on a number of antecedent conditions, for example, the arbitrariness of the frustrator, his power to retaliate against agression, and the presence of internalized values against aggression. In effect, the individual evaluates complex social cues, and the coping process is dependent on this evaluation.

In my view, it is not as useful to say that anger is caused by the stimulus situation, and that anger, the intervening variable, modified by personality factors, then causes the behavior, as it is to say that the objective stimulus situation is appraised on the basis of its characteristics as well as traits of personality, this cognitive activity of appraisal being the intervening process. If both external and internal controls permit it, the outcome will be the emotion, anger, and the behavior of aggression. If internal controls permit anger, but the appraisal of the objective situation is that aggression would be dangerous, and assuming the individual has the capacity to control impulses, then the outcome will be anger but no direct aggression. If internal personality prohibitions against aggression are especially strong, then the appraisal may lead to other emotions and behaviors, for example, fear or depression but not anger or aggression. In this view, depression should be regarded as based on the appraisal of a frustrating or threatening condition in which externally directed anger and retaliation are not viable alternatives.

The same reasoning must apply to coping processes other than aggression, for example, flight, the choice of defense, and efforts to prepare against the harm—as when graduate students study for threatening examinations and plan strategies for coping with the anticipated danger of failing, as observed by Mechanic (1962). The personal and social consequences of any action tendency are appraised by the individual and thus shape the coping strategy which is selected out of many alternative possibilities. Let me give you a further example of this principle from the sociological literature.

Attempting to distinguish between the conditions producing panic or riot, Smelser (1963) has pointed out that these outbursts depend on widely shared beliefs about how the harmful social condition is being caused and how it can be modified or eliminated, and that the hostile action will be condoned, or at least not retaliated against. In the riot, there is the identification of dangerous or evil persons who are held responsible for the damaging situation, and there is the belief that the problem can be overcome by hostile action. In the case of panic a very different appraisal is involved. Discussing the kinds of escape possibilities, for example, that permit panic, Smelser quotes Quarantelli (1954) as follows:

> The important aspect is the belief or feeling of *possible* entrapment. This is reiterated again and again in the remarks of panic participants. It is not that affected individuals believe or feel they are definitely trapped. In such instances panic does not follow ... The flight of panic arises only when being trapped is sensed or thought of as a possibility rather than an actuality ... (p. 273).

> [Smelser adds:] In addition, people who panic sense that this "limited number of escape routes" is "closing" (not closed) so that escape must be made quickly (1963, p. 136).

> [And further:] ... reactions such as terror or infantile regression can occur in such settings (when escape routes are conceived to be completely blocked), but not panic. Marshall (1947) notes that in amphibious attacks during World War II immobility in the face of enemy fire was a common response: ... the sea was at (the troops') back; there was no place to run even had they been capable of movement. They sat there dumbly in the line of fire, their minds blanked out, their fingers too nerveless to hold a weapon (1963, p. 136).

Analysis of mine and submarine disasters also supports the idea that only when there is the possibility of escape which may be closed will there be panic. In other words, one particular kind of appraisal encourages panic rather than some other form of coping reaction.

The well-known experiments of Mintz (1951) on "bottlenecks" or "traffic jams" as groups of subjects must withdraw corks on the ends of strings from a narrow-necked bottle also suggest the importance of appraisal of alternatives, even though Mintz emphasizes the reward structure of the situation. Recent studies by Kelley and others (1965), extending Mintz's work, support the role of appraisal of what others in the group will do in panic situations in determining the coping strategy selected by the individuals in those settings. If we take one traditional view of emotion and coping, we would have to say that Mintz's subjects in the panic-engendering conditions became frightened, and as a consequence, could not properly assess the futility of precipitous "escape." They attempted "escape," although it was maladaptive, because emotions superseded rational thought and action. The view that I think is more fruitful is that the dangers or gains are apprehended by the individual, and this leads to the decision to act in accordance with this appraisal. Fear, or some other emotion, is the *consequence* of this appraisal and the action tendency or coping impulse it activates. If Mintz is correct in his observation that the reward structure is important, then this structure must have been appraised by his subjects on the basis of the stimulus configuration and on the basis of shared motivational characteristics and beliefs about how others will react in such a situation. No effort was made by Mintz to study individual differences in reaction that might have highlighted some of the personality determinants of varieties of appraisal and coping.

Although I have argued that the cognitive process of appraisal underlies the coping process and the observed stress reaction pattern, empirical research must be directed at the interactive role of observable antecedent conditions in the stimulus configuration and personality traits in determining that reaction. Wolff and others (1964) have shown that parents of children dying of leukemia who exhibited strong denial defenses showed significantly less evidence of adrenal cortical secretions than those without such defenses. The parental reactions were treated as a defense because information about the child's outlook had been forcibly brought home to the individual by the physicians and others around him. However, in many situations, failure to interpret dangers realistically can occur simply because the cues of danger are not made available to the individual, as when a physician withholds threatening information. Whether it is withheld or not is often determined by the physician's reading of the patient's reaction to minimal information of disaster. The physican senses (or believes) that the patient will react badly to threatening cues. He responds to these inferred defensive needs on the part of the patient with behaviors that are, from his point of view, protective. In this kind of interchange between the stimulus situation, as represented by the physician's behavior and the personality of the patient, we see a clinical example of the complexity of the problem and the importance of emphasizing the cognitive transactions between a person with a particular personality and the variable kinds of cues of danger the stimulus configuration contains. What the individual will do in the way of coping with the threat is also influenced by a variety of social constraints based on anticipated environmental reactions. For example, in the same study of parents of children with cancer, if the parents did not appear to suffer visibly, they often were exposed to severe criticism from relatives and friends who might regard them as heartless or indifferent to the plight of their child—social pressures which not only added to their already heavy burden but also served to shape their coping reactions as well. The evidence is strong that the observed reaction pattern depends on intervening cognitive processes involving complex interplays between particular personalities and stimulus patterns.

With respect to laboratory studies of personality traits and coping, a fascinating experiment by Conn and Crowne (1964) supports the principle that motivation for approval as a trait results in the inhibition of aggressive behavior as a method of coping when the individual is threatened, by virtue of his appraisal of the consequences of assertive acts that could lead to social disapproval. They observed the amount of euphoria following a strong provocation to anger. First, a measure of need for approval was obtained from male undergraduate students, based on a standardized questionnaire scale in which the subject attributes to himself or denies culturally disapproved statements. In the experimental situation, the subject is joined with an accomplice of the experimenter and introduced to a situation in which he could win considerable money (up to $5.00) along with the accomplice who is his partner. The experimenter is unexpectedly called out of the room, whereupon the accomplice proposes that the two of them enter into collusion in order to maximize their winnings. However, when the experimenter returns and the game begins, the accomplice exasperatingly violates his agreement leading to minimal payments for the subject.

At the conclusion of the game, the subject and accomplice are escorted into another room to wait until the apparatus is ready for the next part of the experiment. In a fashion comparable to that of the Schachter and Singer study (1962), a euphoria-stimulating condition is then created by the accomplice, who makes bad jokes, laughs uproariously, plays makeshift games in which he attempts to involve the subject and generally acts exuberantly and enthusiastically. If the subject mentions the violation of the agreement by the accomplice, the latter laughs and replies, "Well, that's the way it goes."

The authors find that approval-oriented subjects exhibited significantly more euphoria in the experimental condition than did subjects assumed to be low in need for approval, a difference that did not occur in the control condition, in which there was no previous experience of treachery. The behavior of the subjects is described by the authors as follows:

> After being treated in a dastardly manner by the experimental accomplice, approval-striving Ss endorsed by word and action the simulated jubilation of the accomplice and interacted with him as a friend and admirer. In dramatic contrast is the reaction of the low need for approval Ss. Following the same instigation to anger, they became sullen and resentful in facial expression and communication and refused to endorse the accomplice's "ode of joy." Instead, they directed derogatory comments at him and spurned his invitations to play (Conn and Crowne, 1964, p. 177).

For the relationship found by Conn and Crowne to take place, the individual must have taken into account the meaning of the social situation—the potential dangers to his social status were he to act assertively. The subject low in need for approval selects a coping strategy (in this case conformity to social pressure and lack of assertiveness) on the basis of having evaluated what is called for in the situation to preserve needed social relationships. If the subject had really believed the partner would like him better if he acted assertively, a totally different outcome would have to be predicted. The approval-seeking subjects would have acted even more assertively than those low in need for approval.

APPRAISAL AND IRRATIONALITY

I must return briefly to my initial assertion that we should regard threat and coping with threat as the consequences of cognitive processes. At first glance, it would seem that this focus on appraisal places an undue emphasis on cognitive processes in the psychodynamics of stress. It is as if the individual is continually making rational judgments about coping processes, for example, judgments of what course of action is viable or imposes the possibility of further threats. Have we placed ourselves in the position of no longer being able to comprehend irrationality?

It might appear that cognitive appraisal, to which so much importance is attached, is a conscious, rational, balanced consideration of the evidence, leading to a conclusion justified by the facts that a given situation is actually threatening or benign and shaped by the requirement that a given solution will be successful in eliminating or reducing the threat. But the term *cognitive* does not imply awareness, good reality testing, or adaptiveness. It only implies that thought processes are involved, not the kind or quality of the thought. What is meant is that beliefs, expectations, perceptions, and their motivations underlie how a threat stimulus is reacted to. Furthermore, the cognitions involved need not be reportable.

The point is that the stress reaction is the effect of these cognitive appraisal processes and the conditions that determine them. The irrationality or maladaptiveness does not come primarily from the intervention of emotions in thought processes, but rather from the fact that threat places the psychological system in jeopardy and that the alternatives for coping with threat are tied to motives, beliefs, and expectations concerning the situation, which differ from person to person.

It is true that one finds abundant clinical examples of individuals who have acted "irrationally" under accompanying intense emotional disturbance. A lay tradition has grown up which makes emotional disturbance the cause rather than effect of maladaptive behavior. Since negatively toned emotion is an inevitable accompaniment or correlate of threat and coping, it only *seems* as though the emotion is "causing" the trouble. The culprit is really the recognition of threat or danger, and the cognitions that underlie the effort to cope with it. The correlation between threat and emotion makes it easy to confuse cause and effect, especially since the emotional state is the most obtrusive feature of the entire psychological event. The hypothetical construct has mistakenly become the literally conceived cause.

CONCLUDING REMARKS

What we must do in psychological stress analysis is to identify the cognitions that underlie threat, and the specific appraisals that lead to each form of coping, with its observable behavioral and physiological response pattern. Particular appraisals underlie attack which is expressed behaviorally; somewhat different appraisals underlie the impulse to attack which is inhibited. Still different appraisals underlie flight patterns. The same might be said for each form of defense as well. Time does not permit me to do more than make the general point here. These appraisals are, in turn, shaped by the stimulus configuration and personality as they interact.

Two fundamental assumptions must be made if what I have said is to make sense, and these assumptions have made up the two interrelated themes of this chapter. First, the observed pattern of reaction depends on intervening psychological activities, such as the coping process. Secondly, underlying each type of coping is a particular kind of appraisal in which the consequences of cues are interpreted. This appraisal leads to the selection of a coping process that is appropriate to it, though not necessarily to what is required for good adaptiveness or reality testing. I believe that research on the conditions that determine the coping process and the observed patterns of stress reaction would proceed faster and more fruitfully if we sought to conceptualize the appraisals involved in each type of coping, if we ceased to fear phenomenological terms and concepts and used them to the fullest extent to locate the empirical conditions accounting for varieties of stress reaction.

REFERENCES

ARNOLD, M. B. 1960. *Emotion and Personality*, 2. vols. New York: Columbia.
  1967. "Stress and Emotion," in M. H. Appley and R. Trumbull, eds., *Psychological Stress*. New York: Appleton-Century-Crofts.
BENEDICT, R. 1946. *The Chrysanthemum and the Sword*. Boston: Houghton Mifflin.
BERKOWITZ, L. 1962. *Aggression*. New York: McGraw-Hill.
BERNSTEIN, A. S. 1965. "Race and Examiner as Significant Influences on Basal Skin Impedance." *Journal of Personality and Social Psychology*, 1:346–49.
BLOCK, J., and BLOCK, J. 1952. "An Interpersonal Experiment on Reactions to Authority." *Human Relations*, 5:91–98.
CONN, L. K., and CROWNE, D. P. 1964, "Instigation to Aggression, Emotional Arousal and Defensive Emulation." *Journal of Personality*, 32:163–79.
ERIKSON, E. H. 1950. *Childhood and Society*, (rev. ed., 1963). New York: Norton.
GLICKSTEIN, M., CHEVALIER, J. A., KORCHIN, S. J., BASOWITZ, H., SABSHIN, M., HAMBURG, D. A., and GRINKER, R. R. 1957. "Temporal Heat Rate Patterns in Anxious Patients. *AMA Archives of Neurology and Psychiatry*, 78, 101–06.
JANIS, I. L. 1958. *Psychological Stress*. New York: John Wiley.
JOHNSON, L. C., and CORAH, N. L. 1963. "Racial Differences in Skin Resistance." *Science*, 139:766–67.
KELLEY, H. H., CONDRY, J. C., DAHLKE, A. E., and HILL, A. H. 1965. "Collective Behavior in a Simulated Panic Situation." *Journal of Experimental Social Psycholgoy*, 1:20–54.
LACEY, J. I., KAGAN, J., LACEY, B. C., and MOSS, H. A. 1963. "The Visceral

Level: Situational Determinants and Behavioral Correlates of Autonomic Response Patterns," in P. H. Knapp, ed., *Expression of the Emotions in Man.* New York: International Universities.

LAZARUS, R. S. 1965. "An Inspirational View of Response Patterning." Paper given at the Western Psychological Association Meetings in a symposium entitled, "The Dynamics of Emotion: Autonomic and Behavioral Effect." Honolulu (June 17).

——— 1966. *Psychological Stress and the Coping Process.* New York: McGraw-Hill.

LAZARUS, R. S., and ALFERT, E. 1964. "The Short-circuiting of Threat," *Journal of Abnormal and Social Psychology,* 69:195–205.

LAZARUS, R. S., SPEISMAN, J. C., MORDKOFF, A. M., and DAVISON, L. A. 1962. "A Laboratory Study of Psychological Stress Produced by a Motion Picture Film." *Psychological Monographs,* 76 (whole no. 553), p. 35.

LAZARUS, R. S., TOMITA, M., OPTON, E. M., JR., and KODAMA, M. 1966. "A Cross-cultural Study of Stress Reaction Patterns in Japan. *Journal of Personality and Social Psychology,* 4:622–633.

MARSHALL, S. L. A. 1947. *Men against Fire.* New York: Morrow.

MECHANIC, D. 1962. *Students under Stress.* New York: Free Press.

MINTZ, A. 1951. "Non-adaptive Group Behavior." *Journal of Abnormal and Social Psychology.* 46:150–59.

MORDKOFF, A. M. 1964. "The Relationship between Psychological and Physiological Response to Stress." *Psychosomatic Medicine,* 26:135–49.

PERSKY, H., KORCHIN, S. J., BASOWITZ, H., BOARD, F. A., SABSHIN, M. A., HAMBURG, D. A., and GRINKER, R. R. 1959. "Effect of Two Psychological Stresses on Adrenocortical Function." *AMA Archives of Neurology and Psychiatry,* 81:219–26.

PETERS, H. N. 1963. "Affect and Emotion," in M. H. Marx, ed., *Theories in Contemporary Psychology.* New York: Collier-Macmillan.

QUARANTELLI, E. L. 1954. "The Nature and Conditions of Panic." *American Journal of Sociology,* 60:267–75.

SCHACHTER,S. and SINGER, J. E. 1962."Cognitive, Social, and Physiological Determinants of Emotional State." *Psychological Review,* 69:379–99.

SMELSER, N. J. 1963. *Theory of Collective Behavior.* New York: Free Press.

SPEISMAN, J. C., LAZARUS, R. S., MORDKOFF, A. M., and DAVISON, L. A. 1964. "The Experimental Reduction of Stress Based on Ego-defense Theory." *Journal of Abnormal and Social Psychology,* 68:367–80.

WEINER, H., SINGER, MARGARET T., and REISER, M. F. 1962. "Cardiovascular Responses and Their Psychological Correlates: I. A Study in Healthy Young Adults and Patients with Peptic Ulcer and Hypertension." *Psychosomatic Medicine,* 24:477–98.

WHITE, ELNA. 1965. "Autonomic Responsivity as a Function of Level of Subject Involvement." *Behavioral Science,* 10:39–50.

WOLFF, C. T., FRIEDMAN, S. B., HOFER, M. A., and MASON, J. W. 1964. "Relationship between Psychological Defenses and Mean Urinary 17-hydroxycorticosteroid Excretion Rates: I. A. Predictive Study of Parents of Fatally Ill Children." *Psychosomatic Medicine,* 26:576–91.

6. Experimental Studies of Conflict-Produced Stress

ANDREW CRIDER

AS PRESENTLY employed, the notion of stress has little systematic behavioral meaning. In borrowing the term from physics and engineering, psychologists have often implicitly drawn an analogy between steady states and deviations of physical systems and presumed correspondences in behavioral states. Thus, "stress" research typically examines deviations in perceptual, cognitive, visceral, or behavioral activity from some normative or "nonstress" condition, the assumption being that the observed change represents an anomalous and nonfunctional response to environmental demands. The problem here is that a categorization of such deviations as stress reactions simply in terms of their form or topography introduces theoretical presuppositions that can interfere with a more neutral analysis of the behavior in terms of its functional significance for the economy of the individual.

Andrew Crider is assistant professor of psychology at Williams College, Williamstown, Massachusetts.

For example, an increase of heart rate during the performance of a laboratory task is often taken as an a priori operational definition of stress, following Cannon's (1929) view linking sympathetic nervous system arousal with threats to the organism's survival. As pointed out below, however, this topographical approach is embarrassed by such findings as the superior problem-solving performance of individuals who respond to intellectual tasks with marked increases in heart rate as compared with the poorer performance of those who show little or no heart rate change. In another situation generally considered an exemplar of a stressful environment—the conditioning paradigm in which a warning signal precedes some aversive event—the human heart rate response to the signal is actually deceleratory (Wood and Obrist, 1964). In light of such problems, a functional analysis eschews the assignment of meaning to psychophysiological deviations from resting conditions in favor of examining the environmental control of these changes and their effects on the subsequent behavior of the individual. In the latter portion of this discussion, we will suggest some guidelines for interpreting the instrumental significance of physiological arousal under "stress" conditions.

The term "stress" is probably most appropriately used to denote a broad area of research, rather than a theoretical notion. Historically, this research area has shown a concern for examining the control of multiple response systems—verbal, physiological, and behavioral—by *aversive* environmental events. Aversiveness is not a quality that resides in a stimulus, but refers to a type of contingency obtaining between behavior and its environmental context. Thus an aversive event is defined as one whose removal will strengthen any immediately preceding response. A common experimental example involves the actual or threatened *presentation* of a noxious, biologically damaging stimulus to an organism. When the organism is able to remove the stimulus by an appropriate behavioral maneuver, high and sustained rates of responding are produced, accompanied by physiological arousal which can result in ultimate impairment. In the well-known "executive monkey" study of Brady and others (1958), electric shocks were regularly presented to two animals unless one of them (the "executive") pressed a lever, postponing the shock for a short interval. If the response were not forthcoming, both the executive and his cohort received the shock. Under certain conditions of rest and subsequent stress, the executive or avoidance monkey developed gastric ulcers. No such debilitation was observed in the passive cohort who had nonetheless received an equivalent number of noxious electric shocks. Thus the behavioral contingency was of primary importance in determining the aversiveness of the electric shock.

Similarly, an aversive condition can be created by the actual or threatened *removal* of a positively reinforcing stimulus. The stimulus may be the reinforcer which maintains the behavior under question, in which case the operation is known as "extinction," or it may be some independent event, as in the case of the child whose misbehavior leads to the withdrawal of future privileges to engage in satisfying activity. Although it has been demonstrated that behavior that avoids such contingencies will be strengthened, their psychophysiological effects are less well understood. Clinical experience suggests, however, that a number of disorders ranging from depression to cancer may arise from the removal of sources of environmental support and gratification (Engel, 1962; Schmale, 1958).

A third category of aversive conditions are so-called conflict situations in which two or more incompatible responses of approximately equal strength are simultaneously aroused. In the best understood case, conflict is created by both reinforcing and punishing a given behavior (approach-avoidance conflict), although other methods of producing response incompatibility are possible, as in approach-approach or avoidance-avoidance conflicts. A classic experiment done in Pavlov's laboratory produced conflict by creating an insoluble discrimination between one stimulus signaling food reinforcement and a second stimulus signaling its absence. Pavlov's description of the ensuing "experimental neurosis" has been widely quoted:

A projection of a luminous circle on to a screen in front of the animal was repeatedly accompanied by feeding. After the reflex had become well established a differentiation between the circle and an ellipse with a ratio of the semi-axes 2:1, of the same luminosity and the same surface area, was obtained by the usual method of contrast. A complete and constant differentiation was obtained comparatively quickly. The shape of the ellipse was now approximated by stages to that of the circle (ratios of the semi-axes of 3:2, 4:3, and so on) and the development of differentiation continued through the successive ellipses. The differentiation proceeded with some fluctuations, progressing at first more and more quickly, and then again slower, until an ellipse with ratio of semi-axes 9:8 was reached. In this case, although a considerable degree of discrimination did develop, it was far from being complete. After three weeks of work upon this differentiation not only did the discrimination fail to improve, but it became considerably worse, and finally disappeared altogether. At the same time the whole behaviour of the animal underwent an abrupt change. The hitherto quiet dog began to squeal in its stand, kept wriggling about, tore off with its teeth the apparatus for mechanical stimulation of the skin, and bit through the tubes connecting the animal's room with the observer, a behaviour which never happened before. On being taken into the experimental room the dog now barked violently, which was also contrary to the usual custom; in short it presented all the symptoms of a condition of acute neurosis. On testing the cruder differentiations they also were found to be destroyed, even the one with the ratio of the semi-axes 2:1 (1960, pp. 290–91).

Subsequent work in the Pavlovian mold demonstrated such conflict-produced aberrations in animals as hyperactivity, convulsions, sexual anomalies, and visceral dysfunction (Gantt, 1944). There is little question that conflict is aversive and will strengthen behavior that avoids it (Hearst and Sidman, 1961). With human subjects it is also found that conflict situations entail the sort of behavioral reactions of interest to stress researchers: autonomic nervous system arousal, feelings of distress, distortions of thinking and perceiving, and impaired performance. These sorts of outcome behaviors have made conflict situations especially appropriate as stress paradigms, as the following discussion illustrates.

The physiologically arousing effects of Pavlovian discrimination conflict have been convincingly demonstrated on the human level in experiments by Johnson (1963) and Wilson and Duerfeldt (1967). In the Johnson study, subjects were punished with an unpleasant electric shock for failing to execute a simple motor response to one metronome beat or for failing to inhibit the same response to a second beat several steps removed in frequency. In the Wilson and Duerfeldt study, the task was simply to verbally report which of two light intensities would be followed by shock. In both studies, continuous polygraphic measurements of heart-rate and palmar electrodermal activity (skin conductance) were taken. After the initial discrimination had been established, conflict was induced in both experiments by gradually converging the two signals to the point of identity. Under these conditions, heart-rate and palmar skin conductance levels rise with increasing difficulty of discrimination (Johnson), and the specific responses evoked by the two signals and by the shock are augmented (Wilson and Duerfeldt). In the case of heart-rate, this augmentation consists of increasingly greater *deceleration* to the signals but greater *acceleration* to the shock which follows the positive signal. This nicely illustrates the fact that the physiological reaction to a preaversive event does not necessarily mimic the response to the event itself and may even be in a direction opposite to that specified by traditional views linking stress reaction to sympathetic nervous system arousal.

Two additional points of interest can be drawn from these experiments. First, Johnson demonstrated that the heightened physiological activity was attributable to conflict per se, rather than to the increasing frequency of shocks received by subjects as errors in discrimination became more frequent over time. Control subjects matched for shock exposure with the experimental subjects but without the discrimination requirement actually showed declining physiological levels over time and complained of boredom. Secondly, both studies reported that as the discrimination became increasingly insoluble, subjects evinced a variety of untoward behavioral reactions, including reports of anxiety, intropunitiveness, annoyance, and anger. These reactions varied from subject to subject, in line with Pavlov's (1960) observation that behavioral reactions to conflict depend on the basic "temperament" of the animal. This may reflect genetic differences, as Pavlov thought, or may be due to the arousal of behavior patterns that the individual has previously found effective in coping with states of heightened tension (Johnson, 1963). In any case, behavioral reactions to conflict are notably difficult to predict, obviously depending on as yet poorly understood individual differences.

A series of elegant studies of real-life stress by Epstein and Fenz have treated sport parachuting as essentially a temporal approach-avoidance conflict (Epstein and Fenz, 1962; Fenz, 1964; Fenz and Epstein, 1967). Their model derives from Miller's gradient analysis of conflict (Miller, 1944), which postulates increasing strengths of both approach and avoidance tendencies as a function of nearness to a goal. The strength of approach is assumed to be greater than that of avoidance distant from the goal but to increase less rapidly than the strength of avoidance with increasing closeness to the goal. Thus conflict becomes increasingly severe as the net approach tendency decreases closer to the goal. The goal-act of sport parachuting is, of course, the actual jump, with approach represented by the anticipated pleasure and avoidance by the threat of mishap or injury.

Epstein and Fenz assume that physiological arousal is a function of response strength regardless of directionality, so that net arousal at any point prior to the jump can be represented as the sum of both approach and avoidance tendencies at that point. Summation of these tendencies yields an essentially positively accelerated curve of arousal with increasing proximity to the jump. This deduction was tested by measuring heart-rate and palmar skin conductance with a portable apparatus in a group of novice parachutists during a sequence of events leading up to and just following a jump. A group of ostensibly less conflicted experienced jumpers was also tested for comparative purposes. In addition, continuous ratings of subjective anxiety over the same time sequence were obtained from groups of novice and experienced jumpers.

As seen in Figure 6.1, the positive acceleration in heart-rate and skin conductance curves for the novice jumpers is remarkably close to the theoretically expected trends. In contrast, the curves for experienced jumpers are seen to be inverted V-shaped, that is, an initial rise followed by a decline. The time trends for self-rated anxiety are only superficially similar to the physiological data, since a notable downtrend occurs in the novice data just prior to the jump, and the beginning of the downtrend for the experienced jumpers occurs much earlier in time than for the autonomic measures. Without belaboring these discrepancies, it is worth noting that anxiety and physiological arousal among novices do tend to covary with increasing conflict, but their points of divergence suggest two functionally distinct systems. This point will be pursued later. Figure 6.1 also shows an interesting rebound of subjective anxiety just following the jump for the experienced group. This and related evidence leads the authors to speculate that mastery of conflict is not a simple matter of extinction of arousal and anxiety with repeated exposure, but involves instead an active coping process involving learned techniques of anxiety inhibition. With increasing experience these inhibitory processes would be keyed off at increasingly lower levels of arousal, yielding the observed peaking of anxiety and autonomic arousal very early in the sequence for the experienced jumpers. Finally, Fenz (1964) found conflict-produced deviations among novice parachutists in other areas besides physiological arousal and rated anxiety. When tested on the day of a jump and compared with a control day, novices show a decrease in sensory acuity, an increase in reaction time, misperceptions of anxiety-related cues, and deficits in memory and associative processes.

To recapitulate the discussion thus far, we have suggested that stress research should not be diffusely concerned with behavioral deviations from a priori norms of adequacy of functioning, but rather with the multiple effects of behavior under the control of aversive events. Aversive conditions are defined behaviorally as those events an organism will work to escape or avoid, such as the imposition of a

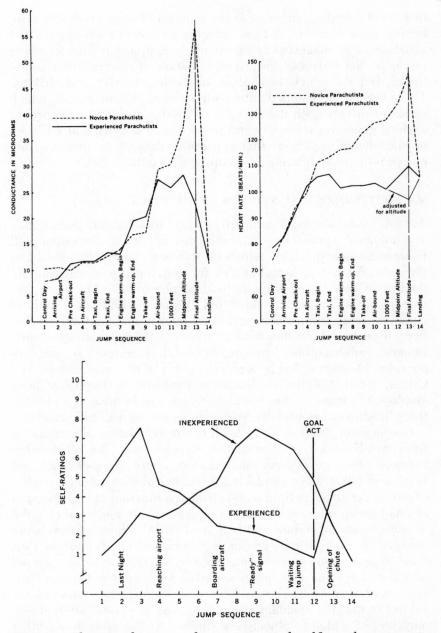

Fig. 6.1. Skin conductance, heart rate, and self-rated anxiety in novice and experienced parachutists as a function of the sequence of events leading up to and after a jump. (From Fenz and Epstein, 1967).

biologically noxious stimulus or the removal of some positively reinforcing state of affairs. A third category of aversive events, conflict
situations, was suggested as a particularly appropriate area for stress
research. Not only has the aversive nature of conflict been established, but the effects of conflict are both extensive and striking.
These include heightened autonomic nervous system arousal, which
varies positively with the severity of conflict, subjective reports of
anxiety, generalized sensory and performance deficits, and a variety
of idiosyncratic reactions that apparently depend on innate or acquired individual differences in coping with tension states.

SOCIOPHYSIOLOGICAL STUDIES OF CONFLICT

As this volume deals primarily with sociological and social-
psychological approaches to stress, the following discussion will
be devoted to a specialty which combines social-psychological and
physiological research techniques in studying the modulating influence of social factors on individual physiology. The term "so-
ciophysiology," coined by Boyd and DiMascio (1954) in a study of
autonomic changes in a patient during psychotherapy interviews, has
been used to denote this field of inquiry. Although an apparently
esoteric subdiscipline, its experimental literature is not in-
considerable, as testified by a recent review of the area (Shapiro and
Crider, 1969). Conflict models have explicitly or implicitly been
employed in much of this research, which can be treated under the
three headings of conformity, status ambiguity, and attitude conflict.

Conformity. Starting with the hypothesis relating alterations in
lipid metabolism to cardiovascular disease (as in the relationship
between blood cholesterol and coronary artery disease), Back and
Bogdonoff (1964) have conducted a number of experimental studies
examining changes in lipid metabolism as a function of various types
of small group interaction. The basic experiment made use of serial
measurements of plasma free-fatty acid (FFA) while subjects were
engaged in an Asch type conformity situation. The release of FFA
from adipose tissue can be stimulated by several hormones, among
which epinephrine and norepinephrine are under autonomic nervous system control. The Asch conformity situation requires the
subject to match a standard stimulus to one of several alternatives,
only one of which is objectively similar. At the same time, other
group members have been preprogrammed by the experimenter to
make a prior choice of one of the incorrect alternatives on a high
proportion of the trials. The subject's degree of independence or

conformity of judgment following the group decision is the major dependent variable of interest. It is known that a significant percentage of subjects will conform to group pressure in this situation by endorsing the majority opinion even though counter to veridical perception.

As Back and Bogdonoff point out, the situation is operationally equivalent to an approach-approach conflict, with conformity defined as a preference for the social stimulus over the competing physical stimulus. In addition, the intensity of conflict can be manipulated by varying the attractiveness of the group for the individual or, conversely, varying the ease with which the physical stimuli can be matched with an alternative. In general an increase in FFA levels is observed during conformity trials, although the magnitude of the response is strongly influenced by the impact of these latter variables. For example, FFA levels rise when the individual is confronted with a perceptually incorrect judgment on the part of acknowledged friends, but show no change or decline when he is similarly confronted by a group of strangers. Furthermore, individuals who conform least in a group of friends show greater increases in FFA level than those who conform most. Thus deviation from the group consensus appears conflictful only when the group has psychological meaning for the individual, that is, when group norms have been established through prior interaction. Secondly, conformity to group consensus in a conflict situation is a stress-reducing maneuver in that it leads to a decrease in FFA arousal. On the other side of the coin, it was also demonstrated that, independently of group composition, the more clearly defined and less ambiguous the correct choice among the alternatives, the greater was the physiological arousal and the more tension-reducing the act of conformity.

Similar findings were reported in a now classic study by Smith (1936). The technique here was to elicit from a class of students individual agreement or disagreement, along with a rating of degree of conviction, to a series of then controversial issues, for example, "Divorce should be granted only in the case of grave offense," "The Soviet experiment in government should be encouraged." Some weeks later, each subject was again asked to express his opinion on each issue after having been confronted with fictitious majority opinions, half of which coincided with the subject's stand and half of which ran counter. Galvanic skin response (GSR) magnitude at the point of response was taken as a measure of "emotional" reaction. Among other things, the GSR was found to be positively related to

degree of conviction, whether with or against the group. More im-
portantly, opinions contrary to the majority elicited larger GSR's than
those coinciding with the majority. Interestingly, individual opinions
held with *absolute* conviction that ran counter to the group consensus elicited smaller GSR's than those held with a lesser degree of
surety. Conflict is by definition not present when one of two alternative responses is of significantly greater strength, and thus when an
opinion is strongly held, contrary group judgments will have little
impact on the individual. Finally, in agreement with the Back and
Bogdonoff research, Smith found that changes in opinion from first to
second testing in the direction of conformity to group norms was
accompanied by less autonomic arousal than changes in the direction
of greater independence.

Status ambiguity. In small-group studies, status ambiguity is engendered when the habitual role behavior of the individual in the
group is threatened by nonsupport or active punishment on the part
of other group members, thus establishing the conditions for an
approach-avoidance conflict. The physiologically arousing effects of
this species of conflict have been demonstrated in a number of
sociophysiological studies. The psychotherapeutic dyad involves a
specialized relationship between a client under an obligation to
discuss any and all matters of personal significance and a therapist
under a complementary obligation to receive the information in a
permissive and nonpunishing manner. If the relationship is
efficacious, we should expect a decrease over time of the emotional
impact of the issues brought up for discussion by the patient. Thus
Dittes (1957a) found that as psychotherapy progressed, the percentage of "embarrassing" statements accompanied by a galvanic
skin response declined. If, on the other hand, the normatively permissive therapist relinquishes this role and adopts instead a nonper-
missive or judgmental manner, we would expect the patient's normatively confessorial behavior to conflict with the threat generated by
the therapist, with subsequent autonomic arousal. These were precisely the results of a second study by Dittes (1957b), who reported a
substantial negative correlation between GSR frequency in successive therapy hours and the rated permissiveness of the therapist
during the session. A similar lack of validation by the therapist of the
patient's normative behavior has been shown to lead to increased
muscular tension (Malmo and others, 1957) as well as heightened
heart rate (DiMascio and others, 1957).

Status relationships can be considered more stable in groups of acknowledged friends with a history of mutual interaction than in groups of strangers interacting for the first time or in groups of sociometrically antagonistic individuals. A conflict hypothesis would predict greater levels of physiological arousal in the latter examples as opposed to the already functioning group. This appears to be the case. Back and Bogdonoff (1964) report higher FFA levels in four-man groups of individually recruited subjects than in natural groups of friends, even while resting prior to an experimental session. This was corroborated by Kaplan and others (1964), who comprised three four-man discussion groups of individuals who had expressed sociometrically positive, neutral, or negative preferences for each other. A GSR measure presumed to indicate "consensual affective investment in the stimulus field" was higher in the subjects constituting the negative group. This could not be accounted for by either greater activity or greater expressions of negative feeling in this group. Rather, it appeared to be correlated with a heightened "sensitivity" of the negative group members both to their own initiatives and to those of the other members.

In an experimental situation in which the individual is manipulated into a group leadership role by reinforcing his decisions, little physiological change is observed. If, however, he is subsequently punished by group disconfirmation of his initiatives, a status conflict is produced which leads to marked increases in FFA levels (Back and Bogdonoff, 1964), as well as other autonomic indicators (Shapiro and Leiderman, 1964). Further differentiating between groups of "friends" and groups of "strangers," it is found that agreement among friends or disagreement among strangers has little arousing effects over the already differential resting levels in these two groups, presumably because agreement is normative among friends as is disagreement among strangers. If, however, friends are experimentally made to disagree or strangers made to agree, increased physiological activity is observed, attributable to a heightening of status uncertainty among members of both groups (Back and Bogdonoff, 1964). As indicated by these authors, disruption of patterns of group relationships, whether toward breakdown in friends or cohesion in strangers, will produce a negative response to the attempted change.

In a slightly different context, Shapiro and Leiderman (1967) were able to create shared or single roles in three-man groups by (1) punishing two members and reinforcing the third for decision-making, or (2) reinforcing two members and punishing the third.

Regardless of the success-failure dimension, it was found that individuals in shared roles had higher electrodermal levels (palmar skin potentials) than those in single roles. These results were referred to Festinger's (1954) social comparison hypothesis, according to which the individual will attempt to assess his group status by evaluating his performance relative to that of other group members. The paired roles, whether successful or unsuccessful, were imbedded in a group context in which one cohort performed similarly and the other dissimilarly, making the comparison somewhat ambiguous. In post-experimental interviews, paired subjects expressed more uncertainty about their relative performance than did single subjects, signaling the presence of a discrimination conflict of the sort investigated in the Johnson (1963) and Wilson and Duerfeldt (1967) studies.

Attitude conflicts. The formation and change of attitudes has been a traditional concern of sociology and social psychology. The contribution of psychophysiology to this field began with the demonstration that symbolic stimuli are capable of arousing a variety of physiological effects in the individual and that the magnitude of the reaction varies with ratings of the intensity of the stimuli along various dimensions of meaning, such as semantic relatedness, emotional intensity, or evaluation (Shapiro and Crider, 1969). The underlying mechanisms for these observations apparently lie in processes of classical conditioning and response generalization. In a rather literal translation of Pavlovian methods to this problem, for example, Razran (1939) conditioned subjects to salivate to the words "style," "urn," "freeze," and "surf" by flashing them on a screen while the subjects ate salty foods. In a second session, the conditioned salivation response was found to generalize more to the synonyms "fashion," "vase," "chill," and "wave" than to the homophones "stile," "earn," "frieze," and "serf." In a similar manner, subjects have been conditioned to respond physiologically to the word "good" and to inhibit responding to the word "bad" by pairing "good" with the aversive stimulus of loud sound. In subsequent tests, generalization occurs to concepts or sentences heavily loaded with positive evaluation but not to concepts or phrases loaded with negative meaning (Acker and Edwards, 1964; Volkova, 1953).

Although physiological responses can thus be demonstrated to vary along dimensions of meaning, a notable increase in the level of responsiveness is observed when symbolic material contains conflicting meanings. Lanier (1941) had subjects rate words in terms of their pleasantness, unpleasantness, or simultaneous pleasantness and unpleasantness, after which the magnitude of the GSR to the presen-

CRIDER : *Experimental Studies* 177

tation of each word was assessed. While unpleasant words evoked somewhat larger responses than pleasant words, the largest responses were evoked by the mixed words producing simultaneous and conflicting meanings. Berlyne (1961) used an information-theory measure of response uncertainty to rank stimulus words in terms of the degree of associational conflict produced by their presentation. Subjects were then instructed to respond to six high and six low uncertainty words with the first association that came to mind. With the GSR again used as an arousal index, high uncertainty words were found to produce greater responsiveness than those of low uncertainty.

In studies of prejudicial attitudes, it is often found that prejudiced subjects show greater physiological reaction to objects of their prejudice (e.g., a Negro experimenter) than do unprejudiced subjects (Rankin and Campbell, 1955; Westie and DeFleur, 1959). More striking changes are obtained, however, when prejudicial attitudes are brought into conflict with contrary opinions. A series of studies along these lines was reported by Cooper (1959), who turned to conflict models after finding that degree of prejudice towards specific ethnic groups was poorly correlated with the magnitude of the GSR elicited by their mention. The basic procedure required subjects to rank 20 ethnic or national groups from most to least liked. For each subject the name of his most-liked group was then inserted into a derogatory statement (e.g., "People can be divided into two groups; the good and the bad. Close to the bottom of the list are the _____."). The name of the least-liked group was inserted into a complimentary statement (e.g., "The world over, no single group of people has done as much for us, for our civilization, as the _____."). Each statement was then read to the subject and the GSR recorded. For comparative purposes, the GSR was measured to complimentary and derogatory statements containing the names of groups toward which the subject was neutral. With this as a baseline, it was found that 14 of 20 subjects responded more to derogatory statements concerning groups toward which they had reported positive attitudes and 19 to 20 subjects responded more to complimentary statements involving negatively evaluated groups.

As Brown (1965) points out, attitude conflict is a psychologically unstable and distressing condition which, like any other conflict situation, motivates the search for techniques of dissonance reduction. A successful avoidance response should then lead to a reduction of physiological arousal. This was nicely demonstrated in a psychophysiological study informed by cognitive dissonance theory (Zimbardo and others, 1966). Subjects were asked to learn a list of nine words by the serial anticipation method while being given two unavoidable shocks per trial until reaching the criterion of two successive errorless trials. Several different conditions were then tested in a second phase of the experiment. As subjects were preparing to leave, they were asked to volunteer for a second part of the experiment. A low-dissonance group was given various justifications for continuing—its importance to science, to the experimenter, to the space program, and so on. A high-dissonance group was given minimum justification. The authors predicted that the high-dissonance group would reduce the dissonance by reevaluating the painfulness of the shock and thus appear to react as if shock intensity had been reduced from high to moderate levels. The results substantially confirmed this prediction. High-dissonance subjects tended to show a decrease in their perception of the painfulness of the shock and electrodermal reactivity to the shock, while low-dissonance subjects showed heightened electrodermal reactivity. The reduced reactivity of the high-dissonance subjects was comparable to that shown by a control group in which the shock level was reduced by 20 volts in the second phase of the experiment. It was concluded that committing oneself to an experience without justification in line with the individual's usual motives can limit the impact of the experience on both behavioral and autonomic responses.

FUNCTIONAL SIGNIFICANCE OF CONFLICT-PRODUCED AROUSAL

Up to this point we have hesitated to ascribe psychological meaning to the physiological changes produced by conflict situations. Rather, the intention has been to outline behavioral models of conflict, indicate their relationship to a variety of social-psychological studies of stress, and to describe the rather consistent psychophysiological effects observed. The problem remains, however, of going a step beyond the use of physiological data as a simple "indicator" of stress in order to examine its significance for the overall functioning of the individual.

The classic position on this problem is, of course, James' (1890) view that autonomic nervous system arousal is the physical basis of emotional experience. It is the individual's discrimination of his own visceral excitation that transforms a purely sensory experience into a full-blown emotional reaction: "If we fancy some strong emotion, and then try to abstract from our consciousness of it all the feelings of its bodily symptoms, we find we have nothing left behind, no 'mind-stuff' out of which the emotion can be constituted, and that a cold and neutral state of intellectual perception is all that remains (James, 1890, p. 451)." Thus the visceral arousal of the individual in conflict presumably provides the substrate for the reports of distress and anxiety observed in these situations. Two major criticisms have traditionally been leveled at this position: (1) in order to account for the variety of emotional states known to psychologists, it is necessary to postulate an equal number of discrete types of visceral patterning in aroused states, which physiologists have been loath to do (e.g., Cannon, 1929), and (2) it is necessary to assume that any state of physiological arousal will necessarily produce emotional reactions, which would appear to be contradicted by specific examples such as the nonemotionality of the aroused condition produced by strenuous exercise.

A contemporary restatement of the visceral theory of emotion that is able to deal with these problems has been provided by Schachter (1964), who sees subjective emotional experience as a resultant of perceived physiological arousal and the characteristics of the social environment in which the individual finds himself. The formation is summarized in the following major propositions:

1. Given a state of physiological arousal for which an individual has no immediate explanation, he will "label" this state and describe his feelings in terms of the cognitions available to him. The same physiological state could be labeled "fear," "joy," "anger," or otherwise, depending on the situation as defined by the individual.

2. If the individual has an appropriate explanation for his aroused bodily state (e.g., "I feel aroused because I have taken a drug which makes my heart beat faster") there will be no need to label his feelings in terms of the alternative cognitions available (e.g., "I feel aroused because I am amused by this comic scene").

3. Given the same situation, the individual will react emotionally or describe his feelings as emotional only to the extent that he experiences a state of physiological arousal.

An emotional sequence begins, therefore, with the discrimination of a state of autonomic excitation that leads to a search for an appropriate explanation through the arousal of an "evaluative need" (Schachter, 1959). The problem is resolved with the information supplied by the social environment. A state of autonomic arousal for which the individual has an a priori explanation, or the same social environment without the autonomic component, will give rise to neither evaluative needs nor emotional experiences.

Although the attention that Schachter's theory has attracted has revivified visceral theories of emotion, there are still two major embarrassments to this psychophysiological stance. In the first place, there is only a poor correlation between the intensity of measured autonomic arousal and the intensity of the coincident subjective experience. Early psychophysiologists almost universally condemned measures of autonomic activity as indices of reported emotion. Syz (1926), for example, complained of the "unreliability" of electrodermal measures in predicting subjective experience, while Landis (1926) pointed out that "emotion" could not be accounted for by the sum of the measured visceral changes coincident with such states. More recently, the data of Fenz and Epstein (1967), alluded to earlier, compelled them to conclude that anxiety and physiological arousal in conflict situations represented two covarying but distinct behavioral processes.

Secondly, while there is no question that visceral changes are fed back to the central nervous system via afferent visceral nerves, there is a surprising lack of evidence that these changes can be verbally identified, or discriminated, by the individual. With the exception of some well-known examples — such as the presence of "visceral pain" in various disease states — there is little reason to dispute Cannon's (1929) original critique of James that the viscera are relatively insensitive structures whose changes are unlikely to serve as cues for judgments of emotionality. Although the lack of evidence may be due to want of trying, Mandler and Kahn (1960) specifically failed in an attempt to train a subject to identify changes in his own heart-rate. The experiment required the subject to "guess" which of two lights would be illuminated on any one trial, with one light contingent on heart-rate decelerations, the other on accelerations. After 5,000 trials there was no evidence of more than random guessing.

Further evidence on this point suggests a rather low correlation (about .30) between individual differences in the amount of reported visceral activity and the actual amount of physiological activity measured in a stress situation (Mandler and Kremen, 1958). While language is replete with references to "racing hearts," "butterflies in the stomach," and so forth, Skinner (1963) has suggested that such verbal reports are more likely under the control of external environmental stimuli than the autonomic effector in question. Skinner bases this on the observation that the verbal community is unable to reinforce discriminations of internal events, so that the individual is less likely to correctly identify his own covert behavior than socially shared stimuli. Several interesting case histories report that sensations of visceral activity can be conditioned regardless of the actual state of the organ in question (Jones, 1956; Razran, 1961). In Jones' report, a patient with the complaint of excessive frequency of micturation was first trained to associate her urinary urges with the readout from a pressure transducer introduced into the bladder. The experimenter was then able to depress artificially the readout device without the patient's knowledge, resulting ultimately in a tolerance for bladder distention without subjective discomfort.

Thus while both subjective anxiety and physiological arousal characterize conflict situations, they appear to be uncorrelated and independent phenomena. This negative conclusion necessarily leads to other approaches to understanding the behavioral significance of conflict-produced arousal. For example, Lacey (1967; Lacey and Lacey, 1958) has proposed that increases in cardiovascular activity promote a dampening of the individual's reactivity to aversive or distracting environmental stimulation. According to this formulation, increases in heart-rate and blood pressure feed back to the brain stem via arterial pressure receptors and exert a behaviorally "inhibitory" influence by reducing cortical activation, decreasing sensory acuity, and raising motor thresholds. As Lacey points out, this sort of mechanism would be especially adaptive where the individual is either confronted with intense and painful stimuli or engaged in problem-solving tasks that demand freedom from environmental distraction. Conversely, situations in which the individual is required to attend actively to environmental inputs are characterized by decreases in cardiovascular activity whose net effect would be a diminution of pressure receptor firing and a corresponding increase in cortical activation, sensory acuity, and motor readiness. In a test of this formulation, Lacey and others (1963) devised a series of tasks varying along a behavioral continuum of environmental intake-environmental rejection. It was found that situations in which the subject was required to attend to external stimuli were indeed correlated with decelerating heart-rates, while the application of aversive stimuli or tasks requiring mental effort and freedom from distraction resulted in marked accelerations.

Lacey's formulation illuminates a long research tradition linking problem-solving activity with physiological arousal. In a classic paper, Gley (1881) studied his own cardiovascular activity while he either rested or engaged in mental activity. Using a simple tambour and kymograph arrangement to record the pulsations of the carotid artery, he found that solving arithmetic problems and perusing philosophical texts led to an increase in heart rate and blood pressure and a corresponding dilatation of the arteries supplying blood to the head region. A half century later, Darrow (1929) reported that tasks calling for associational or cognitive processing were accompanied by increased cardiovascular activity, which contrasted with decreases in cardiovascular activity with simple sensory inputs.

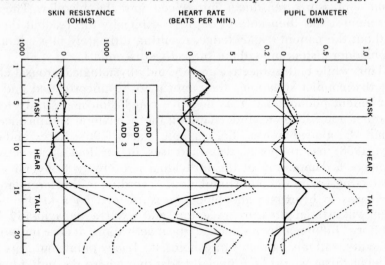

Fig. 6.2. Pupil dilatation, heart rate, and skin resistance changes during information intake (Hear) and report (Talk) phases of a mental task as a function of difficulty level. (From Kahneman and others, 1969).

These findings were extended in a study by Kahneman and others (1969) that examined changes in pupil diameter, palmar skin resistance, and heart-rate during a mental task. The task was graded in difficulty by requiring subjects to add either 0, 1, or 3 to each of four serially presented digits and to read out the transformed series after a 2-second pause. The procedure was paced by background pulses occurring once per second, so that the ready signal occurred at second 1, the instructions to add either 0, 1, or 3 at seconds 5 and 6, the digits at seconds 10–13, and the answer at seconds 15–18. Each subject was given five trials at each level of difficulty. The results appear in Figure 6.2, which shows a similar increase in the three measures during information intake and processing and a corresponding decrease during the report phase, with the amount of change a function of task difficulty. Consonant with Lacey's hypothesis, it has been found that the increase in physiological activity up to the point of problem solution in this task is accompanied by an increasing degree of functional blindness. That is, the ability to recognize an intermittent visual signal is increasingly impaired while the individual is directing attention to problem solution (Kahneman and others, 1967). Thus the physiological arousal is a correlate of a functional desensitization of the organism to environmental stimuli.

The instrumental advantage of physiological arousal during problem-solving is also suggested by studies of individual differences. Blatt (1961) found, for example, that the most efficient problem solvers also showed the greatest changes in heart rate during the task. Similarly, subjects of above average intelligence who are both intellectually oriented and confident of their ability, show greater cardiovascular activity during problem-solving than do less intelligent, less intellectually confident individuals (Kagan and Moss, 1962).

The strong implication of the foregoing, then, is that the physiological arousal characteristic of conflict situations, rather than representing a simple index of stress or a sign of debilitation, can be regarded as part of an active attempt by the subject to cope with the "problem" posed by the conflict. We have suggested one way in which this arousal could facilitate coping — by dampening sensitivity to aversive or distracting environmental inputs, either by feedback to the central nervous system, as is the case with cardiovascular functions, or by direct action on receptors, as with pupillary dilatation. A corollary of this view is that more highly aroused individuals should be able to cope more effectively with conflict than less responsive subjects. In fact, Fenz (1964) noted that novice parachutists who showed an excessive inhibition of prejump arousal were likely to perform poorly at the time of the jump.

Other data, though not specific to conflict situations, points in this same direction. Mandler and others, (1961) found that individuals who showed the greatest psychological disorganization in response to threatening verbal material showed *less* physiological reactivity than did those who successfully dealt with the threat. The subjects were instructed to respond to phrases depicting areas of sex, aggression, dependency, and competition with the first phrase or association that came to mind. Responses were rated as to the manner in which the material was assimilated along a dimension of acceptance-rejection. Subjects who became personally involved with the import of the material showed greater autonomic reactivity than did those who avoided the meaning of the stimuli through misperception, rationalization, or denial of the implied threat.

In another study, a group of students was subjected to a presumably stressful experience with various physiological and psychomotor indices as dependent measures. Those who showed the greatest arousal were rated as psychiatrically better adjusted and also performed most efficiently on the psychomotor task. The investigators concluded that the absence of reactivity represented defensive behavior resulting in less successful adaptation to the stress (Schachter and others, 1965). In a similar fashion, Weiner (1962) suggests that physiological reactivity is a normal concomitant of an adaptive approach to experimental tasks, with nonreactors falling into a class characterized as impersonal, distant, uninvolved, listless, and apathetic.

The theme running through this research is that autonomic reactivity on initial exposure to stressors is correlated with active engagement leading to mastery of the imposed stress. A study by Kagan and Moss (1962), designed to investigate the physiological components of psychological threat by presenting subjects with taped monologues depicting areas of interpersonal conflict, found that the least threatened individuals responded with the greatest autonomic change. For example, those who showed the greatest response to a "peer aggression" monologue rated themselves as aggressive and were in fact openly competitive with peers during adolescence and adulthood. Kagan and Moss propose that the *absence* of autonomic reactivity to imposed stressors be taken as a sign of psychological impairment, a notable suggestion in being diametrically opposed to the significance usually attributed to physiological arousal under conditions of stress.

In sum, then, we have suggested that experimental studies of stress deal in fact with behavioral and physiological responses under the control of aversive events. The conflict paradigm, defined as any situation in which two or more incompatible responses of equal strength are elicited, was proposed as an exemplar of a behaviorally aversive environment. Experiments on both the individual and social-psychological level have demonstrated that conflict generates both subjective distress and physiological arousal as a function of conflict severity. Individual differences in physiological arousal, however, do not appear to be correlated with indices of behavioral deficit nor with reports of emotionality and subjective distress. Rather, the behavioral and the physiological reactions to conflict are independently organized systems. Thus the use of physiological measures as "indices" of stress is a dubious procedure. Indeed, it appears that physiological arousal plays an adaptive role in supporting the individual's attempts to master or cope with aversive environments.

REFERENCES

ACKER, L. E., and EDWARDS, A. E. 1964. "Transfer of Vasoconstriction over a Bipolar Meaning Dimension." *Journal of Experimental Psychology,* 67:1-6.

BACK, K. W., and BOGDONOFF, M. D. 1964. "Plasma Lipid Responses to Leadership, Conformity, and Deviation," in P. H. Leiderman and D. Shapiro, eds., *Psychobiological Approaches to Social Behavior.* Stanford: Stanford University Press.

BERLYNE, D. E. 1961. "Conflict and the Orientation Reaction." *Journal of Experimental Psychology,* 62:476-83.

BLATT, S. J. 1961. "Patterns of Cardiac Arousal during Complex Mental Activity." *Journal of Abnormal and Social Psychology,* 63:272-82.

BOYD, R. W., and DiMASCIO, A. 1954. "Social Behavior and Autonomic Physiology: A Sociophysiologic Study." *Journal of Nervous and Mental Disease,* 120:207-12.

BRADY, J., PORTER, R., CONRAD, D., and MASON, J. 1958 "Avoidance Behavior and the Development of Gastrointestinal Ulcers." *Journal of the Experimental Analysis of Behavior,* 1:69-72.

BROWN, R. 1965. *Social Psychology.* New York: Free Press.

CANNON, W. B. 1929. *Bodily Changes in Pain, Hunger, Fear, and Rage,* 2nd ed. New York: Appleton-Century-Crofts.

COOPER, J. B. 1959. "Emotion in Prejudice." *Science,* 130:314-18.

DARROW, C. W. 1929. "Differences in the Physiological Reactions to Sensory and Ideational Stimuli." *Psychological Bulletin,* 26:185-201.

DiMASCIO, A., BOYD, R. W., and GREENBLATT, M. 1957. "Physiological Correlates of Tension and Antagonism during Psychotherapy: A Study of 'Interpersonal Physiology'." *Psychosomatic Medicine,* 19:99-104.

DITTES, J. 1957a. "Extinction during Psychotherapy of GSR Accompanying 'Embarrassing' Statements." *Journal of Abnormal and Social Psychology,* 54:187-91.

  1957b. "Galvanic Skin Response as a Measure of Patient's Reaction to Therapist's Permissiveness." *Journal of Abnormal and Social Psychology,* 55:295-303.

ENGLE, G. L. 1962. *Psychological Development in Health and Disease.* Philadelphia: Saunders.

EPSTEIN, S., and FENZ, W. 1962. "Theory and Experiment on the Measurement of Approach-avoidance Conflict." *Journal of Abnormal and Social Psychology,* 64:97-112.

FENZ, W. D. 1964. "Conflict and Stress as Related to Physiological Activation and Sensory, Perceptual, and Cognitive Functioning. *Psychological*

Monographs, 78, no. 8 (whole no. 585).

FENZ, W. D., and EPSTEIN, S. 1967. "Gradients of Physiological Arousal in Parachutists as a Function of an Approaching Jump." *Psychosomatic Medicine,* 29:33–51.

FESTINGER, L. 1954. "A Theory of Social Comparison Processes." *Human Relations,* 7:117–40.

GANTT, W. H. 1944. *Experimental Basis for Neurotic Behavior.* New York: Hoeber.

GLEY, C. 1881. "Essai critique sur les conditions physiologiques de la pensée." *Archives de Physiologie,* 13:742–59.

HEARST, E., and SIDMAN, M. 1961. "Some Behavioral Effects of a Concurrently Positive and Negative Stimulus." *Journal of the Experimental Analysis of Behavior,* 4:251–56.

JAMES, W. 1890. *The Principles of Psychology,* vol. 2. New York: Holt.

JOHNSON, H. J. 1963. "Decision Making, Conflict, and Physiological Arousal." *Journal of Abnormal and Social Psychology,* 67:114–24.

JONES, H. G. 1956. "The Application of Conditioning and Learning Techniques to the Treatment of a Psychiatric Patient." *Journal of Abnormal and Social Psychology,* 52:414–19.

KAGAN, J., and MOSS, H. A. 1962. *Birth to Maturity: A Study in Psychological Developments.* New York: John Wiley.

KAHNEMAN, D., BEATTY, J., and POLLACK, I. 1967. "Perceptual Deficit during a Mental Task." *Science,* 157:218–19.

KAHNEMAN, D., TURSKY, B., SHAPIRO, D., and CRIDER, A. 1969. "Pupillary, Heart Rate, and Skin Resistance Changes during a Mental Task." *Journal of Experimental Psychology,* 79:164–67.

KAPLAN, H. G., BURCH, N. R., and BLOOM, S. W. 1964. "Physiological Covariation and Sociometric Relationships in Small Peer Groups," in P. H. Leiderman and D. Shapiro, eds., *Psychobiological Approaches to Social Behavior.* Stanford: Stanford University Press.

LACEY, J. I. 1967. "Somatic Response Patterning and Stress: Some Revisions of Activation Theory," in M. H. Appley and R. Trumbull, eds., *Psychological Stress.* New York: Appleton-Century-Crofts.

LACEY, J. I., KAGAN, J., LACEY, B. C., and MOSS, H. A. 1963. "The Visceral Level: Situational Determinants and Behavioral Correlates of Autonomic Response Patterns," in P. J. Knapp, ed., *Expression of the Emotions in Man.* New York: International Universities Press.

LACEY, J. I., and LACEY, B. C. 1958. "The Relationship of Resting Autonomic Activity to Motor Impulsivity." *Research Publications. Association for Research in Nervous and Mental Disease,* 36:144–209.

LANDIS, C. 1926. "Studies of Emotional Reactions. V. Severe Emotional Upset." *Journal of Comparative Psychology,* 6:221–42.

LANIER, L. H. 1941. "An Experimental Study of Affective Conflict." *Journal of Psychology,* 11:199–217.

MALMO, R. B., BOAG, T. J., and SMITH, A. A. 1957. "Physiological Study of Personal Interaction." *Psychosomatic Medicine*, 19:105-19.

MANDLER, G., and KAHN, M. 1960. "Discrimination of Changes in Heart Rate: Two Unsuccessful Attempts." *Journal of the Experimental Analysis of Behavior*, 3:21-25.

MANDLER, G., and KREMEN, I. 1958. "Autonomic Feedback: A Correlational Study." *Journal of Personality*, 26:388-99.

MANDLER, G., MANDLER, J. M., KREMEN, I., and SHOLITON, R. D. 1961. "The Response to Threat: Relations among Verbal and Physiological Indices." *Psychological Monographs*, 75, no. 9 (whole no. 513).

MILLER, N. E. 1944. "Experimental Studies of Conflict," in J. M. Hunt, ed., *Personality and the Behavior Disorders*. New York: Ronald.

PAVLOV, I. P. 1960. *Conditioned Reflexes*, trans., G. V. Anrep. New York: Dover.

RANKIN, R. E., and CAMPBELL, D. T. 1955. "Galvanic Skin Response to Negro and White Experimenters." *Journal of Abnormal and Social Psychology*, 51:30-33.

RAZRAN, G. 1939. "A Quantitative Study of Meaning by a Conditioned Salivary Technique (Semantic Conditioning)." *Science*, 90:89-91.

——— 1961. "The Observable Unconscious and the Inferable Conscious in Current Soviet Psychophysiology: Interoceptive Conditioning, Semantic Conditioning, and the Orienting Reflex." *Psychological Review*, 68:81-147.

SCHACHTER, J., WILLIAMS, T. A., ROWE, R., SCHACHTER, J. S., and JAMESON, J. 1965. "Personality Correlates of Psychological Reactivity to Stress: A Study of Forty-six College Males." *American Journal of Psychiatry*, 121:XII-XXIV.

SCHACHTER, S. 1959. *The Psychology of Affiliation: Experimental Studies of the Sources of Gregariousness*. Stanford: Stanford University Press.

——— 1964. "The Interaction of Cognitive and Physiological Determinants of Emotional State," in P. H. Leiderman and D. Shapiro, eds., *Psychobiological Approaches to Social Behavior*. Stanford: Stanford University Press.

SCHMALE, A. H. 1958. "Relationship of Separation and Depression to Disease." *Psychosomatic Medicine*, 20:259.

SHAPIRO, D., and CRIDER, A. 1969. "Psychophysiological Approaches in Social Psychology," in G. Lindzey and E. Aronson, eds., *Handbook of Social Psychology*, vol. 3. Reading, Mass.: Addison-Wesley.

SHAPIRO, D., and LEIDERMAN, P. H. 1964. "Acts and Activation: A Psychophysiological Study of Social Interaction," in P. H. Leiderman and D. Shapiro, eds., *Psychobiological Approaches to Social Behavior*. Stanford: Standord University Press.

——— 1967. "Arousal Correlates of Task Role and Group Setting." *Journal of Personal and Social Psychology*, 5:103-07.

SKINNER, B. F. 1963. "Behaviorism at Fifty." *Science*, 140:951-58.

SMITH, C. 1936. "A Study of the Autonomic Excitation Resulting from the Interaction of Individual Opinion and Group Opinion." *Journal of Abnormal and Social Psychology*, 31:138–64.

SYZ, H. C. 1926. "Observations of the Unreliability of Subjective Reports of Emotional Reactions." *British Journal of Psychology*, 17:119–26.

VOLKOVA, V. 1953. "On Certain Characteristics of the Formation of Conditioned Reflexes to Speech Stimuli in Children." *Fiziologicheskii Zhurnal SSSR*, 39:540–48.

WEINER, H. 1962. "Some Psychological Factors Related to Cardiovascular Responses: A Logical and Empirical Analysis," in R. Roessler and N. S. Greenfield, eds., *Physiological Correlates of Psychological Disorder.* Madison: University of Wisconsin Press.

WESTIE, F. R., and DEFLEUR, M. L. 1959. "Autonomic Responses and Their Relationship to Race Attitudes." *Journal of Abnormal and Social Psychology*, 58:340–47.

WILSON, R. S., and DUERFELDT, P. H. 1967. "Cardiac Responsiveness and Differential Conditioning." *Journal of Comparative and Physiological Psychology*, 63:87–94.

WOOD, D. M., and OBRIST, P. A. 1964. "Effects of Controlled and Uncontrolled Respiration on the Conditioned Heart Rate Response in Humans." *Journal of Experimental Psychology*, 68:221–29.

ZIMBARDO, P. G., COHEN, A. R., WEISENBERG, M., DWORKIN, L., and FIRESTONE, I. 1966. "Control of Pain Motivation by Cognitive Dissonance." *Science*, 151:217–19.

7. Physical Illness in Response to Stress

JOHN CASSEL

THE DRAMATIC changes that have occurred in the nature of the diseases afflicting Western society over the last hundred years has been well documented, but the extraordinary regularities with which these changes have occurred in countries undergoing industrialization have been less well recognized. For all those countries for which we have data, it would appear that the earliest health consequences of industrialization and the accompanying urbanization has been an exacerbation of those diseases that have been the plagues of mankind since antiquity, namely the infectious diseases. Thus, in Great Britain and the United States industrialization was accompanied initially by an increase in the rates of tuberculosis. This disease reached its peak over a period of some 50 to 75 years and then began to decline. It is worth noting that this decline occurred prior to the discovery of the tubercle bacillus and several decades before any organized anti-tuberculosis program was in-

John Cassel is professor of epidemiology in the School of Public Health, University of North Carolina, Chapel Hill.

itiated. Furthermore, the decline in incidence has continued at about the same rate for the last 75 to 80 years, notwithstanding the discovery of new and important drugs for the treatment of this disease (Grigg, 1958). As tuberculosis began to decline it was replaced as a central health problem in both Britain and the United States by major malnutrition syndromes. In Britain rickets was the scourge; in the United States, pellagra. These disorders in turn reached a peak and declined for reasons that are also only partially understood, and were themselves replaced by some of the diseases of early childhood. These, too, waxed and then waned largely, but not entirely, under the influence of improvements in the sanitary environment and through the introduction of immunization programs, to be replaced between the world wars by an extraordinary increase in the rate of duodenal ulcer, particularly in young men. This phenomenon, while more marked in Britain, occurred in the United States as well and was accompanied by a marked shift in the male-female ratio of the disease (Susser and Stein, 1962). Gradually, for totally unknown reasons these rates have declined and have been replaced by our modern epidemics of coronary heart disease, hypertension, cancer, arthritis, diabetes, mental disorders and the like. There is some evidence that some of these disorders have reached a peak and are now declining. Death rates from hypertensive heart disease, for example, apparently have been declining in the United States since about 1940–50 (Paffenberger and others, 1966).

Despite intensive research, the explanations for the genesis of these changes in diseases patterns has so far proved to be relatively unsatisfactory. Attention has been focused on the introduction of new pollutants and toxicants into the air and water and on the reduction of old ones, on the increasing amount of ionizing radiation, and on the hazards associated with pesticides and food additives. Changes in plant and animal life and the changing nature of the microorganisms with which man comes into contact, have also received considerable attention. The influence of certain aspects of behavior—exercise, diet, cigarette smoking, alcohol consumption—have been studied in some detail. None of these changes, however, has afforded a very satisfactory explanation for the occurrence of the new diseases nor for the decline of the old ones. One of the consequences of this dissatisfaction with the more orthodox explanations has been a reawakening of interest in the possible role of social and cultural "stress" factors as determinants of disease. This reawakened interest has been reinforced by the realization that the changes in the social structure, and in values, attitudes, and beliefs that have accompanied the industrial revolution have occurred equally as rapidly as have the changes in technology and in the physical and biological environment, and that they may have equal importance in determining the types of health problems manifest in any society. Graham Wallace, for example, posed the problem half a century ago: "How does human nature respond to the conditions of the complex urbanized life, which industrial and mechanical civilization has created?" (Wolman, 1965, p. 2) and despite the research endeavors over the intervening decades, Anthony Payne was forced to conclude in 1965 that ". . . we have tended to regard man as a biological animal with biological needs . . . we have largely ignored the fact that he is a social animal and that it may be at least as important to his health to satisfy his social needs and behavioral urges as his purely biological ones (p. 3)."

The evidence supporting this point of view is at the best fragmentary and equivocal. Which social processes are deleterious as far as human health is concerned? How many such processes are there? What are the intervening links between these processes and disturbed physiological state? These questions remain largely unanswered and in many instances have never been appropriately asked. It is the purpose of this chapter to review some of the evidence supporting the contention that social factors are important as determinants of health status and to indicate the further steps needed to augment our current knowledge in this field and to increase the efficiency of future research endeavors.

Somewhat paradoxically, some of the more convincing evidence concerning the role of social factors as determinants of disease comes from animal studies. To a large extent these have been concerned with variations in the size of the group in which the animals interact and in situations that lead to confusion over territorial control. A number of investigators have shown quite convincingly that as the number of animals housed together increases—with other factors such as diet, temperature, and sanitation kept constant—maternal and infant mortality rates rise, incidence of arteriosclerosis increases, resistance to insults, including drugs, microorganisms, and x-rays, is reduced, and there is an increased susceptibility to alloxan-produced diabetes, to convulsions, and to certain types of cancer (Ader and Hahn, 1963; Ader and others, 1963; Andervont, 1944; Calhoun, 1962; Christian and Williamson, 1958; David and Read, 1958; King and others, 1955; Ratcliffe and Cronin, 1958; Swinyard and others, 1961). Lack of territorial control has been shown to lead to the development of marked and persistent hypertension in mice, to increased maternal and infant mortality rates in rats, and also to reduced resistance to bacterial infection and decreased longevity (Henry, manuscript). Studies by others, particularly Conger (1958), have demonstrated that the efficacy with which an electric shock can produce peptic ulcers in rats is determined to a large extent by whether the subjects are shocked in isolation (high ulcer rates) or in the presence of litter mates (low ulcer rates). The elegant studies of Mason (1959) have indicated that many of these changes could possibly be explained by changes that occur in the pituitary and the adrenal cortical system which accompany changes in group membership and the quality of group relationships. Some of these hormones, such as the 17-hydroxycorticosteroids (17-OH-CS), and epinephrine, increase regularly as the size of the group increases, while others such as norepinephrine are lower in grouped than in single mice.

While the specific findings of these types of studies cannot necessarily be extrapolated directly to man, some of the more general formulations may have extreme importance in human studies. In particular, three such formulations appear to be worth emphasizing. The first is that the stimuli that lead to changes in the pituitary and adrenal cortical axis are not necessarily manifestly emotionally disturbing. Mason has reported that the activity of this axis in monkeys sensitively reflects subtle, everyday differences in the "level of environmental activity" in a manner that could not be interpreted as reflecting emotionally disturbing elements in the environment. He took about fifty observations of urinary 17-OH-CS on five monkeys kept only one at a time in a biochemistry laboratory where the activity of two persons performing routine analyses was rather constant and stereotyped in pattern from Monday to Friday. The room was usually vacant on weekends. The Monday value was markedly elevated over the weekend values, before subsiding to a relatively stable excretion level Tuesday through Friday. Lighting, room temperature, and feeding were more or less constant seven days a week. The only apparent difference was the higher level of general activity in the laboratory during the working week (1959). Other studies have shown that mean 17-OH-CS level can be raised or lowered over at least a twofold range depending upon whether the monkeys are kept in a laboratory occupied by other people or kept in a quiet private room with a minimum contact with people, and that keeping monkeys in open-wire mesh cages leads to higher levels of these hormones than if similar monkeys are kept in solid wall cages (Mason and Brady, 1965).

The second formulation is that within the group there are systematic differences in the level of hormone excretion between those animals which are the habitual receivers of aggression and those which are markedly aggressive or more dominant. In other words, the physiological differences between individuals are enhanced because they are together and because they occupy different positions in the social field of force. Not only do animals become different physiologically because of this social gradient, but paradoxically when living as a group, they also become more alike because of the common social environment they share, tending to respond in a similar fashion to similar stimuli. Under such circumstances, animals in subordinate positions tend to respond in a more extreme fashion than those in dominant positions (Mason, 1959; Welch, 1964; Welch and Klopfer, 1961). This similarity in response has also been found in human subjects. Hill and others (1956) have reported a marked uniformity in the eosinophil depression and the 17-OH-CS secretion of a rowing team working together as a highly organized group in a competitive race. The noted changes were apparently not attributable to common involvement in physical exercise, for the coxswain and the coach showed changes during the race similar to those exhibited by the eight members of the crew. Although comparable physical exercise to that in competition was experienced on practice rowing days, the metabolic response in practice was not nearly so uniform as in competition and did not differ markedly from control days in which there was no exercise.

The implications of this set of findings may well be of profound importance to future research on the role of social factors in disease etiology. At the very least, they provide a rationale for the influence of group membership and position within that group on the individual's response to various stimuli, and would suggest that attempts to assess the effects of presumptive disease "agents" will be inadequate unless the modifying influence of such group factors are taken into account.

The third important formulation is that there is good evidence to indicate that the affect of a given stimulus upon the level of activation will be determined not only by the strength of the stimulus but by the past history of stimulation and by the present state of activation and cumulative inhibition. Sharpless has considered it almost a law of nervous action that a radical and sustained change in the level of stimulation of an excitable structure results in compensatory changes that tend to alter its excitability in such a way that the initial level of activity is easily restored. By implication, therefore, individuals in social isolation or experiencing sensory deprivation should not only exhibit a lowered state of central activation and consciousness, but they should be hyperexcitable to those stimuli they do not receive (Welch, 1964). This has been found to be true for both humans and animals. King and others (1955), for example, found long term isolation made mice so excitable that 50 percent or more had spontaneous convulsions when disturbed by such routine procedures as weighing, cage cleaning, feeding, or opening the cage door for inspection. This hypersensitivity could be largely relieved by housing in groups of twenty. Previous experience, therefore, can exert a marked influence on the type of intensity of subsequent response to a given stimulus. In other words, it is possible for animals and humans to develop an adaptation to stimuli that will lead them to respond in a fashion different from those who are not adapted. These findings are supported by studies done by Mason and others (1959, p. 432), who reports that "laboratory naive monkeys participating in their first experiment showed much higher responses to given stimuli than did veteran monkeys who had had experience over several months of the same stimuli."

As applied to humans, particularly in attempts to explain variations in disease manifestations between populations, such findings emphasize the need to consider the degree to which such populations are exposed to situations for which they are unprepared by previous experience, in addition to assessing the differences in the situations or stimuli themselves.

In summary, these studies taken together suggest that the group takes on an identity as a distinct entity that tends to be distinguishable physiologically not only from other groups larger and smaller than itself but also from other groups of the same size, and that while every physical environment may elicit its own characteristic mean level of environmental stimulation, social factors become the predominant determinants of this stimulation above a certain population density.

These stimuli, while not necessarily emotionally disturbing, can produce important physiological changes and alteration in susceptibility to disease manifestations, and while undoubtedly responses to such stimulation will be determined in part by genetic factors, they will also be influenced by position in the group as well as by previous experience.

The epidemiological data are more fragmentary and less clear-cut than is the experimental evidence. To a large extent the confusion that surrounds much of these data stems from the difficulty in defining the appropriate social processes and from the difficulties in measuring these when defined. A further source of confusion, however, resides in the fact that the majority of studies have failed to distinguish between the effects of social processes and those of other emotional or personality factors. Thus, it is not uncommon to find studies concerned with the relationship between various personality types and/or affective states and physical disease manifestations being advanced as evidence for the role of social factors in its determinants of disease. This confusion between social processes and psychological processes is unfortunate for at least two reasons. On the one hand, the animal experimental work quoted above indicates that social processes may affect physiological functioning in the absence of any marked emotional disturbance. In fact, there is suggestive evidence which would indicate that under certain circumstances marked alteration in affective states may be regarded as an alternative response to social stresses and that the physiological responses in such individuals may be less marked than those who do not display such emotional responses. Wolff and others (1964), reports a study concerned with a group of parents of leukemic children. In a number of the mothers there was an inverse relationship between the amount of affective distress and the level of the 17-OH-CS. Only when signs of affective distress disappeared did the 17-OH-CS levels rise. Secondly, this confusion between the emotional and social factors can lead to a degree of circularity of reasoning. The presence of unpleasant affective states is taken as evidence that the subjects are under some form of social "stress," on the one hand, and the presence of the same states is taken as evidence that the social factors are important in producing disease, on the other. For these reasons the review of the epidemiological studies concerned with the impact of social factors will be restricted to those in which some aspects of the social situation have been clearly delineated and will exclude the majority of studies concerned with emotional or psychological factors.

Holmes in his studies on tuberculosis in Seattle has shown that the disease occurs more frequently in "marginal" people, that is, those individuals deprived of meaningful social contact (1956). He found, for example, higher rates in those ethnic groups who were distinct minorities in the neighborhoods in which they lived, in people living alone in one room, in those who had had multiple occupational and residential moves, and who were more often single or divorced than was true of the general population. It is interesting to note in passing that individuals deprived of meaningful human contact or group membership are also at higher risk of schizophrenia, accidents, suicide, and other respiratory diseases (Dunham, 1961; Durkheim, 1957; Holmes, personal communications; Mishler and Scotch, 1963; Tillman and Hobbs, 1949). Social factors have also been shown to be important in rheumatoid arthritis, level of blood pressure, coronary heart disease, and level of serum cholesterol. As the literature pertaining to rheumatoid arthritis and hypertension has been well and exhaustively reviewed by Scotch and Geiger (1962, 1963), no attempt will be made here to review this in any detail. It is important to note, however, that despite the weaknesses of each study taken individually a rather extraordinary concordance of results is obtained when reviewing all the studies simultaneously. Thus, studies on the level of blood pressure conducted over the last 30 years in many countries across the world including China, Panama, Yucatan, Cuba, Alaska, Navaho and Zuni Indians, Bushmen of the Kalahari Desert, Central and East African Africans, West Africa, and South Africa, Ceylon and India, Fiji, and South Sea Islands have universally shown populations living in small cohesive societies "insulated" from the changes that are occurring in the Western industrializing countries, with low blood pressures that do not differ in the young and the aged (Abrahams and others, 1960; Alexander, 1949; Bibile and others, 1949; Donninson, 1929; Fleming, 1924; Fulmer and Roberts, 1963; Kaminer and Lutz, 1960; Kean, 1941, 1944; Kilborn, 1937; Krakower, 1933; Levine, 1942; Lowell and others, 1960; Maddocks, 1961; Mann and others, 1964; Murphy, 1955; Murril, 1949; Padmayati and Gupta, 1959; Saunders, 1933; Scotch, 1960, 1963; Whyte, 1958). In a number of these studies, groups who have left such societies and had contact with Western culture were also studied and found to have higher levels of blood pressure and to exhibit the familiar relationship between age and blood pressure found in studies of Western populations (Cruz-Coke and others, 1964; Hoobler and others, 1965; Lowenstein, 1961). In one particularly important group of studies in this area (conducted among the Zulu), it was found that blood pressures were higher in urban than in rural dwellers, and that those traditional cultural practices such as membership in an extended family, belief in sorcery and witchcraft, low income and a large number of children, that might be viewed as adaptive in the rural setting but nonadaptive for urban living, were associated with low blood pressure under the former condition, but with elevated blood pressure in the latter setting (Scotch, 1963). In two independent studies, Syme and others (1964, 1965), have demonstrated that occupationally and residentially mobile people have a higher prevalence of coronary heart disease than have stable populations, and that those individuals displaying the greatest discontinuity between childhood and adult situations, as measured by occupation and place of residence, have higher rates than those in which less discontinuity could be determined. Tyroler and Cassel (1964) designed a study in which death rates from coronary heart disease, and from all heart disease, could be measured in groups who were themselves stable but around whom the social situation was changing in varying degree. For this purpose they selected rural residents in the various counties of North Carolina and classified those counties by the degree of urbanization occurring in that locality. Rates for coronary heart disease and all heart disease measured at two points in time, around 1950 and again around 1960, increased dramatically as did the index of urbanization of the county.

This group of studies thus tends to lend support in humans to at least two of the formulations derived from animal work, the work on tuberculosis, schizophrenia, accidents, and suicide providing some evidence of the importance of group membership, while the data on distribution of blood pressures and coronary heart disease may indicate the potential importance of degree of "preparedness" of populations to new and unfamiliar situations. This latter theme has been the basis for a number of additional studies. Cassel and Tyroler (1961), for example, studied two groups of rural mountaineers, one of which was composed of individuals who were the first of their family to engage in industrial work, while the second comprised workers in the same factory drawn from the same mountain coves and doing the same work for the same wages as the first group, but who were the children of previous workers in this factory. The underlying hypothesis was that the second group, by virtue of their previous experience would be better prepared for the expectations and demands of industrial living than the first, and would thus exhibit fewer signs of ill health. Health status was measured by responses to the Cornell Medical Index and by various indices of sick absenteeism. As predicted, the first group had higher Cornell Medical Index scores (more symptoms) and higher rates of sick absenteeism, after the initial few years of service (i.e., after the initial impact of the new situation had "worn off") at each age than had the second.

In a study initially designed to quantify the importance of length of exposure to atmospheric pollution, Haenzel and his coworkers (1962) made the surprising discovery that death rates from lung cancer in the U.S., when controlled for degree of cigarette smoking, were considerably higher in the farm-born who had migrated to cities than they were in lifetime urban dwellers. While not necessarily demonstrating the importance of social factors in disease, this is an important contribution indicating the significance of the adaptive powers of the human organism.

Perhaps one of the more important studies in this series are those conducted by Hinkle and his coworkers (1961). In studying groups of men all working for the same company and all holding similar positions as managers, they found marked differences in the disease prevalence in those groups who had completed college as opposed to those who had not completed college prior to coming to the industry. Those who had completed college, were, with few exceptions, fourth-generation Americans, sons of managers, proprietors, and white-collar workers, and had grown up in families with middle to high incomes and in good neighborhoods. In contrast, the group who had not completed college were hired as skilled craftsmen and later advanced to managerial status. They were sons and grandsons of immigrants, their fathers were skilled or unskilled laborers with an average of grammar school education or less, and they had grown up in families of low income in modest to substandard neighborhoods. This latter group shared a significantly greater number of illness of all sorts than did the former group. It is important to note that they were more susceptible to major as well as minor illnesses, to "physical illness" as well as "emotional illness," to illnesses affecting every organ of the body, and to long-term as well as to short-term illness.

In addition, therefore, to supporting the notion of the importance of "preparedness" for a situation (in this instance measured by educational level in relation to job demands), this study of Hinkle's raises a further possibility. The clustering of so wide a variety of disease syndromes in the unprepared group would suggest that to the extent exposure to unfamiliar situations is important as a determinant of disease or as a factor leading to increased susceptibility to disease, it need not be expected that it will necessarily be related specifically to any particular disease classified according to current clinical nomenclature. In other words, the possibility must be entertained that social factors may increase the risk of ill health by increasing general susceptibility to disease. The manifestation or form of the disease may well be due to an entirely different set of factors (including genetic make-up and the physical and biological pathogens with which the susceptible groups come into contact).

These studies, while providing some support for the influence of group membership on health (in both positive and negative fashion), and for the importance of prior experience or degree of preparedness for new situations, do not make very explicit those attributes of group membership or the nature of the social situations that strain the adaptive mechanisms and lead to variations in physiological response. A potentially fruitful approach to identifying those relevant attributes can be found in a number of studies concerned with the degree to which individuals occupy positions that expose them to ambiguous or conflicting stimuli. Research in this area is still in its infancy and the results, while tantalizing, are only suggestive.

Kahn and his group (1961), for example, in an extensive series of studies in industrial plants have developed techniques to assess the degree to which any given role in the industry is associated with conflict or ambiguity. While no measurements of physiological response or occurrence of "physical" disease were included, individuals occupying such roles were found to have significantly higher symptom scores than did those occupying roles in which there was no, or minimal, evidence of conflict or ambiguity. (It is important to note in this connection that these investigators were able to categorize the various roles, in terms of conflict and ambiguity, independently of the views and perceptions of the occupants of these roles, thus avoiding the danger of circularity—an individual's dissatisfaction being taken as evidence of both role conflict and high symptoms.)

In a similar vein, Jackson (1962) has been concerned with the concept of status inconsistency. This has been measured by the concordance of scores given to the occupational level, education, and racial ethnic background of individuals. Here, too, the only measurement of health status was a symptom query that was found to be highest in those inconsistent status patterns where ascribed status was superior to achieved status. These results have been replicated, and to a large extent confirmed, by Abramson (1966) in Israel, who found that Cornell Medical Index Scores were highest (when controlled for age and sex) when there was a discrepancy between occupational status and educational level.

It seems reasonably clear that advances in this field are going to be limited until the nature of those social processes influencing physiological response (and thus, presumably, susceptibility to disease) can be more precisely defined and quantitated. The need for further understanding of these processes is accentuated by the limited utility of current concepts of etiological factors in disease. Even for that group of diseases about which most is known, the infectious disease, Rene Dubos, a pioneer microbiologist states:

The sciences concerned with microbial diseases have developed almost exclusively from the study of acute or semi-acute infectious processes caused by virulent microorganisms acquired through exposure to an exogenous source of infection. In contrast, the microbial diseases most common in our communities today arise from the activities of microorganisms that are ubiquitous in the environment, persist in the body without causing obvious harm under ordinary circumstances, and exert pathological effects only when the infected person is under conditions of physiological stress. In such a type of microbial disease, the event of infection is of less importance than the hidden manifestations of the smouldering infectious process and than the physiological disturbances that convert latent infection into overt symptoms and pathology (1965, p. 164).

From the data summarized thus far, it would appear not unreasonable to expect that the more precise identification of some of the social processes hinted at could yield important new information on some of the sources of physiological stress that Dubos maintains "convert latent infection into overt symptoms and pathology."

To accomplish such an objective, two major steps must now be taken. First of all, as indicated above, the general formulation that social factors are important in disease genesis can only be made useful if it can be translated into terms capable of being tested and refuted. As in all scientific endeavors, the major prerequisite for such tests is that the relevant variables be susceptible to measurement. The problems of quantitating these social and cultural processes are great and are closely akin to the problems faced by psychologists in their attempts to measure some of the relatively intangible aspects of personality. Perhaps for this reason, the advice of Cattel on the measurement of anxiety seems particularly appropriate.

To the physical scientist the measurement of so intangible an entity as anxiety may seem a bit of a wild goose chase. Yet he will also be the first to recognize that until we can define and measure it, the emergence and testing of any laws or theories about causes and consequences of anxiety is the merest vanity. Fortunately, when they are too oppressed by intangibles, psychologists can hearten themselves by the words of the pioneer, E. L. Thorndyke, that "Whatever exists, exists in some quantity and can therefore be measured."

Even thus encouraged, however, there remains the difficulty that one has to define what has to be measured. However, in science it often turns out that a better procedure than that of defining something is to discover something (1964, p. 396).

These remarks would suggest in this field that the "discovery" necessary is that of more efficient or more effective conceptualization; that until the proposition can be more clearly conceptualized, quantification will be premature and lead to the danger of superficiality and sterility. Various types of social processes have been invoked either implicitly or explicitly in the studies reviewed above. These include concepts such as cultural discontinuity, role incongruity, status crystallization, social integration, role conflict, and frustration. Other studies have concentrated on the concept of adaptation, implying the ability of the human organism to adapt in a variety of fashions to environmental stimuli, including those symbolic stimuli stemming from a society in which he interacts. Few, if any, studies have invoked these concepts simultaneously and it would thus appear to be important in future studies to consider not only the nature of the social situation but also the degree to which the individuals in such a situation have been prepared for it by previous experience or circumstances.

It would appear useful, therefore, to attempt to identify social situations characterized by the number of factors which on a priori grounds can be considered to be deleterious. Ostfeld (personal communication) has suggested that one such set of circumstances would be situations in which (1) the outcome of important events in the lives of individuals is uncertain; (2) that flight or fight are inappropriate mechanisms for helping to determine such an outcome; and (3) that the outcome will be dependent upon constant vigilance on the part of the individuals concerned. In addition to such circumstances, those situations in which aspirations are blocked and in which meaningful human intercourse is restricted might be important for these purposes. In such situations, then, it would be important to determine the degree to which the individuals so exposed were prepared or not prepared. In addition, it is presumably important to determine whether differences exist in the exposed individuals in the degree to which they can tolerate the situation. Presumably, personality differences may be important determinants of the degree to which tolerance exists.

Given this definition of the situation and the degree of susceptibility of the individuals so exposed in terms of their preparedness and in terms of their degree of tolerance, the next question would be the type of outcome that should be anticipated. Here it becomes important to examine the models of causality to which we subscribe, as these will determine the types of outcome accepted as evidence that the social situation is important in the genesis of disease. In most of the research in this field, the model of causation subscribed to by the investigator is implicit, but examination of the studies suggests that those most commonly invoked fall into three categories which can perhaps best be described by the analogy to infectious disease concepts.

The first category includes the studies in which the relationships to be anticipated are of the same order as those found between the tubercle bacillus and tuberculosis. According to this assumption, a social "stress' should be found which will be the cause, say, of coronary heart disease. (While it is no longer considered fashionable to subscribe to a mono-etiological model, it is surprising how frequently this still occurs. Witness, for example, in the field of cardiovascular epidemiology the current controversies as to whether behavior type *or* altered serum lipids are the cause of coronary disease.) Such a model, which by extension would ascribe to social "stress" the same role as a pathogenic microorganism, overlooks the key role played in the infectious disease model by the classificatory system. The classification of infectious diseases is on a so-called etiological basis in which the consequences of exposure to a given organism are defined as a specific disease. Using such a system, the discovery of individuals with identical clinical, x-ray, and pathological manifestations to those found in tuberculosis patients but without the presence of tubercle bacillus does *not* provide evidence against the causative role of the bacillus. Rather, such manifestations are reclassified (by definition) as a disease other than tuberculosis, namely atypical tuberculosis. The point is that such a tautology has been extremely useful for certain purposes (particularly for therapeutic purposes), but its use as a model to guide the search in the discovery of the antecedent social factors in diseases classified on the basis of anatomical location, such as heart disease, or altered function, such as elevated blood pressure, is at best doubtful.

The second category of causation invoked is based on the type of relationship found to exist between height above sea level and malaria. The assumption is that social "stress" situations are indirect indications of some other processes responsible for the diseases. These processes common to both the social situation and the diseases would include the possibility of selection and/or physical factors. While it is obviously important to determine whether such a formulation is appropriate, both the discovery of the possible processes indirectly indicated by the social situation and the documentation of their causative role require the elaboration of a further explicit model. Subscription to this model, therefore, merely defers but does not eliminate the need for a direct formulation.

The third type of model implicit in much of the work is the analogue of the relationships known to exist between polluted water and gastrointestinal diseases. Inherent in these studies is the assumption that certain social situations are "vehicles" containing the causative "agents" of diseases. While such a formulation avoids many of the pitfalls common to the first model, in that it allows for multiple factors and, by analogy at least, is more appropriate for the anatomical type of classificatory scheme used in identifying the dependent variables, it still has several shortcomings. Of these, perhaps the most important is the possibility that the consequences of exposure to these social situations may vary at different times and at different places and that these differences may be a function both of the processes involved in the situation and the attributes of the people exposed. Exposure to polluted water, to return to the analogy, does under certain circumstances lead to high rate of gastrointestinal disease; but alternatively, it may lead to high rates of liver disease (infectious hepatitis) or central nervous system disease (poliomyelitis). In this instance the specific manifestations that are a consequence of exposure are a function both of the nature of the agents contained in the same vehicle and the antibody levels of the exposed population. In the same way, exposure to urbanization at one point in time has been shown to be correlated with an increase in tuberculosis and other infectious diseases and, at a later point in time, to an increase in coronary heart disease and lung cancer. Alternatively, studying two groups differing in many important respects but both exposed to similar situations at the same point in time has been shown to be related to different manifestations of disease. Indians and Africans both living in similar housing, eating similar diets, in the slums of Durban, South Africa, for example, have both been found to be infested with entomeba histolytica. Despite the high infestation rate, the occurrence of marked symptoms of dysentery is very rare among the Indians, among whom mild diarrhea is the most dramatic symptom, but common among the Africans.

In my view a more satisfactory working model would result if this last category of assumptions could be expanded to include the possibilities suggested initially by Claude Bernard and elaborated on by Chapman and others (1960). Chapman suggests that disease should be viewed as occurring when the adaptive responses by the organism to stimuli are inappropriate in kind or amount or both. Logically, then, the problem can be formulated as two interrelated, but from a research point of view separate, questions. First, would be the identification of situations that are likely to evoke inappropriate adaptive responses. Populations exposed to such situations would be expected to manifest a wide spectrum of disease consequences which may or may not "fit" the existing clinical classificatory schemes. The nature or form of these manifestations would be the second type of question. Answers to this will not come from the identification of the processes involved in the situation alone, but must take into account the determinants of the particular adaptive devices utilized by various segments of the population. These determinants presumably will be functions of the genetic endowment and previous experience of the population at risk and, it is to be hoped, will be assessed by various biological indicators.

Such a formulation, by allowing for multiple alternative options to any particular situation and by indicating the need to identify situations likely to evoke inappropriate adaptive responses, can provide leads as to what it is that needs to be quantified and what sorts of relationships would be acceptable as evidence of importance of these situations.

One further caution must be advanced in considering the model of causation subscribed to. This is the concept first pointed out by Halliday (1943) that the causes of any illness may be different from the causes of lack of recovery from that illness. In searching for clues as to the nature of those phenomena likely to lead to the disease as a response — that is, those phenomena that will be labeled as "stress" — the traditional approach is to compare the attributes and life experience of sick people with control groups. The possibility exists, however, that the factors which differentiate these two groups are the reasons why some people are still sick rather than why they became sick.

While the translation of the concepts presented in this chapter into feasible research projects will be no easy task, and may indeed be beyond our current ingenuity, it seems important that the issues be raised and discussed as an essential prelude to further productive inquiry. Failing this, there appears to be the serious danger that future research will continue in the existing repetitive mold, documenting an association between certain social conditions and disease states without illuminating the processes involved or indicating further directions for research or improving our ability for informed intervention, either preventive or therapeutic.

REFERENCES

ABRAHAMS, D. G., ABLE, C. A., and BERNART, G. 1960. "Systematic Blood Pressure in a Rural West African Community." *West African Medical Journal*, 9:45.

ABRAMSON, J. H. 1966. "Emotional Disorder, Status Inconsistency and Migration." *Milbank Memorial Fund Quarterly*, 44:23–48.

ADER, R., KREUTNER, A., and JACOBS, H. L. 1963. "Social Environment, Emotionality and Alloxan Diabetes in the Rat" *Psychosomatic Medicine*, 25:60–68.

ADER, R., and HAHN, E. W. 1963. "Effects of Social Environment on Mortality to Whole Body X-Irradiation in the Rat." *Psychological Reports*, 13:24–215.

ALEXANDER, F. 1949. "A Medical Survey of the Aleutian Islands." *New England Journal of Medicine*, 240:1035.

ANDERVONT, H. B. 1944. "Influence of Environment on Mammary Cancer in Mice." *Journal of National Cancer Institute* 4:579–81.

BIBILE, S. W., CULLUNDINE, H., WATSON, R. S., and WIKRAMANAYAKE, T. W. 1949. "Variation with Age and Sex of Blood Pressure and Pulse Rate for Ceylonese Subjects." *Ceylonese Journal of Medical Science*, 6:80.

CALHOUN, J. B. 1962. "Population Density and Social Pathology." *Scientific American*, 206:139.

CASSEL, J. T., and TYROLER, H. A. 1961. "Epidemiological Studies of Culture Change, I: Health Status and Recency of Industrialization." *Archives of Environmental Health*, 3:25.

CATTELL, R. B. 1964. "Psychological Definition and Measurement of Anxiety." *Journal of Neuropsychiatry*, 5:396–402.

CHAPMAN, L. F., HINKLE, L. E., and WOLFF, H. G. 1960. "Human Ecology Disease and Schizophrenia." *American Journal of Psychiatry*, 117:193.

CHRISTENSON, W. N., and HINKLE, L. E., JR. 1961. "Differences in Illness and Prognostic Signs in Two Groups of Young Men." *Journal of the American Medical Association*, 177:247–53.

CHRISTIAN, J. J., and WILLIAMSON, H. O. 1958. "Effect of Crowding on Experimental Granuloma Formation in Mice." *Proceedings of the Society of Experimental Biology and Medicine*, 99:385–87.

CONGER, J. J. 1958. "The Role of Social Experience in the Production of Gastric Ulcers in Hooded Rats Placed in a Conflict Situation." *Journal of Abnormal and Social Psychology*, 57:216.

CRUZ-COKE, R., ETCHEVERRY, R., and NAGEL, R. 1964. "Influence of Migration on Blood Pressure of Easter Islanders." *Lancet*, 1:697–99.

DAVIS, D. E., and READ, C. P. 1958. "Effects of Behavior on Development of

Resistance in Trichinosis." *Proceedings of the Society for Experimental Biology and Medicine*, 99:269–72.

DONNINSON, C. P. 1929. "Blood Pressure in the African Native." *Lancet*, 1:56.

DUBOS, R. 1965. *Man Adapting*. New Haven: Yale University Press (pp. 164–65).

DUNHAM, H. W. 1961. "Social Structures and Mental Disorders: Competing Hypotheses of Explanation." *Milbank Memorial Fund Quarterly*, 39:259–310.

DURKHEIM, E. 1957. *Suicide*. Glencoe, Ill.: Free Press.

FLEMING, H. C. 1924. "Medical Observations on the Zuni Indians." *Contribution to Museum of American Indians*, 7: no. 2. New York: Heye Foundation.

FULMER, H. S., and ROBERTS, R. W. 1963. "Coronary Heart Disease among the Navajo Indians." *Annals of Internal Medicine*, 59:740–64.

GRIGG, E. R. N. 1958. "The Arcana of Tuberculosis." *American Review of TB* 78:151–72, 426–53, 583–603.

HAENZEL, W., LOVELAND, D. B., and SIRKEN, M. G. 1962. "Lung-Cancer Mortality as Related to Residence and Smoking Histories." *Journal of National Cancer Institute*, 28:947–1001.

HALLIDAY, J. L. 1943. "Principles of Aetiology." *British Journal of Medical Psychology*, 19:367.

HENRY, J. P. Manuscript. "Systemic Arterial Pressure as a Measure of Stressful Social Interaction."

HILL, S. R., GOETZ, F. C., FOX, H. M., MURAWSKI, B. J., KRAKAUER, L. J., REIFENSTEIN, R. W., GRAY, S. J., REDDY, W. J., HEDBERG, S. E., ST. MARC, J. R., and THORN, G. W. 1956. "Studies on Adrenalcortical and Psychological Response to Stress in Man." *AMA Archives of Internal Medicine*, 97:269–98.

HOLMES, T. H. 1956. "Multidiscipline Studies of Tuberculosis," in P. J. Sparer, ed., *Personality Stress and Tuberculosis*. New York: International Universities Press.

HOOBLER, S. W., TEJADA, G., GUZMAN, M., and PARDO A. 1965. "Influence of Nutrition and 'Acculturation' on the Blood Pressure Levels and Changes with Age in the Highland Guatamalan Indian." *Circulation*, 32:4.

JACKSON, E. F. 1962. "Status Consistency and Symptoms of Stress." *American Sociologal Review*, 27:469–80.

KAHN, R. L., WOLFE, D. M., QUINN, R., SNOEK, J. D., and ROSENTHAL, R. A. 1961. *Organizational Stress: Studies in Role Conflict and Ambiguity*. New York: John Wiley.

KAMINER, B., and LUTZ, W. P. 1960. "Blood Pressure in Bushmen of the Kalahari Desert." *Circulation*, 22:289.

KEAN, B. H. 1941. "Blood Pressure Studies on West Indians and Panamanians Living on Isthmus of Panama." *AMA Archives of Internal Medi-*

cine, 68:466.
1944. "Blood Pressure of the Cuna Indians." *American Journal of Tropical Medicine*, 24:341.
KILBORN, L. G. 1937. "A Note on the Blood Pressure of Primitive Races with Special Reference to the Maio of Kiweichaw." *Chinese Journal of Physiology*, 11:135.
KING, J. T., LEE, Y. C. P., and VISSCHER, M. B. 1955. "Single Versus Multiple Cage Occupancy and Convulsion Frequency in C₃H Mice." *Proceedings of the Society for Experimental Biology and Medicine*, 88:661–63.
KRAKOWER, A. 1933. "Blood Pressure of Chinese Living in Eastern Canada." *American Heart Journal*, 9:376.
LEVINE, V. E. 1942. "The Blood Pressure of Eskimos." *Federation Proceedings*, 1:121.
LOWELL, R. R. H., MADDOCKS, I., and ROGERSON, G. W. 1960. "The Casual Arterial Pressure of Fijeans and Indians in Fiji." *Australasian Annals of Medicine*, 9:4.
LOWENSTEIN, F. W. 1961. "Blood Pressure in Relation to Age and Sex in the Tropics and Subtropics: A Review of the Literature and an Investigation in Two Tribes of Brazil Indians." *Lancet*, 1:389.
MADDOCKS, I. 1961. "Possible Absence of Hypertension in Two Complete Pacific Island Populations." *Lancet*, 2:396.
MANN, G. V., SHAFFER, R. D., ANDERSON, R. S., and SANDSTEAD, H. H. 1964. "Cardiovascular Disease in the Masai." *Journal of Atherosclerosis Research*, 4:289.
MASON, J. W. 1959. "Psychological Influences on the Pituitary-Adrenal-Cortical System," in G. Pencus, ed., *Recent Progress in Hormone Research*, 15:345–89.
MASON, J. W., BRADY, J. V., POLISH, E., BAUER, J. S., ROBINSON, J., and DODSON, E. 1959. "Concurrent Measurement of 17-hydroxycorticosteroids and Pepsinogen Levels during Prolonged Emotional Stress in the Monkey." *Psychosomatic Medicine*, 21:432.
MASON, J. W., and BRADY, J. V. 1965. "The Sensitivity of the Psychoendocrine System to Social and Physical Environment," in D. Shapiro, ed., *Psychobiological Approaches to Social Behavior*. Stanford, Calif.: Stanford University Press.
MISHLER, E. G., and SCOTCH, N. A. 1963. "Sociocultural Factors in the Epidemiology of Schizophrenia. A Review." *Psychiatry*, 26:315–51.
MURPHY, W. 1955. "Some Observations on Blood Pressures in the Humid Tropics." *New Zealand Medical Journal*, 54:64.
MURRIL, R. I. 1949. "A Blood Pressure Study of the Natives of Ponape Island." *Human Biology*, 21:47.
PADMAYATI, S., and GUPTA, S. 1959. "Blood Pressure Studies in Rural and Urban Groups in Delhi." *Circulation*, 19:395.

208   PART THREE : *Consequences of Stress*

PAFFENBERGER, R. S., JR., MILLING, R. N., POE, N. D., and KRUEGER, D. E. 1966. "Trends in Death Rates from Hypertensive Disease in Memphis, Tennessee 1920-1960." *Journal of Chronic Disease,* 19:847-56.

PAYNE, A. M. M. 1965. "Environmental Determinants of Community Well-Being," in *Pan American Health Organization Scientific Publication No. 123.* p. 3.

RATCLIFFE, H. L., and CRONIN, M. T. I. 1958. "Changing Frequency of Arteriosclerosis in Mammals and Birds at the Philadelphia Zoological Garden." *Circulation,* 18:41-52.

SAUNDERS, G. M. 1933. "Blood Pressure in Yucatans." *American Journal of Medical Science,* 185:843.

SCOTCH, N. A. 1960. "A Preliminary Report on the Relation of Sociocultural Factors to Hypertension among the Zulu." *Annals of the New York Academy of Science,* 86:1000.

———. 1963. "Sociocultural Factors in the Epidemiology of Zulu Hypertension." *American Journal of Public Health,* 52:1205-13.

SCOTCH, N. A., and GEIGER, H. J. 1962. "The Epidemiology of Rheumatoid Arthritis. A Review with Special Attention to Social Factors." *Journal of Chronic Diseases,* 15:1037-67.

———. 1963. "The Epidemiology of Essential Hypertension II. Psychological and Sociocultural Factors in Etiology." *Journal of Chronic Diseases.* 16:1183-1213.

SUSSER, M., and STEIN, Z. 1962. "Civilization and Peptic Ulcer." *Lancet,* 1:115-19.

SWINYARD, E. A., CLARK, L. D., MIYAHARA, J. T., and WOLF, H. H. 1961. "Studies on the Mechanism of Amphetamine Toxicity in Aggregated Mice." *Journal of Pharmacology and Experimental Therapy,* 132:97-102.

SYME, S. L., HYMAN, M. M., and ENTERLINE, P. E. 1964. "Some Social and Cultural Factors Associated with the Occurrence of Coronary Heart Disease." *Journal of Chronic Diseases,* 17:277-89.

———. 1965. "Cultural Mobility and the Occurrence of Coronary Heart Disease." *Health and Human Behavior,* 6:178-89.

TILLMAN, W. A., and HOBBS, G. E. 1949. "Social Background of Accident Free and Accident Repeaters." *American Journal of Psychiatry,* 106:321.

TYROLER, H. A., and CASSEL, J. C., 1964. "Health Consequences of Culture Change: The Effect of Urbanization on Coronary Heart Mortality in Rural Residents of North Carolina." *Journal of Chronic Diseases,* 17:167-77.

WELCH, B. L. 1964. "Psychophysiological Response to the Mean Level of Environmental Stimulation. A Theory of Environmental Integration," in *Symposium on Medical Aspects of Stress in the Military Climate.* Walter Reed Army Institute of Research. p. 51.

WELCH, B. L., and KLOPFER, P. H. 1961. "Endocrine Variability as a Factor in the Regulation of Population Density." *American Naturalist,* 95:256-60.

WHYTE, W. M. 1958. "Body Fat and Blood Pressure of Natives of New Guines: Reflections on Essential Hypertension." *Australasian Annals of Medicine*, 7:36.

WOLFF, C. T., FRIEDMAN, S. B., HOFER, M. A., and MASON, J. W. 1964. "Relationship between Psychological Defenses and Mean Urinary 17-hydroxycorticosteroid Excretion Rate." *Psychosomatic Medicine*, 26:592–609.

WOLMAN, A. 1965. "Environmental Determinants of Community Well-Being," in *Pan American Health Organization Scientific Publication No. 123*, p. 2.

8. Mental Illness in Response to Stress

E. GARTLY JACO

STRESS has become a generally accepted link in the etiological process of mental illness, particularly after the notion of anxiety became regarded as a basic component of the psychoneuroses (Laughlin, 1967). Stress is also compatible with the widespread idea that psychic conflict is the root of all functional mental illness since the writings of Meyer (Lief, 1948) and Freud (1924). Consequently, the examination of mental illness in response to stress as a process related to psychic conflict and anxiety is based upon many studies and much theorizing in contemporary psychopathology and psychiatry. Many conceptual and theoretical problems and issues are involved in any treatise on the topic of stress and its relationship to mental illness and related conditions, however, and this chapter can only present a few facets and will thus perforce be somewhat selective. The major so-called "functional" mental illnesses will be discussed, with the exception of the psychophysiologic (psychosomatic)

E. Gartly Jaco is professor of sociology at the University of California, Riverside.

diseases, which are discussed elsewhere in this volume. (Since the concept of stress is also presented in other chapters, no elaboration is needed here.)

For the purposes of this presentation, stress will be regarded as a force or stimulus, whatever its form may be, which provokes the individual organism to respond in a condition of disturbance. Stress thus is more demanding of a response than a "press" (Murray, 1938), and may lead to harm, impairment, or even destruction of the individual, if not alleviated after a period of continuance. This conception thus implies that stress may take various forms—biological, psychological, and sociological—in essence and manifestation, and may have external as well as internal origins.

When mentioning mental illness here, then, we are essentially discussing forms of human behavior in a "disturbed" state. The so-called psychoneuroses, psychoses, personality disorders, psychophysiologic (psychosomatic), and acute and chronic brain disorders as major typologies of mental illness as officially classified by the American Psychiatric Association (1952) all essentially and basically deal with *disturbances* of the individual in his verbal and nonverbal behavior. A much-used textbook in clinical psychiatry (Noyes and Kolb, 1963) expresses this as follows:

> ... mental disorders are not so much diseases as disturbances of persons. It is increasingly clear that, even when anatomical or physiological disturbances in brain elements are known to exist, they cannot adequately explain the behavior which accompanies them. In varying degrees, this behavior will be colored by, and express, the primitive impulses, affective experiences, and other needs and purposes of the patient's inner life. Stresses in interpersonal relations and in the sociocultural field are no less to be considered than stresses in the biophysical sphere (p. 93).

The individual in an episode of mental illness is a "disturbed" person. Whether or not the disturbed individual is "ill," "abnormal," in a "pathological" condition, or is even playing a "game" (Szasz, 1961) is irrelevant to our major topic.

The disturbance aroused by stress conditions is usually known and the individual involved is usually conscious of his disturbed state, although he may not always know why he is aroused or upset. Thus, stress usually involves the self-concept of the individual at some psychic level, either that some part of his body is suffering or being attacked, or his self-identity is being threatened, attacked, or involved in some hazardous and potentially harmful situation or circumstance. Hence, stress is usually "felt" by the individual, an emotional state is aroused, and his defenses and coping mechanisms are mobilized, even though he may not be aware of the source of such threat other than a vague feeling that "something is wrong" and that his guard must be up if he is to survive the pending attack. Maslow and Mittelmann (1951) have summarized this process as follows: "Psychopathology implies that following situations of stress, the individual manifests suffering, symptoms, impaired efficiency, lessened ability for enjoyment, lack of adequate insight (p. 108)."

The relationship between stress and psychopathology or disturbed behavior is described by Noyes and Kolb (1963) as follows:

> It seems most fruitful to look upon most manifestations of psychopathology not as the result or expression of some "disease" but as a mode of behavior or of living which is the logical, although socially maladjusted, outcome of the particular individual's original endowment, of the molding influences of the home, of traumatic experiences which modified personality development, of the stresses and problems springing from within his emotional and instinctive life, of his inability to meet these strains, of the type of self-defensive reactions habitually utilized for minimizing anxiety, and of any bodily ailments which impair the integrity or efficiency of his biological organism. *Mental disorders should, therefore, be regarded as patterns of human reaction set in motion by stress* (p. 53, emphasis added).

THE ETIOLOGICAL MODEL OF STRESS AND MENTAL ILLNESS

It has become almost traditional to regard three somewhat nebulous groups of etiological agents in the causation or etiology of mental disease: the biological, the psychological, and the social. The interplay of these sets of factors in the etiology of mental illness is generally accepted (Maslow and Mittelmann, 1951). Their relationship in terms of "predisposing" and "precipitating" or "exciting" factors is also a popular conceptualization (Burgess, 1953; Coleman, 1950; Pearson, 1963; Rennie, 1953). *Predisposing factors* are those which develop a susceptibility, tendency, or predilection toward acquiring a mental breakdown, while *precipitating factors* accelerate or "trigger off" the onset of the aberration. Stress can be involved in both precipitating and predisposing factors, and can occur in the realms of biological, psychological, and sociological categories. A brief summary of the total etiology of mental disturbance in terms of these factors is presented as follows, drawing heavily from the author's previous writings on this topic (Jaco, 1959a):

A *predisposing population* contains inherent biogenic and emergent psychogenic deficiencies which set different internal limits on the development of defenses and coping mechanisms against stress and tension for its component human organisms. A *predisposing social system* is that which causes such internal limits of populations to be reached or exceeded more frequently by its incumbents in the process of interacting in or being exposed to that system than would occur in other social systems. A social structure can predispose to mental breakdown by subjecting individuals in that system to a high frequency of stresses. For example, in meeting the responsibilities and requirements of a social role, the role-player may be required frequently to cope with situations that create anxiety, such as the salesman awaiting a decision on each contract he is negotiating. In necessitating his performance of such a role over a long span of his life in a social organization containing excessive stress elements, and by continually subjecting him to these stress conditions, that social system may predispose him and others to a mental breakdown in time. Thus, the individual becomes susceptible or "set up" for the final precipitating event that triggers off a mental breakdown. A predisposing population and social system, therefore, possess a large quantity of potential precipitators, that is, stress inducers, for a large portion of its members.

Social precipitating factors (or "precipitators") are elements in social acts of which an individual becomes aware by being required, compelled, or obliged to cope with or to adapt to. This accelerates a demand on him to adapt, readjust, or at least to cope with the demand and thereby induces stress. The sudden loss of a loved one followed by the necessity to change many habits and patterns of daily living may induce stress and subsequent mood disturbances such as a reactive depression. Added to this may be a failure to develop ways for preventing or relieving stress reactions in a socially appropriate manner. *Personal precipitating factors* involve the perceptive ability and "psychological set" of the individual's personality which affect his reactions to stress (stress reactors). These reactions are expressed in terms of his own defenses, coping mechanisms, and related personality attributes.

Thus, when predisposing elements of the social structure confront a predisposed member of the population with a crisis, threat, or disturbing force to his self or ego that demands simultaneously a reaction from him that he is unable or inept to cope with in terms of his defenses, a stressful reaction is precipitated. Defense mechanisms may be set into motion. The stress elements may serve as sources of rationalization. The subject may attempt to suppress them from his conscious thoughts; he may try to avert stress by projecting his problems on to others with hostility or by creating anxiety in his "method of prevention" or reduction of stress. This may lead to (1) a loss of personal identity, as in situations of "anomie"; (2) a confusion of identity, as in ambivalence and conditions of cultural conflict; or (3) a distortion of identity, as in inappropriate responses, delusions, and fantasies. All three types of reactions are manifested in some form of disturbed behavior. The final outcome may be the onset of a form of mental illness. A suggested conceptual outline of this model of the *total etiology* of mental illness is presented in Figure 8.1.

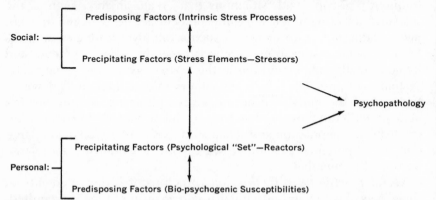

Fig. 8.1. Conceptual outline of the total etiology of mental illness.

Figure 8.1's etiological model, with its interplay of social and personal predisposing and precipitating factors, can be illustrated as follows: In contemporary American society, the conjugal marriage institution may be regarded as a *social* predisposing factor in the induction of many anxieties, stresses, and subsequent forms of mental illness by the fact that one component of this system is the expectation that marital partners choose each other. Such choices often run the risk of incompatible, unhappy marriages, often due to disparities in sociocultural backgrounds of the marital partners, divergent status and role expectations, conflicting child-rearing norms, etc., leading to increasingly frequent conflicts between spouses and making a harmonious marital relationship difficult. Such conflicts may lead to separation or divorce. The break in the marital relationship may precipitate a mood disturbance in the form of a mental depression in one or both of the spouses. Thus, the marriage system may be viewed as the social predisposing factor, while the event of divorce can be termed the social precipitating event inducing the onset of the psychiatric disorder. Furthermore, the conjugal marriage institution may predispose to a greater frequency of a particular mental illness in a population than another type of marriage system.

On the other hand, not everyone getting divorced in American society becomes mentally ill with a depression, in that not every person reacts to such precipitating events in the same manner or degree. It is at this point that the *personal* predisposing and precipitating factors become etiologic agents. Biogenic and psychogenic factors could predispose certain individuals to fail to acquire appropriate means of coping with marriage as well as withstanding the loss of a spouse following divorce. Attitudes toward marriage and divorce, and certain perceptions and evaluations of stressful experiences during marriage and following its breakup may precipitate a psychiatric disorder in that particular individual, a disorder that other persons might be able to defend their self-identity against.

The foregoing theoretical model in which social and personal predisposing and precipitating factors are delineated as conducive to psychopathology and mental illness implies that social and psychological stresses are operating in all of these factors. Stress thus is regarded as both external and internal to the individual, and by its simultaneous and continuous and overwhelming demands eventuates into some form of mental aberration and disturbed behavior. This assumption underlies by and large the studies of stress and their relation to the production of psychopathology. Cameron (1963) in discussing the neuroses states categorically "that certain persons are predisposed to develop neurotic behavior under stress by the kind of internal, psychological equilibrium which they establish during their first five years. This may have its roots in a congenital hypersensitivity to anxiety-provoking stimulation. It certainly has its roots in early environmental experiences, particularly those having to do with interrelationships with other persons (p. 450)." Cameron (1963, pp. 468-69) also lists five major precipitating factors common to all psychoses, each of which is essentially a stress condition: (1) loss or threatened loss of a major source of gratification; (2) loss or threatened loss of basic security; (3) an upsurge of erotic or hostile drive; (4) a sudden increase in unconscious, preconscious, or conscious guilt; and (5) reduced general effectiveness of the defensive organization. Such considerations of the etiological factors, in the numerous theories of psychopathology and mental illness have guided many, but by no means all, of the research and clinical studies involving social and psychological stress conditions that might be linked to the onset of mental illnesses or involved in the life histories of mentally disturbed individuals.

SOME SOURCES OF SOCIAL AND PSYCHOLOGICAL STRESS

To attempt to encompass all of the specific types and sources of stress would require several large volumes, since a large and varied literature exists on this topic. We will here present only some of the more representative studies and topics on social and psychological stress, and attempt to assess the contributions of such studies to the existing body of knowledge on the relationship between stress and mental illness.

The pathogenic effects of *social isolation* have long been recognized and described, particularly in connection with schizophrenia (Faris, 1934), although conclusive evidence is still far from being established (Jaco, 1954; Kohn and Clausen, 1955). Isolation might also be involved in the background of other types of psychopathology, such as the manic-depressive psychoses, since the reactions to reduced social contact might take many aberrant forms. Cameron and Magaret (1951, p. 481) have offered the term "desocialization," which may be regarded as a consequence of social isolation. They define desocialization as being "a reduction in the social articulation of behavior, resulting from the partial or complete detachment of an individual from participation in the activities of the social community." In this relatively anonymous state, the individual is cast adrift in the community without benefit of the stabilizing and socializing forces available to others who are active participants in society. The individual may occasionally attempt to restore relations with others in a compulsive manner and, if failing, may become extremely depressed and suicidal. Other reactions to isolation could encompass such mental states as the "paranoid pseudo-community" (Cameron, 1943) or self-indulgence in autistic daydreams, distrust, aversion, fantasy-thinking, and overt hostility (Weinberg, 1952). Social isolation, therefore, may render stressful the performance of social roles in society, make status relations nebulous and disruptive, and contribute to a possible disturbance in self-identity.

Weinberg (1966) has delineated several forms of social isolation. In a critique of this concept, he concludes that "the isolation resulting from rejection seems more directly instrumental in the schizophrenic onset than the isolation resulting from lack of contacts. The more self-involving and intimate the relationship the more destructive the rejection; and the earlier the more sustained and recurring this rejection the more it bears as a precipitating factor in the schizophrenic onset (p. 40)."

The sources of social isolation are varied and have not been precisely delineated in the literature. Weinberg's aforementioned critique may be helpful in suggesting different types of isolation, but a precise typology is still needed. Thus, while the relationship of social isolation to stress is reasonably established, its etiologic connection to mental illness is still ambiguous, if not in doubt.

Work and the *economic role* of the individual may impose stresses conducive to mental illness as well as exposing the organism to noxious physical agents such as exogenous poisons (Pearson, 1963). Occupations of divergent status levels have been found to exhibit excessive rates of mental illness (Clark, 1949; Jaco, 1960; Ødegaard, 1956). In an economic system in which the individual is forced to compete against others to earn his livelihood, such terms as "economic insecurity" and "cut-throat" competition in the marketplace are given as examples of stresses imposed by this system that have been related to mental illness (Jaco, 1959a; Leavy and Freedman, 1967). The generating of neurotic behavior by economic insecurity has been related to a "threat to subsistence" and to a "threat to self-esteem" by Leavy and Freedman (1967). These investigators conclude that "greater and lesser degrees of neurotic behavior resulted when insecurity and poverty defeated the individuals' attempt to live up to the expectations they made upon themselves. Furthermore, the psychological correspondence existing between economic insecurity and loss of love was illustrated in our cases (p. 118)." Leavy and Freedman (1967) also report the relationship of economic competition to psychoneuroses:

Economic competition operated as a pathogenic agency in several ways. The struggle for achievement liberated in some patients feelings of hostility which were poorly withstood. In other cases, the culturally prescribed standards of success and prestige presented goals impossible of achievement, which augment already existing conflicts. In yet others, economic life offered a new arena for the enactment of competitive struggles which had been going on in one guise or another since early childhood. In all these it may be said that the obligation to compete, like economic insecurity, had a double function: it was a direct threat, since failure might again endanger subsistence, and it was also more subtly involved as a social force, invoking the individual's allegiance in the pursuit of a value not open to criticism (p. 118).

Loss of social status, somewhat related to the competitive work-role, as indicated by downward social mobility, has long been regarded as stressful (Hollingshead and Redlich, 1953; Parsons, 1949), particularly in societies assigning high value to achievement. Somewhat paradoxically, upward social mobility has also been viewed as stressful and may bear some relationship to schizophrenia

(Hollingshead and Redlich, 1958) and to psychoneurosis (Hollingshead and others, 1954). These social factors have been channeled into the concept of "goal-striving behavior" by Kleiner and Parker (1963) in a critical evaluation of studies involving status, social mobility, and mental disorder. Thus, the open-class society where status is lost or gained by goal-striving behavior may be regarded as contributing factors in disturbed behavior in social spheres additional to the economic, but the precise etiologic connection to mental illness is still unclear.

The *family group* that is disrupted or in conflict has been studied extensively as a major source of stress. Such studies have been reviewed in several treatises (Cleveland and Longaker, 1957; Cumming, 1961; Lidz, 1958; Milbank Conference, 1961; Myers and Roberts, 1959). Most studies have emphasized the stressful effects of parental relationships in rearing and socializing their children, beginning with the influence of Freud's writings on the family backgrounds of neurotic patients. Stresses such as maternal deprivation, maternal overprotection, rejection, negligence, abuse, "double-bind" relationships, ambivalence, perversion, and "schizophrenogenic" parents are some examples found in families producing mentally disturbed members. The plethora of family studies in mental illness are of such wide variety and scope that Cumming (1961, p. 177) was led to conclude that "organized study of the area of the family and mental illness is in a state of chaos."

Social change in a variety of forms and consequences has been related to stress and mental illness (Hughes and others, 1960; Leighton, 1965). "Social disintegration" has been particularly singled out by Leighton (1965) as a resultant of change related to mental illness. This condition refers to an array of factors such as "role dissolution, loss and deformation of sentiments and values, confusion regarding the meaning of symbols and cues, failures of communication, the breaking apart of family structure and deterioration of capacity for leadership, followership and conjoint effort (Leighton, 1965, p. 218)." While Leighton prefers to distinguish between cultural change and disintegration, the conditions are nevertheless related. Murphy (1961) has prepared an extensive survey of the epidemiologic literature on social change and mental illness, focusing on such variables as immigration, internal migration, war and peace, and acculturation to Western civilization. The theoretical underpinning of these studies is the assumption that change in the social milieu increases the hazards and threats of human experience and behavior, which in turn are conducive to stress and, hence, mental disorder. Conflicting findings were exhibited by the array of studies reported by Murphy, with perhaps the factor of acculturation to Western modes of living by so-called "underdeveloped" or non-Western societies the most consistently significant factor related to increased rates of mental illness. Although the specific etiologic aspects of social change are not specified in his report, Murphy does present certain types of mental illness that are associated with social change, such as acute confusional states, epidemic hysteria, mild depression, schizophrenia, and arteriosclerotic psychosis. On the other hand, social change has been related to a reduction in certain psychiatric symptoms, such as depression, and the precise etiologic significance of change to mental illness consequently is still vague and open to question.

Life-history approach. Beginning with Freud, the life-history approach to describing and analyzing a sequence of stress experiences and conflicts as they lead toward psychopathology of individuals has been basic to understanding mental illness. Developmental studies and more recently the life cycle of the individual as he passes from infancy to adulthood and old age have become a method of organizing and relating the frequency and types of stresses and reactions to them (Erickson, 1963). As Caudill (1958) points out, stresses of childhood are different from the stresses of adulthood. Consequently, the attempt to relate stresses and conflict in terms of the age-epoch of the individual is increasingly becoming a standard practice in psychiatry (Noyes and Kolb, 1963; Pearson, 1963; Redlich and Freedman, 1966). This effort is further supported by existing epidemiological studies of mental illness in which many major mental disorders are more frequent during certain stages of the life cycle than others — disorders such as sociopathic conditions typical of adolescence, schizophrenia in early adulthood, affective and psychophysiological disorders in middle adulthood, chronic addictions and involutional disorders in later maturity, and cerebral arteriosclerosis and senile dementia in old age (Rose and Stub, 1955). Longitudinal studies with adequate research controls of subjects continuing through various phases of the life cycle have often been cited as an urgent need in order to validate the etiological significance of these factors for mental illness. Beyond sheer cost, however, the methodological obstacles are enormous. The attrition of subjects over a lengthy period of analysis, the proper selection and maintenance of appropriate samples, the delineation of factors related to mental illness from those involving survival to the later stages of the life cycle, and the distinct universes to which generalizations and evaluations of results can be validly referred are only a few of the methodological problems involved in this mode of inquiry.

Attention to stresses related to psychiatric disorders of the elderly population is increasing as earlier notions of exclusively organic etiology of such illnesses are undergoing reevaluation. Discontinuities in the phase of "later maturity" with loss of social status implied in retirement and widowhood (Belknap and Friedsam, 1949), the concept of "disengagement" with aging (Cumming and Henry, 1961), breakdown of channels of communication and the interruption of living routines (Dunham, 1947), and "forced dependency" and "role obsolescence" (Williams and Jaco, 1958) are types of stresses that have been related to mental disorders of later maturity and old age.

Miscellany. A wide variety of many other sources of social and psychological stress have been related to onset of mental and emotional disorder, such as bereavement (Volkart, 1957), social deprivation (Lemkau, 1965), industrial relations (Caravedo and Valdivia, 1961), concentration camps (Trautman, 1964), social or community disintegration (Leighton, 1965), disasters (Tyhurst, 1951), transition states, (Tyhurst, 1957), poverty and deprivation (Rogler and Hollingshead, 1965), and industrialization and urbanization (Duhl, 1963). Perhaps, as new forms and perceptions of stress emerge with future social change, the listing of stress factors as related to disturbed behavior will correspondingly expand.

Finally, only minimum consideration has been given to social and psychological factors that may prevent or reduce stress for individuals (Simmons, 1950). The major effort has been on pathologic, stress-producing factors, while little attention has been devoted to factors conducive to mental health (Opler, 1967). For example, migration and social change might have therapeutic components for certain individuals that might also be pathogenic to other individuals (Murphy, 1961). Groen (1947) found that his Jewish ulcer patients in Amsterdam who lost their ulcer symptoms while in concentration camps during World War II reactivated their ulcer symptoms after returning to their former way of life after the war. The two-edge sword of stress-induction and -reduction to mental illness and health is still an unsolved dimension in stress studies, particularly those involving social and cultural factors, and they may likely be a major contributor to ambiguous and conflicting reports.

DISCUSSION

The study of stress and its relationship to psychopathology and mental illness, while generally accepted in the psychiatric literature, is not in a satisfactory state as yet. The work of Lazarus (1966) and a recent symposium on psychological stress (Appley and Trumbull, 1967) indicate the complexity of the phenomenon of stress and the diverse reactions to it, as do numerous efforts to study stress under an array of experimental and other research conditions. Indeed, most of the chapters in this volume illustrate the variations in definitions and criteria of stress and its multidimensional elements. Thus, when attempting to connect the event of stress or even the accumulation of stresses to specific mental aberrations, many divergent and often conflicting perspectives and points of view are found. Furthermore, while much literature includes the notion of stress in its relationship to mental illness, little consensus exists on the *precise* connection between stress and specific forms of mental illness. Stress, therefore, whether "external" or "internal," in existing psychiatric theories is lacking in specificity concerning its casual linkage to specific mental disorders. King (1963) has summarized succinctly some of the current difficulties in studies of stress and illness as follows:

> The various theoretical approaches leave unresolved a number of issues and problems. The issue is specific emotional conflict leading to specific disease *v.* idiosyncratic response to stress according to previous conditionings. The latter view holds that over-reactivity of tissues rests more on the individual's continuing experience, while the former emphasizes relationships between emotional conflicts and biological patterns which are more or less true for all individuals. Selectivity of causal pathways to disease is therefore more open in the nonspecificity theories. . . . The specificity *v.* nonspecificity issue thus has implications for prediction; that is, who will become ill and with what disease. At the present time the nonspecificity approach seems to be more relevant to the question of who will become ill, while the specificity scheme has more significance for the type of illness that will ensue (p. 105).

Many crucial questions still remain concerning the precise contribution of stress to the overall process of becoming mentally ill for an individual, such as *when* stress occurs, *how much* stress is needed, as well as the *nature* of those stresses that both predispose and precipitate a mental aberration. If anxiety neuroses are the product of stressful experiences before the age of five, as some have claimed, then the *timing* of such stresses as well as their extent and nature are of critical significance in the etiology of this disorder.

Another epistemiological problem lies in existing knowledge of the nature and etiology of mental illness. Psychiatric taxonomy with the heritage of Kraeplelin's pioneering efforts has delineated mental illness essentially upon symptomatology rather than etiology, in contrast to clinical medicine. Since symptoms can vary within and between individual cases of mental aberration and related conditions, this renders difficult and less precise any valid effort to establish specific connections between stress conditions and the mental illnesses. Szasz's (1961) provocative criticism of the existence of "true" mental diseases in the traditional clinical sense may have some merit, but to replace disease conceptions with "problems of living" contributes little to furthering the development of a more valid and precise psychiatric nosology.

Finally, certain methodological issues in the study of stress and mental illness need closer examination. The literature of clinical psychiatry abounds with case studies in which stresses are reported in the life histories of mentally disturbed individuals without accompanying control cases. Indeed, the chances are quite high that every person, even the so-called "normal," will have stresses in their life histories, if vigorously investigated. Epidemiological studies have been properly criticized for lack of field controls and other research design strategies necessary to delineate potential etiological factors (Mishler and Scotch, 1963). The lack of specificity of "stress" itself, and its many likely forms and the variant meaning and response to experimentally devised stress situations, have created difficult methodological conditons for laboratory studies.

Consequently, the conclusion seems warranted that there still remain many basic questions and gaps in our present knowledge of the crucial relationship between stress and mental illness as well as to other forms of illness. Simmons and Wolff (1954) have expressed a similar conclusion as follows:

> A formulation that portrays a sequence such as the following is clearly incomplete and may be misleading: typical situation —►specified stress —►particular reaction pattern —► identifiable structural change (pathology). It leaves significant gaps in the chain of sequences. The missing links may be indicated as: typical situation—►? —►specified stress —► ?—► particular reaction pattern —► ? —► identifiable structural change. The interrogation points represent the possible intervening variables that tie situation to stress, stress to reaction, and reaction to illness. The conclusion emerges that these relatively unknown components play a large part in tipping the scales in the individual-environment balance in ways to aggravate stress, activate reactions, and debilitate some persons and not others. It would appear obvious that these missing links, or puzzling variables, challenge research in the social as well as in the physical sciences (p. 144).

SUMMARY

The concept of stress has become entrenched in current theories of the etiology of mental and emotional illnesses, especially the so-called "functional" disorders, with only a minimum of critical evaluation. A wide array of social and psychological stresses have been related to many forms of psychopathology and mental illnesses in epidemiological, clinical, and laboratory studies, some of which have been mentioned here. Certain of these stresses have been regarded as predisposing individuals to mental aberration, while others were viewed as precipitating factors. These stresses have been related to various phases of the life cycle, to certain forms of mental illness, and to various conditions of living and maintaining a self-identity in human society.

Nevertheless, the current status of knowledge of the precise connection between stress, anxiety, psychopathology, and mental illness is unsatisfactory. There still remain many basic questions, gaps, and ambiguities in fully and precisely understanding the crucial relationship between stress and mental illness.

REFERENCES

AMERICAN PSYCHIATRIC ASSOCIATION. 1952. *Diagnostic and Statistical Manual of Mental Disorders.* Washington, D.C.: American Psychiatric Association.

APPLEY, M. H., and TRUMBULL, R., eds. 1967. *Psychological Stress.* New York: Appleton-Century-Crofts.

BATESON, G., JACKSON, D. D., HALEY, J., and WEAKLAND, J. 1956. "Toward a Theory of Schizophrenia." *Behavioral Science,* 1:251-64.

BELKNAP, I. C., and FRIEDSAM, H. J. 1949. "Age and Sex Categories as Sociological Variables in the Mental Disorders of Later Maturity." *American Sociological Review,* 14:367-376.

BURGESS, E. W. 1953. "Social Factors in the Etiology and Prevention of Mental Disorders." *Social Problems,* 1:53-56.

CAMERON, N. A. 1943. "The Paranoid Pseudo-community." *American Journal of Sociology,* 49:32-38.

1959. "The Paranoid Pseudo-community Revisited." *American Journal of Sociology,* 65:52-58.

1963. *Personality Development and Psychopathology.* Boston: Houghton Mifflin.

CAMERON, N. A., and MAGARET, A. 1951, *Behavior Pathology.* Boston: Houghton Mifflin.

CARAVEDO, B., and VALDIVIA, O. 1961. "A Study on Mental Health of a Cross-section of Industrial Population." *International Journal of Social Psychiatry,* 7:269-82.

CAUDILL, W. 1958. *Effects of Social and Cultural Systems in Reactions to Stress.* New York: Social Science Research Council.

CLARK, R. E. 1949. "Psychoses, Income and Occupational Prestige." *American Journal of Sociology,* 54:433–40.

CLEVELAND, E. J., and LONGAKER, W. D. 1957. "Neurotic Patterns in the Family," in A. H. Leighton, J. A. Clausen, and R. N. Wilson, eds., *Explorations in Social Psychiatry.* New York: Basic Books.

COLEMAN, J. C. 1950. *Abnormal Psychology and Modern Life.* Glenview, Ill.: Scott, Foresman.

CUMMING, E., and HENRY, W. E. 1961. *Growing Old.* New York: Basic Books.

CUMMING, J. H. 1961. "The Family and Mental Disorder: An Incomplete Essay," in Milbank Conference, *Causes of Mental Disorders: A Review of Epidemiological Knowledge, 1959.* New York: Milbank Memorial Fund.

DUHL, L. J., ed. 1963. *The Urban Condition.* New York: Basic Books.

DUNHAM, H. W. 1947. "Sociological Aspects of Mental Disorders in Later Life," in O. J. Kaplan, ed., *Mental Disorders in Later Life.* Stanford, Calif.: Stanford University Press.

ERIKSON, E. H. 1963. *Childhood and Society.* New York: Norton.

FARIS, R. E. L. 1934. "Cultural Isolation and the Schizophrenic Personality." *American Journal of Sociology,* 39:155–69.

FRIED, MARC. 1964. "Effects of Social Change on Mental Health." *American Journal of Orthopsychiatry,* 34:3–28.

FREUD, S. 1924. *Collected Papers.* New York: International Psychoanalytic Press.

GRINKER, R. R., and SPIEGEL, J. P. 1945. *Men under Stress.* New York: Blakiston.

GROEN, J. 1947. "Psychogenesis and Psychotherapy of Ulcerative Colitis." *Psychosomatic Medicine,* 9:151–74.

HALLOWELL, A. I. 1936. "Psychic Stresses and Cultural Patterns." *American Journal of Psychiatry,* 92:1291–1310. Reprinted in M. K. Opler, ed., *Culture and Mental Health,* 1959. New York: Macmillan.

HOCH, P. H., and ZUBIN, J., eds., 1964. *Anxiety.* New York: Hafner.

HOLLINGSHEAD, A. B., ELLIS, R. A., and KIRBY, E. C. 1954. "Social Mobility and Mental Illness."*American Sociological Review* 19:577–84. Reprinted in S. K. Weinberg, ed., *The Sociology of Mental Disorders,* 1967. Chicago: Aldine Publishing Company.

HOLLINGSHEAD, A. B., and REDLICH, F. C. 1953. "Social Stratification and Psychiatric Disorders." *American Sociological Review,* 18:163–69.
1958. *Social Class and Mental Illness.* New York: John Wiley.

HUGHES, C. C., TREMBLAY, M. A., RAPOPORT, R. N., and LEIGHTON, A. H. 1960. *The People of Cove and Woodlot.* New York: Basic Books.

JACKSON, D. D. 1960. *The Etiology of Schizophrenia.* New York: Basic Books.

JACO, E. G. 1954. "The Social Isolation Hypothesis and Schizophrenia." *American Sociological Review,* 19:567–77.

1957. "Social Factors in Mental Disorders in Texas." *Social Problems*, 4:322–28.

1959a. "Social Stress and Mental Illness in the Community," in M. B. Sussman, ed., *Community Structure and Analysis*. New York: Crowell.

1959b. "Mental Health of the Spanish-American in Texas," in M. K. Opler, ed., *Culture and Mental Health*. New York: Macmillan.

1960. *The Social Epidemiology of Mental Disorders*. New York: Russell Sage Foundation.

JANIS, I. L. 1951. *Air War and Emotional Stress*. New York: McGraw-Hill.

KING, S. H. 1963. "Social Psychological Factors in Illness," in H. E. Freeman, S. Levine, and L. G. Reeder, eds., *Handbook of Medical Sociology*, Englewood Cliffs, N. J.: Prentice-Hall.

KLEINER, R. J., and PARKER, S. 1963. "Goal-striving, Social Status, and Mental Disorder: A Research Review." *American Sociological Review*, 28:169–203. Reprinted in S. K. Weinberg, ed., *The Sociology of Mental Disorders*, 1967. Chicago: Aldine Publishing Company.

KOHN, M. L., and CLAUSEN, J. A. 1955. "Social Isolation and Schizophrenia." *American Sociological Review*, 20:268–69.

LANGNER, T. S., and MICHAEL, S. T. 1963. *Life Stress and Mental Health*. New York: Free Press.

LAUGHLIN, H. P. 1967. *The Neuroses*. Washington: Butterworths.

LAZARUS, R. S. 1966. *Psychological Stress and the Coping Process*. New York: McGraw-Hill.

LEAVY, S. A., and FREEDMAN, L. Z. 1967. "Psychoneurosis and Economic Life," in S. Kirson Weinberg, ed., *The Sociology of Mental Disorders*. Chicago: Aldine Publishing Company.

LEIGHTON, A. H. 1965. "Cultural Change and Psychiatric Disorder," in A.V.S. de Reuck and R. Porter, eds., *Transcultural Psychiatry*. Boston: Little, Brown.

LEIGHTON, A. H., CLAUSEN, J. A., and WILSON, R. N. 1957. *Explorations in Social Psychiatry*. New York: Basic Books.

LEIGHTON, A. H., and HUGHES, J. M. 1961. "Cultures as Causative of Mental Disorder," in Milbank Conference, *Causes of Mental Disorders: A Review of Epidemiological Knowledge, 1959*. New York: Milbank Memorial Fund.

LEMERT, E. M. 1951. *Social Pathology*. New York: McGraw-Hill.

LEMKAU, P. V. 1965. "Prevention in Psychiatry." *American Journal of Public Health*, 55:554–60.

LIDZ, T., FLECK, S., and CORNELISON, A. 1966. *Schizophrenia and the Family*. New York: International Universities Press.

LIEF, A., ed. 1948. *The Commonsense Psychiatry of Adolf Meyer.* New York: McGraw-Hill.

MASLOW, A. H., and MITTLEMANN, B. 1951. *Principles of Abnormal Psychology: The Dynamics of Psychic Illness*. New York: Harper.

MILBANK CONFERENCE. 1961. *Causes of Mental Disorders: A Review of Epidemiological Knowledge, 1959*. New York: Milbank Memorial Fund.

MISHLER, E. G., and SCOTCH, N. A. 1963. "Sociocultural Factors in the Epidemiology of Schizophrenia." *Psychiatry*, 26:315–51.

MURPHY, H.B.M. 1961. "Social Change and Mental Health," in Milbank Memorial Fund Conference, *Causes of Mental Disorders: A Review of Epidemiological Knowledge, 1959*. New York: Milbank Memorial Fund.

MURRAY, H. A. 1938. *Explorations in Personality*. New York: Oxford University Press.

MYERS, J. K., and ROBERTS, B. H. 1959. *Family and Class Dynamics in Mental Illness*. New York: John Wiley.

NOYES, A. P., and KOLB, L. C. 1963. *Modern Clinical Psychiatry*, 6th ed. Philadelphia: Saunders.

ØDEGAARD, Ø. 1956. "The Incidence of Psychoses in Various Occupations." *International Journal of Social Psychiatry*, 2:85–104.

OPLER, M. K. 1959, ed. *Culture and Mental Health*. New York: Macmillan. 1967. *Culture and Social Psychiatry*. New York: Atherton Press.

PARSONS, T. 1949. *Essays in Sociological Theory*. New York: Free Press.

PEARSON, M. M. 1963. *Strecker's Fundamentals of Psychiatry*. Philadelphia: Lippincott.

PROVENCE, S., and RITVO, S. 1961. "Effects of Deprivation on Institutionlized Infants." *The Psychoanalytic Study of the Child*, 19:189–205.

REDLICH, F. C. and FREEDMAN, D. X. 1966. *The Theory and Practice of Psychiatry*. New York: Basic Books.

RENNIE, T. A. C. 1953. "The Yorkville Community Mental Health Research Study," in Milbank Conference, *Interrelations Between the Social Environment and Psychiatric Disorders*. New York: Milbank Memorial Fund.

ROGLER, L. H., and HOLLINGSHEAD, A. B. 1965. *Trapped: Families and Schizophrenia*. New York: John Wiley.

ROSE, A. M., and STUB, H. R. 1955. "Summary of Studies on the Incidence of Mental Disorders," in A. M. Rose, ed., *Mental Health and Mental Disorder*. New York: Norton.

ROSEN, G. 1959. "Social Stress and Mental Disease from the Eighteenth Century to the Present: Some Origins of Social Psychiatry." *Milbank Memorial Fund Quarterly*, 38:5–32.

SIMMONS, L. W. 1950. "The Relations between the Decline of Anxiety-inducing and Anxiety-resolving Factors in a Deteriorating Culture and Its Relevance to Bodily Disease." *Proceedings of the Association for Research in Nervous and Mental Disease*, 29:127–36.

SIMMONS, L. W., and WOLFF, H. G. 1954. *Social Science in Medicine*. New York: Russell Sage Foundation.

SZASZ, T. S. 1961. *The Myth of Mental Illness*. New York: Paul B. Hoeber.

THOMAS, R. C. 1955. *Mother-Daughter Relationships and Social Behavior*. Washington, D.C.: Catholic University of America Press.

TITCHENER, J. L., ZWERLING, I., GOTTSCHALK, L., and LEVINE, M. 1958. "Psychological Reactions of the Aged to Surgery." *AMA Archives of Neurology and Psychiatry*, 79:63–73.

TRAUTMAN, E. C. 1964. "Fear and Panic in Nazi Concentration Camps: A Biosocial Evaluation of the Chronic Anxiety Syndrom." *International Journal of Social Psychiatry*, 10:134–41.

TYHURST, J. S. 1951. "Individual Reactions to Community Disaster." *American Journal of Psychiatry*, 107:764–69.

1957. "The Role of Transition States — Including Disasters — in Mental Illness," in Walter Reed Army Institute of Research, *Symposium on Preventive and Social Psychiatry*. Washington, D. C.: U. S. Government Printing Office.

VOLKART, E. H. 1957. "Bereavement and Mental Health," in A. H. Leighton, J. A. Clausen, and R. N. Wilson, eds., *Explorations in Social Psychiatry*. New York: Basic Books.

WEINBERG, S. K. 1952. *Society and Personality Disorders*. Englewood Cliffs, N. J.: Prentice-Hall.

1966. "The Relevance of the Forms of Isolation to Schizophrenia." *International Journal of Social Psychiatry*, 13:33–41.

WHEELIS, A. 1958. *The Quest for Identity*. New York: Norton.

WILLIAMS, W. S., and JACO, E. G. 1958. "An Evaluation of Functional Psychoses in Old Age." *American Journal of Psychiatry*, 114:910–16.

WYNNE, L. C., RYCKOFF, I. M., DAY, J., and HIRSCH, S. I. 1958. "Pseudomutality in the Family Relations of Schizophrenics." *Psychiatry*, 21:205–20.

9. Social Pathology and Stress

JAMES E. TEELE

In his book, *On Aggression*, Lorenz (1966) has argued that man, alone of all animals, injures and kills his own kind without sufficient cause and is thereby in grave danger of self-extinction. While one may not agree with Lorenz either in his prediction or in his interpretation, his thesis does call attention to the causes of wide-ranging pathology in human society.

If we consider the array of social pathologies, such as mental illness, poverty, addiction, and crime, virtually everyone is affected by them in his lifetime. In the area of crime alone, one cross-sectional study of 1700 randomly selected adults showed that 91 percent of the respondents admitted having committed one or more offenses for which they could have received a jail or prison sentence (Wallenstein and Wyle, 1947). Short (1954) had similar findings for juvenile and college boys.

James E. Teele is associate professor of sociology in the Harvard School of Public Health, Boston.

The data on Table 9.1 gives a rough estimate of the scope and extent of defined social pathology in the United States.

Table 9.1 The scope of social pathology in the United States

Pathology Area	Year	Prevalence Estimates
Hidden adult criminals (i.e., gambling, tax crimes, desertion, etc.)	1965	90,000,000[a]
Institutionalized adult criminals at end of year	1958	200,000[b]
Hidden juvenile delinquents (between 10 and 20 years old)	1965	15,000,000[c]
Juveniles referred to courts	1965	600,000[d]
Children in outpatient psychiatric clinics (10–19 years old)	1962	194,000[e]
Impaired adult mental health	1965	25,000,000[f]
Hospitalized psychotic persons on any given day		600,000[g]
Alcoholics	1966	6,000,000[h]
Narcotics addicts	1965	57,000[i]
Women having abortions	1967	500,000[j] 1,000,000
Child-abusing adults	1965	2,500,000[k] 4,000,000 families
Adult male homosexuals		2,500,000[l]
Suicides	1962	20,207[m]
Auto death (accidents)	1960	40,000[n]
Auto injury (accidents)	1960	3,000,000[o]
Out-of-wedlock births	1967	300,000[p]
Poverty	1962	35,000,000[q]
Mental retardation	1962	5,400,000[r]
Urban disorders	1967 (First 9 months)	164[s]

[a] Estimated on the basis of findings by Joseph Wallenstein and Clement Wyle, "Out Law-Abiding Law-Breakers," *Probation*, 9 (April, 1944): 185–92.
[b] Based on estimates presented in Edwin Sutherland and Donald Cressey, *Principles of Criminology*, (6th ed.), New York: Lippincott, 1960, p. 33.
[c] Estimated on the basis of findings presented in James Short, "A Report on the Incidence of Criminal Behavior, Arrests, and Convictions in Selected Groups," *Research Studies of State College of Washington*, 22 (June, 1954): 110–18.
[d] From "Juvenile Court Statistics – 1965," Children's Bureau Statistical Series: no. 85, U.S. Government Printing Office, 1966.
[e] From Beatrice Rosen, and others, "Adolescent Patients Served in Outpatient Psychiatric Clinics," *American Journal of Public Health*, 55 (October, 1965): 1563–77.
[f] Estimated on the basis of findings presented in Leo Srole, and others, *Mental Health in The Metropolis: The Midtown Manhattan Study*, New York: McGraw-Hill, 1962.

The footnotes to this table indicate that while some of the estimates are based on adequate sources, others are less well based and must be accepted tentatively. Nonetheless, the breadth and depth of social pathology in the United States depicted in Table 9.1 suggest that virtually everyone would fit into some category of pathology. In this chapter we propose to consider the relationship of social stress to specific forms of pathology. Since it is not possible to consider adequately the relationship of social stress to each of them, we shall discuss only three: (1) juvenile delinquency and crime; (2) suicide; (3) urban disorders. The choice of these problems is dictated by the consideration that they have long been subjects of sociological inquiry and consequently, appreciable data have been collected on them and some theoretical explanations have been posited. There is also some presumptive evidence that they are, in large part, related to social stress.

In studying the causes of these social problems, sociologists have long found it useful to employ the concept of deviance rather than that of pathology. Lemert (1948) raised this issue some years ago. The concept of deviance focuses on the problem of the social causes of variability in behavior; on the individual in the group context rather than on the state of the individual, per se. Becker (1963) has defined deviance as the failure to obey group rules. He qualified this definition by noting that: (1) people's response to a given act as deviant varies greatly over time; (2) the degree to which an act will be treated as deviant depends on who commits the act and on who feels he has been harmed by it; (3) the rules of a society are largely

 g Estimate presented by John Clausen, "Mental Disorders" in Robert Merton and Robert Nisbet, eds., *Contemporary Social Problems*, 2nd ed., New York: Harcourt, Brace and World, 1966.

 h Upper limit of various estimates presented by Richard Blum (assisted by Lauraine Braunstein), "Mind-Altering Drugs and Dangerous Behavior: Alcohol," in *Task Force Report: Drunkenness, The President's Commission on Law-Enforcement and Administration of Justice*, U.S. Government Printing Office, 1967, p. 30.

 i Estimate presented in *Task Force Report: Narcotics and Drug Abuse, The President's Commission on Law Enforcement and Administration of Justice*, U.S. Government Printing Office, 1967, p. 2.

 j Estimate given by Clark Vincent, "Illegitmacy – Problem or Symptom," paper presented at the Conference on Preventive and Helping Services for the Unwed Mother, March 4–5, 1968, Boston. (This conference was co-sponsored by the United Community Services of Boston and the Boston University School of Social Work and was chaired by the present author.)

 k Based on estimates presented by David Gil and John Noble, "Public Knowledge, Attitudes and Opinions About Physical Child Abuse in the United States," *Papers in Social Welfare, Brandeis University*, no. 14 (September, 1967), p. 33.

 l Based on estimates derived from the Kinsey data and presented by Edwin Schur in *Crimes Without Victims*, Englewood Cliffs, N.J.: Prentice Hall, 1965, p. 75.

 m From Jack P. Gibbs "Suicide," chap. 6 in Merton and Nisbet, eds., *Contemporary Social Problems*, 2nd ed.

 n From "Accidental Death and Injury Statistics," U.S. Department of Health, Education and Welfare, Public Health Service Publication no. 111, U.S. Government Printing Office, October 1963, p. 6.

 o Ibid., p. 12.

 p Estimate from Clark Vincent, "Illegitmacy – Problem or Symptom?"

 q From a report prepared by the President's Council of Economic Advisors, 1964, and drawn on by S. M. Miller and Martin Rein in "Poverty, Inequality and Policy," chap. 9 in Howard S. Becker, ed., *Social Problems: A Modern Approach*, New York: John Wiley and Sons, 1966 (see esp. pages 437–42).

 r From the Report of the President's Panel on Mental Retardation, Washington, D.C.: U.S. Government Printing Office, 1962.

 s From the Report of The National Advisory Commission on Civil Disorders (New York: Bantam Books), 1968, pp. 112–13.

dependent upon what group or groups in a society are making them; and (4) the power of enforcement is bound up with the question of who is the deviant. The general framework for our analysis will be a stress model and the concept of deviance will be implicit in our discussion of social stress. Within this framework this chapter will consider the chains of events that lead to deviance or pathology. The model is one of sequential stochastic processes. The sequence includes potentially stressful social situations, perceptions of the events as stressful, reactions to these situations. Scott and Howard (chap. 10 in this volume) have reviewed various stress models and note that there are a number of different referents of the stress concept in these models. They state that "Mechanic (1962) defines stress in terms of responses that individuals have to situations," while "Basowitz and his associates (1955), and to some degree Janis (1954), define it as a quality of a situation that is independent of the reaction of individuals to it." They further note that Selye (1956) and Dohrenwend (1961) define stress as "an intervening state which is the internal reaction to stressors, loads, or noxious stimuli." Scott and Howard present a stress model they call a problem-solving model. The components of stress to be considered in the present chapter approximate the components Scott and Howard include in their problem-solving model. Although they would not confine themselves to the study of traumatic events, they would include "wearing" or long-term events; they would not assume that what is stressful for one person is stressful for another, and they would not exclude second-order problems (when mastery of stress fails) from consideration. Some of these components, it will be seen, are utilized in this chapter—potentially stressful situations that exist over time, the individual perception of events, and the subsequent reactions, both mastery and failure—but this chapter will consider only briefly the mastery of stress. Since this is a chapter on social pathology, however, it will concentrate on the failure to master stress. Scott and Howard indicate the components of mastery as the will to master a problem, the resources for solving a problem, the approach to the problem, and whether or not the problem is solvable. These components, especially the last, are important to keep in mind when we discuss failure to master a problem, since, if important requirements for coping (like intelligence) are not available, or if the problem is not solvable, then the response almost has to be pathological.

Whereas the examples of social pathology to be discussed are viewed as deviant reactions to stress situations, it should be clear that many people have mastered these potentially stressful situations. Indeed, many persons thrive in situations that would greatly distress others, hence the notion of *potentially stressful situations* is central to the present approach.

POTENTIALLY STRESSFUL SITUATIONS

Psychologists and sociologists have theorized about and carried out research on potentially stressful situations. The typical approach of psychologists has been to induce frustration in experimental subjects by setting up a task at such a level of difficulty that failure is inevitable (Crandall, 1951; Dollard and others, 1939; Funkenstein and others, 1957). These experiments have been valuable in producing knowledge on the range of reactions to experimentally induced stress where all the subjects have been placed under stress. Thus, for example, Funkenstein and his colleagues induced frustration in the subjects of their laboratory experiment and then recorded reactions they classified in three groups: anger-out responses, anger-in responses, and anxiety responses. They then assessed the manner in which the men handled stress on a time continuum. "Mastery" was assessed on the basis of the physiological reactions of the subjects. Although such experiments are valuable sources of knowledge about reactions to stress, they are limited by the type of subjects used (healthy college men), by the type of stress situation (laboratory experiment), and by the limits the situation imposes upon the social responses. Moreover, experimental stress situations are not of the wearing kind which are prevalent in the real world and which appear to result in the types of social pathology that here concern us.

It would be useful for our purpose to focus on more realistic potentially stressful situations such as broken family situations, living or working in a hostile environment, poverty (whether due to loss of wealth or being born poor), inconsistency between roles, unemployment (whether due to retirement or temporary loss of job), school or job failure, and social isolation.[1] Most of the research that has been done linking social stress situations to various forms of pathology have suffered from two major limitations: (1) the research

1. A few of these potentially stressful situations have been or could have been included among the forms of pathology shown in Table 9.1. This is because these items (e.g., poverty or school under-achievement) could either induce stress or result from stress. Thus, it is possible to regard the categories of social pathology in Table 9.1 as the potential stress-inducing situations, like poverty, or as apparently unambiguous resultant forms of pathology, such as suicide or crime (even though suicide or crime could be stressful for others in the society). It should also be said of the situations listed that they are not mutually exclusive. For example, the situation of attending school in a hostile environment could result in social isolation.

is correlational, permitting only speculative causal analysis; (2) the methodology does not include the study of stressful situations over a relatively long period of time. The study of potentially stressful situations *over time* would give behavioral scientists the opportunity to learn much more about several aspects of the study of reactions to stress: (1) *characteristics of persons who master stress versus the characteristics of persons who do not master stress;* (2) *the kinds of potential stress situations that most often result in failure to master stress;* and (3) *the forms of pathology* (if any) *which are · typical results of the interaction of (1) and (2).* An obvious difficulty, of course, in such a study would be the stability of situations. *The advantages,* however, of the study of potentially stressful situations over time are obvious. It allows for the close observation of the use of "resources" (Scott and Howard, chap. 10), or "mediating factors" (Dohrenwend and Dohrenwend, chap. 4), and other aspects of the response to potentially stressful situations.

Bearing in mind the limitations of research relevant to the linkage of stress situations and social pathology, we shall analyze juvenile delinquency and crime, suicide, and urban disorders with respect to one or two of the potentially stressful situations with which these are frequently linked. Many of these studies, in spite of their limitations, are excellent.

THE BROKEN HOME SITUATION

Some students, like Monahan, are apparently convinced that delinquency is strongly related to the broken home situation. Broken homes have been theoretically and empirically linked with practically all the forms of pathology to be dealt with here, but the broken home situation is more often linked to juvenile delinquency than to any other type of social pathology. On the basis of his studies in Philadelphia, Monahan (1957a) states:

> The stability and continuity of family life stands out as a most important factor in the development of the child . . . . The relationship is so strong that if ways could be found to do it, a strengthening and preserving of family life, among the groups which need it most, could probably accomplish more in the amelioration and prevention of delinquency and other problems than any other single program yet devised (p. 258).

Monahan (1957b) stresses, however, that it is the lack of family life per se that is associated with delinquency, and points out that his data "give no support to the belief in the overriding importance of socially broken homes – as over and against the orphaned homes – in the persisting pattern of youthful delinquency (p. 364)."

A number of other behavioral scientists have been more conditional in associating types of homes with delinquency. Weeks (1940), for example, has presented findings indicating that broken homes have greater consequences for girls than for boys when type of delinquency is considered. Nye (1958) claims that the relationship between broken homes and delinquency is itself suspect because the courts and other law enforcement agencies are more likely to incarcerate those from broken homes than those from intact homes. Concerned with the definition and measurement of delinquency, Nye worked with the problem as it exists in the general population, studying delinquency among the noninstitutionalized. His data give some support to the idea that broken homes are related to certain types of delinquency, particularly the type he classified as "governability." He included truancy, running away from home, expulsion from school, driving without a license, and drinking alcoholic beverages in this category. He states that, "As to categories, *less* delinquent behavior was found in broken [rather] than in unhappy broken homes. The happiness of the marriage was found to be much more closely related to delinquent behavior in children than whether the marriage was an original marriage or a remarriage, or one in which the child was living with one parent only (p. 51)." In a similar vein, Tait and Hodges (1962) distinguish between a structurally broken home and a functionally broken one. They indicate that, to their knowledge, no evidence exists which contradicts the view that a functionally broken home is a contributing factor in delinquency.

Rodman and Grams (1967), drawing on the research of Monahan, Weeks, Nye, and others point out that, despite the complexity of the relationships among broken homes (i.e., the outward structure), family functioning (i.e., the internal structure), and delinquency, social scientists are not justified in concluding that outward structure is not causally important in the etiology of delinquency. It seems to the present author that one would expect proportionately more unhappy homes among broken homes than among unbroken homes and that therefore the relationship between broken homes and delinquency holds. It is a question of the order of abstraction. One can agree with Nye that the broken home is only a *structural feature* and does not, by itself, generate delinquent behavior. But the dynamic features of this structural feature, the associated conditions, the problem-solving resources available, are likely to be present in such a way in most American communities as to make it unwise to ignore or downgrade the statistical association between delinquency and broken homes, however complex that relationship may be.

The relevance of the social control theories of delinquency, advocated by Reckless (1961), Nye (1958), and Reiss (1951) seem clear in this connection since they emphasize—in a way that Cloward and Ohlin (1960) and Cohen (1955) do not—the likelihood of delinquency when personal and social controls break down. Each of them (Reckless, Nye, and Reiss) conducted research and obtained results that support the idea that family strength is a powerful barrier to delinquent behavior.

HOSTILE ENVIRONMENTS

The notion of the hostile environment as a cause of delinquency is closely related to the situation of the newly arrived immigrant. During the years when the flow of immigrants to the United States was heavy, many persons argued that immigration was the chief cause of crime. According to Sutherland and Cressey (1960), there were a number of loosely related hypotheses about crime among immigrants. These included the notions that the immigrants (1) were of inferior racial stock; (2) were unfamiliar with the codes (culture) of America; (3) were poverty-stricken; and (4) were highly mobile. Sutherland and Cressey cite evidence, however, indicating that the crime rate among white immigrants to the United States in this century is considerably lower than the crime rate among the native white population. Even when corrections are made for the fact that the age and sex distributions are not the same, the immigrant crime rate does not exceed the crime rate for the native-born. Other studies too have produced findings that tend to contradict "theories" about immigrant crime. Thus Taft (1936) has shown that in general the second generation of immigrants had higher commitment rates than their foreign-born parents and a lower commitment rate than the native white of native parentage. Van Vechten (1941) has shown that immigrants who arrive in the United States in infancy or early childhood have higher crime rates than immigrants who arrive in young adult life or middle age. Sutherland and Cressey maintain that studies such as these, showing higher crime and delinquency rates among the sons of immigrants than among their parents, indicate that delinquency behavior patterns are assimilated in America.

If the situation of the immigrant is viewed as a potentially stressful situation, the theoretical framework developed by Merton (1957) provides an explanation for the increase in delinquency and crime rates among the sons of immigrants. According to Merton, American culture tends to indoctrinate all groups in our society in relatively high status aspirations. Success, in terms of material goods and life style, is the goal of all. Different racial, ethnic, and class groupings are unequal in their ability to realize these aspirations by legitimate means, however. Merton then deals with the solutions that result when individuals accept social goals without access to the approved means of achieving such goals. Essentially, Merton holds that when such barriers exist the individuals concerned may look for either a substitute goal, a substitute means of attaining the goal, or both. The employment of the substitute goals or means often involves delinquent or criminal behavior.

The situation described by Merton applied more to the children of the foreign-born than to the foreign-born themselves. More specifically, the foreign-born has left his home country looking for a haven, and when he arrives he is full of hope and the feeling that he has found his haven. Relative to the place he left, he is already, perhaps, better off in the United States. Even when he is unwelcome, which is often, he is not likely to perceive the hostility. The environment is not perceived as hostile because the newly arrived immigrant may be better off than he was and because he is probably too new to the situation to recognize hostility. Consequently, he gratefully takes whatever job is offered. Undoubtedly, not all the foreign-born were happy with their new situation and many may not have been disposed toward viewing the situation as one full of opportunity. It is assumed however, that this was the case for most newly arrived immigrants and that this is what accounts for their having relatively low crime rates. Indeed, mere arrival in the United States was a stress-relieving action for many immigrants.

Their children, on the other hand, came to recognize the contempt and hostility focused on their parents. Moreover, the children, even when well-educated, compared themselves unfavorably with the children of native-born Americans. It may be too that the children of the immigrants came to resent the low positions their parents so willingly occupied in American society and thereupon directed their resentment to the larger society. The perception of a hostile environment could help explain the higher commitment rate for the second generation as opposed to the foreign-born.

The situation of a hostile environment, then, is viewed here as a potentially stressful situation, similar to the situation of the broken family in that it does not necessarily result in the failure to master stress. Perception is a more relevant factor in the case of the immigrant than in the broken-home situation because, it is posited, the immigrant himself did not attribute hostility to, or perceive hostility

in, his surroundings. Indeed, it is believed that the differing perceptions of the foreign-born and his children explain some of the
differences in crime and commitment rates between these generations. The hostile environment as a factor in potential stress situations could be used in an examination of crime and delinquency
rates among ethnic groups. For example, if differing crime and delinquency rates exist among Negroes by birthplace, stability of residence, and age, such differences might be better explained in terms
of the perception of the environment rather than in terms of opportunity theory. The differences in crime and delinquency rates among
various ethnic groups may be attributable not only to the resources
and opportunities available to them in coping with their environment but also to perceptions of the environment over time.

The way in which the law is enforced and justice is administered
creates another type of hostile environment. There have been indications that legal agencies render justice differently to individuals
of different ethnic and racial groups.

The importance of the relationship between race, on the one hand,
and the enforcement of law and the administration of justice, on the
other, was emphasized in the Report of The President's National
Advisory Commission on Civil Disorder (1968). Admittedly, any confrontation with the machinery of justice is a potentially stressful
situation. However, The Advisory Commission on Civil Disorders
has recognized that for a large number of Negroes in the United
States, almost any encounter, at any level, with the machinery for
administering justice is a confrontation with a hostile environment
and represents a potential stress situation above and beyond that
which normally exists for whites. The difference between Negroes
and whites with respect to the stresses created by the machinery of
justice is perhaps comparable to the difference between systematic
and random error. Thus, for blacks, the overused term "police brutality" could be supplemented with such terms as "bail brutality,"
"jury brutality," and "court brutality."

Relevant to this position are the research findings reported by
Piliavin and Briar (1964), who report that among minor offenders
apprehended by police, a youth's "character" was a major criterion
for determining police disposition (ranging from arrest to release).
That is, his "attitude" rather than the evidence proving guilt or
innocence was decisive in disposition. This attitude was apparently
related to the youth's group affiliation, age, race, grooming, dress,
and demeanor. The authors also found that in comparison with other
youths, Negroes and boys whose appearance matched the delinquent
stereotype were more frequently stopped and interrogated by patrol-

men—often even in the absence of evidence that an offense had been committed. The authors found an overrepresentation of blacks among "innocent" juveniles accosted by the police and that the police concentrated their surveillance activities in areas frequented or inhabited by blacks. Thus, it would seem that black youths—whether guilty or innocent—are in a potentially stressful situation in a confrontation with police, assuming that the youths are aware of these police biases (a not unwarranted assumption).

Other recent research extends these findings. In a study of police arrests policies in two cities, Wilson (1968) found that in the city with a nonprofessional[2] police department the probability of court action for black juveniles arrested for selected offenses is three times higher than for whites. No differences by race were found for the city with a professional police department.

Although sociological research on bail practices in the United States is sparse, especially with respect to differences by race, most experts agree that the system discriminates against persons on the basis of their income, with poor people being more liable to be detained pending trial (Freed and Weld, 1964). On the basis of studies in New York and Philadelphia, Foote (1962) suggests that pretrial incarceration is disadvantageous to the accused in case disposition.

The most drastic action a court can take against a person is to sentence him to death, and perhaps nothing is more revealing of the hostility of the machinery of justice toward blacks than the disproportionate sentencing to death of blacks. In 1958 Clinard noted that "Of those persons executed for rape during the past twenty-three years, for example, 89.7 percent were blacks" (p. 155). Others have noted that while a high proportion of black males convicted for rape have received the death sentence, few white males convicted of the same offense have been similarly dealt with (*Playboy*, 1968).[3]

2. James Q. Wilson (1968), defined a "professional" police department as one governed by general, impersonal rules, one that recruits its members on the basis of achievement criteria, and one that enforces laws without respect to person. Nonprofessional departments rely on particularistic judgments, recruit only from among local citizens, and have a less formal sense of justice than professional departments.

3. A dramatic demonstration of the fact that black males are often subjected to unfair prosecution procedures was brought to light recently with the publication of a setting aside of a life term stemming from the charge of rape of a white girl in Rockville, Maryland. Although the details of the case were not published, the story as presented in the *New York Times* (May 16,1967) is that two young black males had been unjustly imprisoned for nearly six years, including twenty-two months in Death Row of the Maryland State Penitentiary in Baltimore. In setting aside the life terms (previously, Governor Tawes had changed their death sentences to life sentences) the judge ruled that the Giles brothers "have been deprived of their liberty without due process of law." The *Times* story concludes: "The ruling was widely regarded here as a vindication of the efforts of the so-called Giles-Johnson Defense Committee, a small group of

The experience of blacks with the administration of justice suggests why they often view the police as hostile. When blacks walk into a police station or a court, they perceive themselves in a hostile environment. Future research may not only be able to link this kind of hostile environment to "primary deviation" (first offenses), but may find it possible to link it to what Lemert (1967) calls "secondary deviation," that is, deviant responses created by society's reaction to deviance.

SUICIDE

Delinquency or crime can be thought of as lying on one dimension of responses to stress situations, with homicide constituting the extreme of that dimension. One could call this the "anger-out" dimension. "Anger-in" then would be an appropriate name for an opposing dimension of stress responses.[4] It might be assumed that suicidal threats and warnings are on this second dimension. If so, then completed suicide might constitute the extreme of the anger-in dimension. These dimensions may be thought of not only as dimensions of intensity but also as dimensions of time with each dimension theoretically subject to intervention. Thus, in terms of intensity, suicide is a more violent act than a threat of suicide. Suicide is also, in many cases, the end of a process that included threats at an earlier stage (Farberow and Shneidman, 1955).

Although a number of social scientists and clinicians have linked suicides and homicides in their studies, the prevailing practice has been to study the two phenomena in isolation from one another. Since I am trying here to link stressful situations to specific types of pathology, I will also treat the two dimensions of anger-in and anger-out separately. Thus delinquency and crime, representing the anger-out dimension, were discussed in the previous section. Suicide, representing anger-in, is discussed in this section. In this section, also, the research on suicidal warnings will also be taken into consideration, since it bears on the issue of the process of suicide.

A great many sociologists, beginning with Durkheim, have addressed themselves to the problem of suicide. Durkheim (1951), utilizing trailblazing correlational techniques, devoted much of his time and energy to the task of explanation. As a result, he is probably best known for the careful and skillful weaving of the concepts of altruistic, anomic, and egoistic suicide. However, as Gibbs (1966) has

white residents of the county who have labored since early 1963 on the case. The Committee's research led its members to believe the three men were innocent."

4. These terms: "anger-out" and "anger-in" were used by Funkerstein, King, and Drolette (1957).

indicated, Durkheim's conceptual scheme was based on variables and conditions which he found to be related to the overall rates of suicide, and not on the separate rates of each of the three types. Thus, it has remained for others to attempt to refine Durkheim's concepts and to test his hypotheses. In recent years, Gibbs and Martin (1964), Henry and Short (1954), and Pierce (1967) are a few of those who have tested some of Durkheim's hypotheses or dealt with his conceptual theme.

Explicitly and implicitly, each of these writers has dealt with the relationship of stress situations to suicide. Indeed, of all the forms of social pathology, none has been more systematically and universally linked to conditions of stress than suicide.

Durkheim, as indicated, linked suicide to a condition of normlessness which occurs during times of rapid economic change. He theorized that sudden depression results in suicide because many persons find the prospect of a lower standard of living intolerable and hence cannot bring themselves to accept the new regulations or controls that are required. Durkheim called this rejection of norms or regulations *anomie*. In Durkheim's theory, prosperity could have the same result as economic depression, especially if the changes were sudden. Durkheim postulates that sudden prosperity increases aspirations beyond the likelihood of fulfillment, and this too may result in the rejection of the old regulatory system.

With respect to Durkheim's other major emphasis — egoistic suicide — some have argued that it is hardly distinguishable, conceptually and empirically, from anomic suicide (Gibbs, 1966). Others, however, apparently agree that Durkheim has achieved a conceptual distinction between "anomie" and "egoism" (Henry and Short, 1954). All would agree, perhaps, that Durkheim was, in the case of the causes of egoistic suicide, once again concerned with stressful situations, even though his situations of stress were inferred from statistical data. Durkheim's statement with respect to egoistic suicide was that "suicide varies inversely with the degree of integration of the social groups of which the individual forms a part 1951, (p. 209)."

He then focused mainly on the "protective" or integrative qualities of domestic life and religious life when discussing the data showing that Catholics and Jews have a lower suicide rate than Protestants and that married persons have a lower suicide rate than single persons. Durkheim's argument strongly suggests that to be an unmarried, widowed, or divorced person is to be, at worst, in a situation of stress (reminiscent of the "broken home") and, at best, poorly equipped to cope with stressful situations. With respect to religious life, he maintained that Protestantism preaches individualism, which, by definition, means that persons are not closely bound to others. Although there is controversy over Durkheim's conceptual clarity and continuing discussion about the testability of his hypotheses, there is universal agreement that his basic ideas have led to much subsequent work. In the present context, it seems clear that Durkheim's work is relevant to the study of stress.

The work of Henry and Short, influenced by Durkheim, is also highly relevant to the consideration of stress and suicide. These two authors (Henry and Short) are explicit in dealing with suicide as a possible response to frustrating (stressful) situations. They have suggested that external restraint, that is, the presence of conformity to the demands of others, legitimized the expression of aggression against others, and, conversely, that the absence of external restraint leads to the consideration of alternative "solutions" (e.g., suicide) to frustrating situations, since other oriented aggression is not legitimized. These authors posited that both a *low social status* and a *strong relational system* are sources of external restraint. They did not utilize empirical measures of social status but described it conceptually in terms of achievement, possession, power and authority. Thus, they assumed that with respect to status in this country, the first named of each of the following five pairs have higher status and thus are subject to fewer external restraints: whites-blacks, males-females, high income-low income, young people-older persons, and army officers-enlisted men.

A repeated criticism of the Henry-Short formulation is that these authors appear to have overlooked the possibility that many high-status persons (e.g., army officers) are subject to strong external restraint by others. Overall, however, their assumptions are interesting, plausible, and highly relevant to a consideration of the relationship between stress situations and suicide. This is especially true in view of the fact that for four of the five pairs they successfully predicted the higher suicide rate; age proved to be the exception. Their low-status age group (persons 65–74 years of age) had a substantially higher suicide rate than the high-status age group (25–34 years of age). In attempting to explain this exception, Henry and Short shifted their focus. Even though they did not specify how they measured the "strength of relational systems," they suggested that the strength of the relational system decreases with age. Drawing on other data (e.g., the higher suicide rate among single, widowed, and divorced persons), they suggested that the strength of the relational system is a more appropriate predictor of suicide among the elderly than is social status. It is especially notable that the Henry-Short "relational system" is comparable to Durkheim's notion of "integration" of social groups, and that both concepts are relevant to the study of stress and suicide. Henry and Short have dealt more clearly with the relationship between hierarchical status and suicide, perhaps, than any other sociologists.

It remained, however, for Gibbs and Martin (1964) to develop Durkheim's notion of the integration of social groups in such a way as to link the suicide rate to a particular pattern of status occupancy. Their theory—called the theory of status integration—is deliberately focused on the population level (i.e., the macrosociological level), and the authors have made no attempt to include assessments of individuals. Following Durkheim's statement that suicide varies inversely with the degree of integration of social groups, Gibbs and Martin postulated that the suicide rate of a population varies inversely with the stability and durability of social relationships. Having no available measure of the "stability and durability of social relationships," the authors moved through a series of additional postulates and assumptions and deduced that "in populations where the occupancy of one particular status tends to be closely associated with the occupancy of certain other statuses, the members are less subject to role conflict, more capable of conforming to the demands and expectations of others, more capable of maintaining stable and durable social relations, and consequently less prone to suicide (Gibbs, 1966, pp. 316–17)." The authors' system of postulates explicitly moved from degree of adherence to *patterned expectations, to role conflict*, to *incompatible statuses*, and then to a societal attribute, the degree of *status integration*. They then indicated that it is possible to measure status integration. Their theorem is: *The suicide rate of a population varies inversely with the degree of status integration.*

Their measure of status integration provides a mathematical assessment of the extent to which members of a population are concentrated in specific status configurations or are scattered haphazardly throughout a large number of such configurations. The stresses, then, are thought to be brought about by the occupancy of peculiar status combinations that involve incompatible role expectations. It is noteworthy that the statuses need not be hierarchical. Societies characterized by a high degree of status integration would be expected to have low suicide rates, while within a given society those status clusters that are infrequently occupied would be expected to have a high suicide rate. As an illustration, Gibbs provides data on marital status by age in the United States:

In 1950, of the males 60-64 years of age, 79.3% were married, 9.6% widowed, 8.6% single, and 2.5% divorced. The corresponding average annual suicide rates during 1949-1951 for the four marital statuses in this group are: . . . 36.2, . . .64.7, . . . 76.4, . . . 111.1. Consistent with the major theorem, there is a perfect inverse relation between the proportion in a marital status and the suicide rate of the status. The prediction of such a relation (and all other predictions generated by the theory) rests on the assumption that the relative frequency with which a cluster of statuses is actually occupied reflects the extent of role conflict among the statuses, with infrequently occupied clusters assumed to be characterized by role conflict, and consequently, weak social relations (1966, p. 317).

Gibbs has urged sociologists not to follow Durkheim blindly since, in many instances, Durkheim's conceptualization is inadequate. While this advice is warranted, it is also true that Gibbs and Martin have provided a splendid example of the value of Durkheim's conceptualization. Indeed, Gibbs and Martin, Henry and Short, and numerous other social scientists have advanced the study of suicide by continuing to question Durkheim's assumptions, to clarify and measure his concepts, and to test his hypotheses.

It is notable that the authors whose works have been discussed in this section have all focused on stressful situations as they are related to suicide. In drawing this section to a close, however, it would be an omission not to emphasize that the foregoing students of suicide have probably dealt with, in most cases, the final act of a process. None of these authors have dealt with the process of suicide.

It is, in fact, of considerable interest that a number of clinicians and social scientists, including Edwin Shneidman and Norman Farberow (1957), have suggested that actual and attempted or threatened suicides are motivationally similar; these authors also suggest that the threat of suicide should be taken seriously. In a similar vein, Calvin Schmid (1960) combined actual and attempted suicides in a recent study "because of their close relationship sociologically (p. 529)." Others have combined threatened and attempted suicides for similar reasons (Teele, 1965). Secondly, although there is no claim that all people who have threatened or attempted suicide go on to commit suicide, two recent studies suggest that sociopsychological studies of persons who threaten or attempt suicide may provide new approaches to the study—and prevention—of suicide. One such study is by Temoche (1961), who found in a population of former mental patients in Massachusetts (hospitalized between 1934-51) that the threat or past attempt at suicide was three to four times more common among the suicides (committed in 1949–51) than among the nonsuicides. The other study by Shneidman and Farberow (1957) found, in a population of former mental patients in Los Angeles County (hospitalized between 1944–53), that 75 percent of the subjects who later committed suicide had a history of having previously threatened or attempted suicide.

Wilkins (1967) in an excellent review of studies bearing on the relationship between attempted and completed suicide, presented data showing that there is some disparity among these studies. He suggested that one reason for these disparities is the use, by some, of samples of formerly hospitalized mental patients (who have larger proportions of completed suicides among those with a prior attempt). Another reason for the disparity, he stated, is the sources the researchers have consulted. Thus, police and public officials have relatively little contact with cases of attempt, and hospitals and private physicians have relatively more. Another point Wilkins made is that not all suicides have made prior attempts. Using these and other considerations, Wilkins tentatively concluded that between 1 and 5 percent of attemptors subsequently filter into the population of completed suicides.

Wilkins also noted the differences between samples in studies of threats of suicide, and indicated that forewarnings may not predict what people will do after they have forewarned (i.e., suicide or not). People who threaten should receive further attention in research since they are, in fact, often a part of the process of completing suicide.

What is needed, it seems, is more intensive study of the conditions linked to suicidal warnings, to suicidal attempts, as well as to suicide. Needless to say, the approach should take into consideration, as possible sources of stress, some of the circumstances studied by Durkheim, Henry and Short, and Gibbs and Martin: social relationships, group cohesiveness, status, and role conflict.

URBAN DISORDERS

As shown in Table 9.1, there were 164 reported cases of "urban disorder" in the United States during the first nine months of 1967 as reported by the President's National Advisory Commission on Civil Disorders (1968). More of these disorders occurred during the remaining months of 1967 and in 1968. Most of these involved northern urban centers, and hundreds of blacks were participants. What caused these outbreaks of violence? In a nine-month span, then, the

United States had experienced more than half as many serious urban disorders as it had in an earlier 50-year span during this century (Lieberson and Silverman, 1965). Moreover, the earlier riots had involved predominantly white violence, while in 1967-68, disorders were characterized mainly by black violence. The President's National Advisory Commission on Civil Disorders, popularly known as the Kerner Commission, frequently referred to the 1967 disorders as riots, and never as revolts or rebellions. Whites, in general, seem to describe the disorders as riots. From the beginning, however, many blacks were referring to these disorders as rebellions and revolts.

What lies behind these differing perceptions? If whites believe or wish to believe that the disorders are "riots," is it because they hope that the disorders are momentary and isolated incidents that can be charged to "hotheads" or "riffraff" and handled appropriately, as one handles the criminal class? If blacks believe that the disorders are "rebellions," is it because they have a deep and abiding desire to be free of the restrictions that have long beset them in America and are convinced that organized violence is the answer? The following analysis and discussion (drawing heavily on the sociological theory of alienation) will suggest that elements of both riot and revolt were present in these disorders.

Theory of alienation. One theory which provides a general description of the process leading to urban disorders is presented in Merton's theory of anomie (1957). The reader will recall that Merton was alluded to earlier in this chapter in connection with the discussion on delinquency and the hostile environment. Briefly, it was noted that Merton dealt with the solutions that resulted when individuals accepted social goals but were denied access to the approved means for achieving them. Merton stated that social structures generated the circumstances that exerted pressures upon certain persons in the society to engage in nonconformist rather than conformist behavior. He developed a typology of various kinds of socially deviant but adaptive behavior that could occur when individuals were frustrated by obstacles placed in the way of reaching a socially desirable goal (e.g., success) by legitimate means. The typology includes (1) innovation—the culture goal is retained but the individual feels called upon to develop new means to the goal; (2) ritualism—the individual, seeing that the goal is unattainable, scales it down or abandons its pursuit altogether but continues to adhere to the institutional or societal means; (3) retreatism—the individual rejects both the goal and the means to it and, in Merton's terms, withdraws from society; (4) rebellion—the individual not only rejects both the goal and the means to it but seeks to institutionalize new methods or means oriented toward new culture goals and *shared* by the members of the society.

Merton presented his scheme primarily in terms of *individual* responses to frustrated aspirations. However, with respect to *rebellion*, Merton introduces the notion of *shared* new values and goals held by members of a subgroup. It is of some interest that after Merton's approach to the issue of rebellion, few sociologists have gone on to exploit it. This lack of attention to rebellion as a subject for study by sociologists is especially notable in view of the substantial attention subsequently given his concept of *innovation* (in the study of crime and delinquency). Thus, although Merton did not deal substantially with the notion of gang delinquency, Cloward and Ohlin (1960) did concern themselves with this topic in their elaboration of Merton's discussion of anomie. In doing so, they drew on several of Merton's types of adaptations, including innovation, retreatism, and rebellion.

By combining features of Merton's discussion of rebellion with his discussion of innovation, and by elaborating upon his discussion of social structural limitations to access by *certain classes or strata of people* to the American culture goal of success, Cloward and Ohlin were able to develop a theory of the origin of deviant subcultures. With respect to Merton's formulation, Cloward and Ohlin (1960) state:

> It helps us to explain, for example, why youth in the lower class are apparently more likely than middle class youth to engage in extreme law-violating behavior. There is every reason to think that persons variously located in the social hierarchy have rather different chances of reaching common success-goals despite the prevailing ideology of equal opportunity. The middle-class person can generally take advantage of educational opportunities despite their cost; his family may be in a position to finance his beginnings in a profession or in business, or at least to put him in touch with established and successful people who can give him an "edge". In these and other ways, middle-class youth enjoy greater access to success-goals (p. 85).

Cloward and Ohlin also reviewed many studies of aspirations and suggested that there was firm evidence that a substantial number of lower-class youth aspire beyond their means, although in absolute terms their aspirations are lower than those of middle-class youth.

They also suggest that *relative* to the middle-class aspirations, the poor or the lower class want more. For example, they want (and need) a proportionately greater income increase than do middle-class persons, although in absolute dollar terms the increase in income sought is far greater among the middle class than among the poor.

Because of the barriers faced by the lower class youth in their attempts to realize their aspirations, and the ensuing failure to attain their goals, Cloward and Ohlin believe that frustrated lower class youth often find other frustrated persons like themselves. These youths then discuss their common dilemmas, arrive at a common conclusion that their failure can be blamed on the social system, and find strengths, rewards and esteem in the group which may develop new—and deviant—avenues to success goals. The delinquent norms developed by the group form what is called the delinquent subculture.

Although Cloward and Ohlin were primarily concerned with social class differentials vis-à-vis delinquent behavior and delinquent subcultures, it seems obvious that were the terms "black" and "white" substituted for "lower class" and "middle class," their discussion would be relevant to the present interest in the alienating process. Moreover, since blacks are more likely to be lower class than whites, and are also discriminated against on the basis of color alone, there would seem to be particularly strong forces pushing them into alienation from the system. And indeed a variety of researchers, using scales that purport to measure psychological anomie, have shown that blacks are more alienated than whites.

For example, Middleton (1963), using representative items from six different measures of alienation, assessed the relationship of race to each type of alienation in a southern community. The types of alienation utilized by Middleton were drawn mainly from the sociological literature and were identified as: *powerlessness, meaninglessness, normlessness, cultural estrangement, social estrangement,* and *estrangement from work.* First, assessing the interrelationship among the six items, Middleton found that cultural estrangement had extremely low correlations to the other five items which were highly intercorrelated. It is clear from Middleton's discussion that these five items more closely reflect the meaning of alienation as used by Merton and Cloward and Ohlin, while the sixth (cultural estrangement) reflects isolation from the popular culture of the mass media. In every case, proportions of blacks giving the alienated response were greater than those of white, although the difference was very slight for the item tapping cultural estrangement.

For each item the black-white proportions of positive responses were as follows: powerlessness, 70 and 40; meaninglessness, 71 and 48; normlessness, 55 and 16; cultural estrangement, 35 and 34; social estrangement, 60 and 27; and estrangement from work, 66 and 18. Moreover, Middleton found that while education reduced the amount of alienation his respondents exhibited, this effect was stronger for whites than for blacks. Middleton concluded that "by far the most striking finding of the study is the pervasiveness of alienation among the Negro population . . . (p. 977)."

Findings in another southern-based study, by Killian and Grigg (1962), are in agreement with Middleton's that blacks are more alienated than whites, although Killian and Grigg found greater racial differences among rural-dwelling respondents than among urban dwellers. For blacks, they found that alienation was high for rural residents, regardless of social class, and for lower-class urban residents. On the northern scene, a more recent study sponsored by the *Chicago Sun-Times* (Braden, 1968) confirms that Chicago blacks are much more likely than whites to score high on a measure of alienation, though data on social class were not presented. These data strongly suggest that blacks in the United States are highly stressed.

As we have seen, then, before the urban disorders took place a number of social scientists, such as Merton and Cloward and Ohlin, had described some of the alienating features in American society and still others, such as Middleton, Killian, and Grigg, have presented data suggesting what should have been obvious: that American blacks were not happy with their positions or their fortunes in the United States.

Alienating situations faced by blacks. The alienating or stress-inducing situations blacks experience are many. A few of the major ones will be discussed. Each of these situations is familiar to a significant number of blacks.

Blacks — even in the earliest days of slavery — protested and fought against what some have regarded as the most vicious form of slavery ever known to man. Both Tannenbaum (1963) and Elkins (1968) found the American brand of slavery particularly destructive as compared with other instances of slavery. Thus, in the United States, slave owners retained absolute authority over their blacks, who were unable to leave their masters' properties without written authorization; slaves could own no property, had no right to assemble in public unless a white person was present, and could not even enter into a contract of marriage. Following the abolition of slavery, blacks were quickly deprived of their rights during the Reconstruction Era. Contemporary blacks have become particularly aware of the cruel and inhuman treatment and of the injustices dealt out to their forebears. Thus when blacks, aware of the cruelties of slavery, are told to emulate nineteenth-century white European immigrants, while at the same time being denied equitable educational and job opportunities, their feelings of alienation and resentment are undoubtedly strengthened.

Another alienating situation faced by blacks was the charge that blacks had no history or culture. Originating in part in the desire to rationalize slavery, this belief is only now being widely repudiated by blacks. In the past this belief had the effect of causing blacks to feel hatred toward themselves. Today, utterance of the charge that they have no history is a sure way to alienate blacks. Now blacks are insisting on the inclusion of black history in the school curricula and on selecting their own heroes. The resistance of whites, regardless of the organizational, political and social causes, to ceding to blacks a substantial voice in their schools is seen by blacks as an attempt by whites to block reforms in both the curriculum and in the selection of teachers.

The past and present use of violence to suppress blacks—yet another alienating situation—is one reason why many blacks wish to have control of the security forces in the black community. Recent writings have increased our knowledge of the historical use of violence by whites in the United States. For example, the United States Commission on Civil Rights (1965, p. 7) has stated, "... emancipated slaves were subjected to acts of cruelty, oppression, and murder, which local authorities were at no pains to prevent or punish." According to Williamson (1965), after the Civil War many South Carolina white citizens organized themselves into "home police" or militia for the sole purpose of keeping the black community under control.

Williamson notes that in Mississippi, by 1875 whites had combined the carefully controlled use of force with the threat of violence to keep the blacks under control. The National Advisory Commission on Civil Disorders notes that violence against blacks was not limited to the South and that anti-black riots occurred in New York, 1900; Springfield, Ohio, 1904; Greensburg, Indiana, 1906; Springfield, Illinois, 1908:

> The latter was a three-day riot, initiated by a white woman's claim of violation by a Negro, inflamed by newspapers, intensified

by crowds of whites gathered around the jail demanding that the Negro, arrested and imprisoned, be lynched. When the sherif transferred the accused . . . to a jail in a nearby town, rioters headed for the Negro section and attacked homes and businesses owned by or catering to Negroes (p. 215).

Throughout this post-emancipation period, especially in the South, blacks found that their security was increased when there were armed black soldiers in town. While white southerners denounced the presence of armed blacks, they saw no harm in armed whites. The suppression of the blacks after the Civil War was completed when federal troops were removed and the blacks were disarmed.

This tendency by whites to welcome the arming of whites and the disarming of blacks apparently prevails today. Thus Robert Williams (1968) describes the ordeal this country has put him through because he believed in the right of Afro-Americans to defend themselves from the violence of the Ku Klux Klan. Williams states that because he armed the blacks of Monroe, North Carolina, in 1957 so that they might defend themselves, he is now in exile.

According to Seale (1968), a similar persecution has befallen the leaders of the Black Panthers, another organization which advocates the arming of the black community. Thus Huey Newton, a leader of the Black Panthers, is in jail and one of the most articulate spokesmen, Eldridge Cleaver, has taken flight rather than be returned to prison. Many blacks (and many whites, also) believe that the Black Panther organization is being politically persecuted because of their advocacy of arms for blacks. Many blacks also believe that others of their leaders — even the advocates of non-violence — have been subjected to persecution, perhaps most dramatically portrayed in the tragic assassination of Dr. Martin Luther King.

Blacks' reactions and interpretations of numerous other social conditions and practices catalogue their alienation in the United States. They feel that many whites value their property more than they do the lives of blacks; they perceive American foreign policy as largely racist; they resent the overrepresentation of blacks among the Vietnam war dead, and they are bitter about the denigration of revered blacks such as Dubois and Malcolm X. They also resent their disenfranchisement, discrimination on jobs and housing, union exclusion policies, the failure of most city and state governments to pursue school integration aggressively, the preference for projects for space over programs for the poor, and the continued resistance to interracial social intercourse.

The conditions that Cloward and Ohlin described as necessary for the development of a delinquent subculture among lower-class youth are present in most of the black ghettos. These are reinforced by the virtual confinement of most blacks in the inner city core areas—due to residential segregation. Briefly reviewing these conditions, they include (1) the presence of barriers that block the attainment of goals, (2) a placing of blame for the failure to attain goals on external sources rather than on oneself, and (3) sharing of the experiences of grievances with others in like circumstances.

Anger and alienation in black ghettos, then, have been growing and many blacks have been discussing their condition and the unsatisfactory results of nonviolent responses for a long time. Kenneth Clark (1965) and James Baldwin (1963) were among those who warned America of the growing alienation of black youth and adults.

Black alienation had reached such heights by 1967 that 164 cities experienced civil disorder, one-fourth of these disturbances being serious. The Kerner Report states that the disorders were a response to "white racism." It would seem that the "riotous" nature of the disorders lies in the fact that there was no apparent coordination or planning and that the mobs often entered into a state of revelry. The "rebellious" nature of the disorders would lie in the fact that such large numbers of the ghetto blacks were generated by a common sense of rage and protest.

That most blacks have alienating experiences and are subjected to stress in this country is borne out by a supplemental study of the Kerner Commission. The report states that the urban riots of the 1960's are a form of social protest by noncriminal elements and are justified as such by a majority of Negroes. Some of the conclusions of this study of riot participation in six cities (Detroit, Newark, New Haven, Dayton, Grand Rapids, and Cincinnati) by Fogleson and Hall (1968) follow:

1. Contrary to the notion that only 1 or 2 percent of the black community actively participated in the disorders, the authors found that about 18 percent of the black residents in the disorder areas, on the average, participated in the disorders;

2. The overwhelming majority of rioters were employed. About three-fourths of those arrested had jobs; and

3. More than two-thirds of those arrested were adults (over 18 years).

On the basis of these and other findings, Fogleson and Hall concluded that the rioters *did not* constitute a tiny minority of the black community, composed of riffraff and outside agitators and opposed by a large majority of the ghetto residents. The authors challenge the riffraff theory that has been so comforting to some white Americans and has supported them in turning away from the basic issue of black-white relations in the United States.

The study by Fogleson and Hall, then, provides the last link in the alienation theory described here: that a black subculture, involving shared negative evaluations of the black experience in the United States, may be in the process of development. This subculture, while composed of only a minority of the blacks at this time, is still substantial enough to constitute a warning to America that the stresses faced by blacks are becoming intolerable to a growing number.

Urban disorders, then, can in large part be understood in terms of the potentially stressful situations blacks have experienced. It is one alternative dissemminated and reinforced by group norms. A tragic commentary upon life in the black ghetto in the United States is that many blacks *believed* that there were no alternative solutions. And, indeed, whatever solutions were in process, appeared to be unfolding at an exceedingly slow pace.

CONCLUSION

In this chapter I have considered the relationship between stressful situations and particular forms of deviance or social pathology. I have focused on what may be classified as individual responses to stress, such as crime and suicide as opposed to group responses to stress in the form of urban disorders. It was noted that not all responses to stress are pathological. Moreover, in discussing crime, suicide, and urban disorders, I have stressed some common themes, such as alienation, the operation of group norms, differential treatment by the society, the perception of a hostile environment, and blockages to the achievement of social goals. It is not my position that most or all pathological behavior is attributable to the social system, but that the social system often tends to generate stress that may sometimes lead to or contribute to pathology. It appears that while our society has been zealous in its pursuit of the control and suppression of delinquency and other forms of deviance, it has been woefully weak in the control (i.e., relief) of stress.

A disease model of crime, of suicide, and even of urban disorders is often preferred by society because it focuses upon the deficits of the "criminal" or the "rioter" and not upon those of the social system; accordingly, it calls for changes in those experiencing the pathology, as opposed to changes in the more pervasive institutions and practices of society. Durkheim (1951), Merton (1957), Szasz

(1961), and Cooper (1967) are only a few of those who have made this point. It is understandable, for example, that many whites perfer to view the "rioter" as sick rather than accept the interpretation of the Kerner Commission, which pointed to white racism and institutional bigotry as the sources of intolerable stresses focused on blacks in America. The usefulness of the stress concept, indeed, is that it helps to clarify the link between the institutional order, on the one hand, and the pathology or deviance, on the other.

It may be hoped that the findings of social scientists on the possible relationship between social stress and pathology will serve to encourage society, to the extent possible, to remove the sources of stress and, in turn, to avoid the high cost of social pathology.

REFERENCES

BALDWIN, J. 1963. *The Fire Next Time*. New York: Dell.
BASOWITZ, H., PERSKY, H., KORCHIN, S. J., and GRINKER, R. R. 1955. *Anxiety and Stress*. New York: McGraw-Hill.
BECKER, H. 1963. *Outsiders*. New York: Free Press.
BRADEN, W. 1968. "Blacks Feel They Don't Count." *Boston Glove*, September 25.
BUSH, G. 1967. "Status Consistency and Right Wing Extremism." *American Sociological Review*, 32 (February):36–92.
CLARK, K. B. 1965. *Dark Ghetto*, New York: Harper and Row.
CLINARD, M. 1958. *The Sociology of Deviant Behavior*. New York: Rinehart and Company, Inc.
CLOWARD, R., and OHLIN, L. 1960. *Delinquency and Opportunity*. New York: Free Press.
COHEN, A. 1955. *Delinquent Boys*. New York: Free Press.
COOPER, D. 1967. *Psychiatry and Anti-Psychiatry*. London: Tavistock.
CRANDALL, V. J. 1951. "Induced Frustration and Punishment, Reward Expectancy in Thematic Apperception Stores." *Journal of Consulting Psychology*, 15:400.
DOHRENWEND, B. P. 1961. "The Social-Psychological Nature of Stress: A Framework for Causal Inquiry." *Journal of Abnormal Psychology*, 62:294–302.
DOLLARD, J. 1939. *Frustration and Aggression*. New Haven: Yale University Press.
DURKHEIM, E. 1951. *Suicide, A Study in Sociology*, trans., John A. Spaulding and George Simpson, New York: Free Press.
ELKINS, S. M. 1968. *Slavery*. Chicago: University of Chicago Press.
FARBEROW, N., and SCHNEIDMAN, E. 1955. "Attempted, Threatened and

Completed Suicide." *Journal of Abnormal and Social Psychology*, 50 (March):230.

FOGELSON, R., and HALL, R. 1968. "Who Riots? A Study of Participation in the 1967 Riots," in *Supplemental Studies for The National Advisory Commission on Civil Disorders*. New York: Frederick A Praeger.

FOOTE, C. 1962. "The Bail System and Equal Justice," in N. Johnson, L. Savitz, and M. Wolfgang, *The Sociology of Punishment and Correction*. New York: John Wiley.

FRANKLIN, J. H. 1967. *From Slavery to Freedom*. New York: Alfred A. Knopf.

FREED, D., and WALD, P. 1964. *Bail in the United States*. National Conference on Bail and Criminal Justice.

FUNKENSTEIN, D., KING, S., and DROLETTE, M. 1957. *Mastery of Stress*. Cambridge: Harvard University Press.

GIBBS, J. P. 1966. "Suicide," chap. 6 in R. Merton and R. Nisbet, *Contemporary Social Problems*, 2nd ed. New York: Harcourt, Brace and World.

GIBBS, J. P., and MARTIN, W. T. 1964. *Status Integration and Suicide*. Eugene, Ore.: University of Oregon Press, p. 17.

HENRY, A., and SHORT, J. 1954. *Suicide and Homicide*. Glencoe, Ill.: Free Press.

HOLLINGSHEAD, A., and REDLICH, F. C. 1958. *Social Class and Mental Illness*. New York: John Wiley.

JANIS, I. 1954. "Problems of Theory in the Analysis of Stress Behavior." *Journal of Social Issues*, 10:12–25.

KILLIAN, L. M., and GRIGG, C. M. 1962. "Urbanism, Race, and Anomia." *American Journal of Sociology*, Vol. LXVII, No. 6, pp. 661–65.

KOHN, M., and CLAUSEN, J. 1955. "Social Isolation and Schizophrenia." *American Sociological Review*, 20 (June):265–73.

LEMERT, E. M. 1948. "Some Aspects of a General Theory of Sociopathic Behavior." *Research Studies of the State College of Washington*, 16:23–29.

1967. *Human Deviance, Social Problems, and Social Control*, esp. chap. 3. Englewood Cliffs, N.J.: Prentice Hall.

LIEBERSON, S., and SILVERMAN, A. R. 1965. "The Precipitants and Underlying Conditions of Race Riots." *American Sociological Review*, 30:887–98.

LORENZ, K. 1966. *On Aggression*, New York: Harcourt, Brace and World.

MECHANIC, D. 1962. *Students under Stress*. Glencoe, Ill.: Free Press.

MERTON, R. 1957. *Social Theory and Social Structure*, esp. pt. 2. Glencoe, Ill.: Free Press.

MIDDLETON, R. 1963. "Alienation, Race, and Education." *American Sociological Review*, 28 (December):973–77.

MONAHAN, T. 1957a. "Family Status and the Delinquent Child: A Reappraisal and Some New Findings." *Social Forces*, 35 (March):250–58.

1957b. "The Trend in Broken Homes Among Delinquent Children." *Marriage and Family Living*, November, pp. 362–5.

NYE, F. 1958. *Family Relationship and Delinquent Behavior.* New York: John Wiley, p. 42.

PIERCE, A. 1967. "The Economic Cycle and the Social Suicide Rate." *American Sociological Review,* 32 (June):457–62.

PILIAVIN, I., and BRIAR, S. 1964. "Police Encounters With Juveniles." *American Journal of Sociology,* 70 (September):206–14.

PLAYBOY. 1968. "Playboy Forum," *Playboy* Magazine, March, pp. 47–48.

PRESIDENT'S NATIONAL ADVISORY COMMISSION ON CIVIL DISORDERS. 1968. *Report of the President's National Advisory Commission on Civil Disorders.* 1968. New York: Bantam Books.

RECKLESS, W. C. 1961. *The Crime Problem,* 3rd ed. New York: Appleton-Century-Crofts.

REISS, A., JR. 1951. "Delinquency as the Failure of Personal and Social Controls." *American Sociological Review,* 16 (April):196–207.

RODMAN, H., and GRAMS, P. 1967. "Juvenile Delinquency and the Family: A Review and Discussion." *Task Force Report: Juvenile Delinquency and Youth Crime,* Appendix L, pp. 188–221. Washington, D.C.: U.S. Government Printing Office.

SCHMID, C. 1960. "Urban Crime Areas: Part I." *American Sociological Review,* 25 (August):527–42.

SEALE, B. 1968. "Selections from the Biography of Huey P. Newton." *Ramparts,* October 26, pp. 21–34.

SELYE, H. 1956. *The Stress of Life.* New York: McGraw-Hill.

SHNEIDMAN, E., and FARBEROW, N. 1957. *Clues to Suicide.* New York: McGraw-Hill.

SHORT, J. 1954. "A Report on the Incidence of Criminal Behavior, Arrests, and Convictions in Selected Groups." *Research Studies of the State College of Washington,* 22 (June):110–18.

SUTHERLAND, E., and CRESSEY, D. 1960. *Principles of Criminology,* 6th ed., pp. 143–48. New York: Lippincott.

SZASZ, T. 1961. *The Myth of Mental Illness.* New York: Harper.

TAFT, D. R. 1936. "Nationality and Crime." *American Sociological Review,* 1 (October):724–36.

TAIT, C. D., and HODGES, E. F. 1962. *Delinquents, Their Families and the Community.* Springfield, Ill.: Charles Thomas.

TANNENBAUM, F. 1963. *Slave and Citizen.* New York: Random House.

TEELE, J. E. 1965. "Suicidal Behavior, Assaultiveness and Socialization Principles." *Social Forces,* 43 (May):510–18.

TEMOCHE, A. 1961. "Suicide and Known Mental Disease." D.P.H. dissertation, Harvard University. School of Public Health.

UNITED STATES COMMISSION ON CIVIL RIGHTS. 1965. *Law Enforcement: A Report on Equal Protection in the South.* Washington, D.C.: U.S. Government Printing Office.

VAN VECHTEN, C. 1941. "The Criminality of the Foreign-Born." *Journal of Criminal Law and Criminology,* 32 (July–August):139–47.

WALLENSTEIN, J., and WYLE, C. 1947. "Our Law-Abiding Lawbreakers."

Probation, 25 (March–April):107–12.

WEEKS, H. A. 1940. "Male and Female Broken Home Rates by Types of Delinquency." American Sociological Review, 5:601–9.

WILKINS, J. 1967. "Suicidal Behavior." American Sociological Review, 32 (April):286–98.

WILLIAMS, E. 1944. Capitalism and Slavery. Chapel Hill, N.C.: University of North Carolina Press.

WILLIAMS, R. F. 1968. "Negroes with Guns," pt. 6, no. 5, in J. Grant, ed., Black Protest. Greenwich, Conn.: Fawcett.

WILLIAMSON, J. 1965. After Slavery: The Negro in South Carolina during Reconstruction, 1861–1877. Durham, N.C.: University of North Carolina Press.

WILSON, J. Q. 1968. "The Police and the Delinquent in Two Cities," chap. 2, in S. Wheeler, ed., Controlling Delinquents. New York: John Wiley.

PART FOUR
Conclusions and Implications

10. Models of Stress

ROBERT SCOTT
AND ALAN HOWARD

THE PRIMARY purpose of this chapter is to survey existing conceptual models of stress in order to evaluate the contribution each has made to our present understanding of stress phenomena. The chapter is divided into four sections. Section I identifies and briefly describes each of the major conceptual models of stress; in Section II each conceptual model is critically evaluated in terms of its contribution to existing knowledge; Section III contains our attempt to derive a unified, comprehensive stress model; and in Section IV we attempt to reinterpret previous stress models in terms of our own model.

I. EXISTING CONCEPTUAL MODELS OF STRESS

Eight basic conceptual models have been proposed to explain the phenomena of stress. Six of these were explicitly formulated by

Robert A. Scott is assistant professor of sociology at Princeton University, and Alan Howard is an anthropologist at the Bernice P. Bishop Museum, Honolulu.

researchers, who then used them as a guide for their own studies of stress; the remaining two exist in the form of implicit assumptions contained in many medical and psychiatric studies of the responses of individuals to conditions of extreme duress. A brief description of each of these eight models follows.

1. Mechanic (1962) has formulated a model of stress for the purpose of interpreting selected problems concerned with the social psychology of adaptation. This model was developed in order to interpret the findings of a study of graduate students while they prepared for and took qualifying examinations for the doctoral program in the department of sociology at a large state university. Mechanic defines stress as "the discomforting responses of persons in particular situations (1962, p. 7)." Whether or not a situation, event or happening produces discomforting responses depends upon four factors: the ability and capacity of a person; skills and limitations produced by group practices and traditions; the means provided to individuals by the social environment; and the norms that define where and how an individual may utilize these means. The successful mastery of a situation, and the feelings that are aroused in the process are termed reversibility. Reversibility depends upon adaptive devices consisting of thoughts and behavior relevant to one's situation or to feelings about it. If behavior is relevant to situational demands, it is termed coping behavior. The term "defense" is used in reference to behavior and thoughts aimed at managing feelings evoked by the situation and the coping behavior. This stress model was developed for, and applies most appropriately to the social and social-psychological level of functioning in the organism.

2. Basowitz and his associates (1955) developed a model of stress based upon a study of men in combat. The central concepts in this model are "anxiety," "stress," and "stress situations" (1955, p. 54). Anxiety is defined as a conscious and reportable experience of intense dread and foreboding. Such feelings typically arise when the integrity of the organism is in some manner threatened. In theory, any stimuli may threaten the integrity of an organism and thereby produce the experience of anxiety; empirically, some stimuli are more likely than others to produce anxiety. Stress refers to this latter class of stimuli. Stimuli form a continuum based on differential meaning to the organism and on the anxiety-producing potential they have. At one end of this continuum are stimuli that have meaning only to a single individual or a few persons; at the other end of the continuum are stimuli that, because of their intensity and their explicit threat to vital functions, are likely to overload the capacity of

most organisms. Basowitz uses this idea to designate as stressful certain kinds of stimuli without regard to response. Such stimuli are regarded as stressful because of their assumed or potential effect, even though it is recognized that they may provoke differing responses. By virtue of their assumed generality, these are referred to as stress situations. This model has been used primarily to interpret the responses of groups of persons who are simultaneously subjected to conditions of extreme duress.

3. Studies by Alexander (1950), Dunbar (1947), and Grinker and Spiegel (1945) have produced the psychosomatic model of stress. The psychosomatic model is based on the premise that the tensions and strains that occur in one system of the body often have pathological consequences for other body systems. Anxiety or fear generated by serious conflicts in a person's life may be expressed not only through subjective feelings of intense dread and discomfort, but through alterations in basic physiological processes as well. Such basic physiological reactions occur when the organism's responses to provoking circumstances are inappropriate. Solvable conflicts handled directly, or in an overtly assertive fashion, are less likely to result in significant, sustained alterations in organic processes, since the tension generated by the initial conflict is externally and not internally dissipated. If, however, such conflicts are not confronted directly, the predicted result is that the tension will be internally dissipated, flowing from one bodily system to another and thereby producing certain characteristic organic changes.

4. A fourth model of stress, developed by Wolff and his associates (1950, 1953), is closely related to the psychosomatic model. The principal concept in this model is the "protective reaction pattern." According to this model, when the body is confronted with insults to its physical integrity, a complex reaction occurs aimed at sealing off and then ridding the body of its threat. This process is illustrated by the nasal adaptive reaction induced by inhaling noxious fumes. The reaction consists of intense mucous secretion and tearing, which is aimed at flushing out the nose and eyes, thereby ridding the body of the noxious agent. This same reaction may be set in motion by symbolic as well as by physical threats, and the reactions thereby induced are similar in both instances. This model differs from the psychosomatic model in that the protective reaction pattern is not conceptualized as a chain reaction beginning with feeling states and then progressing to altered bodily reaction and finally to organic abnormality. Altered feelings, bodily adjustment, and behavior are considered to occur simultaneously and in varying degrees.

5. A biochemical model of stress has been developed by Hans Selye (1956). This model is basically concerned with an analysis of stress at the physiological and biochemical levels of human functioning. Selye defines stress as "a state manifested by a specific syndrome which consists of all of the nonspecifically induced changes within a biologic system (1956, p. 54)." A nonspecifically induced change is one that affects all, or most parts of a system without selectivity. Nonspecifically induced changes are described in terms of the General Adaptation Syndrome, a three-stage process brought about by a specific stressor, or a stress-producing stimulus. The first stage is characterized by an alarm reaction, during which a general mobilization occurs. This phase leads to a stage of resistance, which is characterized by a set of internal responses that stimulate tissue defense. If the stressor continues to affect the organism despite these responses, the third stage – that of exhaustion – is eventually reached.

6. A large number of studies have isolated specific physiological changes that are commonly produced by stressful stimuli. These studies fall into two broad categories: First, there are studies of the effects of stress on such physiological processes as cardiac functioning (Stevenson and Duncan, 1950, pp. 799-817; Wolf, 1948, pp. 1056-76, mucous membrane secretion (Wolff, 1948, pp. 313-34, and gastric functioning (Margolin, 1950, pp. 656-64); second, there are studies of the relationship between stress and the genesis and onset of specific disease syndromes such as cardiovascular disorders (Wolff, 1950), ulcerative colitis (Grace, 1950, pp. 679-91; Lindemann, 1950, pp. 706-23), dermatitis (Kepecs and Robin, 1950, pp. 1010-15), and glaucoma (Ripley, 1950, pp. 523-36). As a rule, these studies do not contain an explicit conceptual model; rather, they are guided by a set of implicit assumptions about stimuli that are stressful, how they operate upon the organism, and why the effects of stress are manifested as they are. An examination of these implicit assumptions suggests a kind of mechanical model of stress. In this model, stress is viewed as the internal response of the organism to an external load placed upon it by some pathogenic agent, stressor, or life crisis. Stress, in turn, produces distinct pathological changes and certain typical disorders of adaptation.

7. Another model of stress, one evolved by Dohrenwend, modifies Selyes' physiological stress model in order to apply it to studies of the prevalence and distribution of mental disorders in the social environment (1961, pp. 294-302). Dohrenwend has isolated five basic sets of factors involved in stress reactions. These are (1) external

stressors that throw the organism into an imbalanced state; (2) factors that mediate or alleviate the effects of the stressor; (3) the experience of stress itself, which is the product of the interaction between the stressor and the mediating factors; (4) the adaptive syndrome, which consists of the organism's attempt to cope with the stressor; and (5) the organism's response, which may be either adaptive or maladaptive.

Mediating factors play a very important role in Dohrenwend's model. Two basic types of mediating factors are identified: those that determine the amount of external constraint associated with stress, and those that determine the amount of inner constraint. External and internal constraint, in turn, produce conditions of external and internal control. External control is experienced when force is exerted in favor of activity that is demanded by outer events. Conversely, internal control is experienced when an individual attempts to inhibit action demanded by outer events in favor of actions demanded by inner events. From this basic paradigm, Dohrenwend then derives eight basic propositions concerning factors that determine the intensity and duration of stress. In this model, stress is defined as a state intervening between antecedent constraints and consequent efforts to reduce constraint. As such, stress is regarded by Dohrenwend as the product of any behavior in response to pressures, regardless of whether the behavior is adaptive or maladaptive.

8. Janis has evolved a model of stress that is basically concerned with psychological responses of individuals to traumatic events. This model is based upon his own studies of victims of air-raid attacks during the war, and of patients undergoing major surgery (1954, pp. 12–25). He also draws heavily on the numerous studies of natural disasters and man-made calamities. His model is comprised of three basic elements: the disaster situation; the psychological responses of individuals to disaster; and intrapsychic and situational determinants of these psychological responses. Janis identifies three major phases of danger found in all large-scale disasters. These are the threat phase, in which persons perceive objective signs of impending danger or in which they receive explicit warnings that some kind of danger might be approaching, but at a time when the immediate environment is still free from the physical impact of the danger; the danger-impact phase, in which persons are actually confronted with physical dangers in their immediate environment such that their chances of escaping injury or death are at least partly contingent upon the speed and efficiency of their protective responses; and the danger-of-victimization phase, which usually occurs immediately af-

ter the actual impact of the danger has subsided or terminated, and in which people perceive the variety and magnitude of the losses sustained by themselves and others.

Five types of reactions are associated with these danger phases. These are apprehensive avoidance, in which individuals attempt to escape the situation psychologically by employing the defense mechanism of denial; stunned immobility, in which there is an almost total absence of motor and mental activity, coupled with disorientation; apathy and depression; docile dependency, in which persons show a distinct lack of independent action; and agressive irritability, in which they are often prepared to lash out at anyone who frustrates or angers them in any way. These reactions, which usually produce distinctly different consequences, do share one common effect: they all result in a marked drop in mental efficiency.

There are two basic factors that determine which of these five basic responses will occur. The first concerns characteristics of the danger stimuli that are perceived and experienced by the individual; the second are situational and predispositional determinants, of which Janis identifies seven. These are: (1) previously institutionalized ideologies and rationales concerning the natural cause of disaster; (2) previously formed expectations concerning the ways .in which danger situations can be avoided or mitigated; (3) self-conceptions of one's social role in the emergency situation; (4) the degree of identification or affiliation with the psychological groups that are threatened by the danger; (5) the social status with respect to the chances of receiving aid, relief, and preferential treatment; (6) the amount of prior training in relevant protective strategies and tactics dealing with the danger situation; and (7) personality characteristics, such as strength of dependency needs and chronic levels of anxiety with respect to body integrity.

There have been a number of other attempts to develop models of stress (Bharucha-Reid and Rodabe, 1962, pp. 147–58; Caudill, 1953, pp. 194–208; Levine and Scotch, 1967; Sarbin, 1962, pp. 324–41). In general, they are all variants on the basic conceptual models we have described in this section.

II. CRITIQUE OF EXISTING MODELS

Each of the models described has made a distinctive and important contribution to existing theory and research. At the same time, each has definite limitations. The purpose of this section is to analyze the nature of these limitations. It is important to understand that many of these shortcomings do not inhere in the models as such; they are created by the perspective we will bring to bear upon them. With only a few exceptions, these models are perfectly adequate conceptualizations of the phenomena they are intended to interpret. Limitations are created when the task switches from the analysis of stress at one level of human functioning to a broader and more integrated view of stress phenomena. Indeed, the task of seeking higher orders of abstraction than now exist is only possible because of the enormous amount of useful research that has been produced by these various models. Our critical discussion of their limitations should not, therefore, be construed to mean that we regard them as unimportant or useless; on the contrary, such a discussion is the logical and desirable outgrowth of the pioneering efforts that have preceded it.

One of the major factors that inhibits the conceptual integration of existing knowledge about stress is that the concept itself is defined differently in different conceptual models. Five different referents of the stress concept can be found in the models we have cited. Mechanic defines stress in terms of responses that individuals have to situations; Basowitz and his associates, and to some degree Janis, define it as a quality of a situation that is independent of the reaction of individuals to it; Selye, Dohrenwend, and several proponents of the mechanical model define stress as an intervening state which is the internal reaction to stressors, loads, or noxious stimuli; Dunbar's version of the psychosomatic model defines stress as an attribute of the stimuli; Alexander's psychosomatic model, and Wolff's model of the Protective Reaction Pattern, define stress both as a quality of the stimulus as well as the individual's response to it. The fact that there are so many different referents to the concept of stress makes it very difficult, and on occasion even impossible to meaningfully interpret and integrate research findings generated by these differing conceptions of the phenomena.

A second limitation of these models is that they are field-specific. By this we mean that they can only be applied to one, or at the most two of the several environmental fields to which the human organism simultaneously adapts. This limitation is a serious one for the reason that studies of stress have shown it to be a phenomenon that largely transcends the arbitrary levels of analysis designated by the terms biochemical, physiological, psychological, and sociocultural. Stress manifests itself in all of the environmental fields to which the organism simultaneously adapts. Traumatic psychological stimuli often

produce basic changes in the organism's physiological and biochemical functions; social crises have been shown to affect the individual both as a psychological and as a biochemical organism. A
major characteristic of an integrative model of stress must therefore
be its ability to conceptualize stress phenomena at all levels of
organism functioning without unduly distorting the specific phenomena of any given level. An analysis of the models we have
described will show that none of them effectively accomplishes this
important task. It would be difficult, for example, to apply Selye's
model to Mechanic's data without seriously altering the meaning of
his study. Mechanic's model, in turn, cannot be applied to the data
Wolff has obtained from his study of the Protective Reaction Pattern
without major modifications on the model itself. Wolff's framework,
in turn, cannot be applied easily to the data obtained by Basowitz,
Janis, and Grinker and Spiegel. By and large, the models we have
described are tailored to phenomena of a biochemical, or a physiological, or a psychological, or a sociological nature, but not for
combinations of these things. Perhaps the most successful effort in
this regard is Dohrenwend's adaptation of the Selye model, and its
application to the study of stress in the social environment. The
success of this effort lies in the fact that Dohrenwend's model can be
applied both to the biochemical and the social psychological levels
of analysis without unduly distorting the phenomena of either level.

A third limitation of most stress models is that they deal exclusively with events of an extreme and highly traumatic nature,
although the framework Janis has proposed, for example, applies to
the study of natural disasters or personal crises. Both the psychosomatic model and the model of the Protective Reaction Pattern
are efforts to conceptualize psychological and physiological responses of the organism to dramatic and noxious stimuli. The Basowitz
model applies only to situations a majority of persons are likely to
find threatening, and therefore anxiety-producing. Selye's model
deals almost entirely with traumatic stimuli, although it does have
the merit of taking into account certain less noxious stimuli as well.
In short, the concept of stress has been too closely equated with
extreme trauma and duress. This association has had the effect of
diverting attention away from the study of stimuli that are wearing to
the organism, and that have important physiological and psychological consequences for it, but which are neither dramatic nor
especially unusual. The relevance of such stimuli for the study of
stress is suggested by the findings of an investigation by Scott of
patterns of illness in a group of female employees in a large com-

mercial enterprise (1963). The study revealed that traumatic events such as the sudden death of a family member or friend, a recent divorce, or similar personal crises often produced acute illnesses. It was also clear, however, that such events were comparatively rare, and therefore of little value in helping to explain the very large amount of illness that routinely occurred on a day-to-day basis. An analysis of the data revealed that the life style of the individual, and especially the quality of her social role relationships with others, was much more determinative of the amount and severity of illness she suffered than the occasional traumatic situations that arose. In effect, both traumatic and nontraumatic but wearing events are stressful in the sense that they both produce the same types of physiological and psychological responses. With two notable exceptions, this fact is ignored in existing models of stress. These exceptions are the models by Mechanic and Dohrenwend. The basic problem with both models is, however, that they go too far in the other direction. Mechanic uses the concept of stress both to refer to the initial responses of persons to challenging situations and to their reactions to the failure to meet these challenges in any effective way. By this definition the concept of stress loses much of its meaning, since almost all situations or stimuli to which individuals respond could be considered stressful. In the Dohrenwend model, stress is described as a state of the organism which results from the interaction between any antecedent constraint and the consequent efforts to reduce it. Here again, the definition encompasses virtually all stimuli to which the organism may be subjected.

Fourth, most of these models are incomplete. By this we mean that they do not take into account all of the relevant variables that produce stress. If we consider the phenomena of stress in terms of the complex of factors explicitly suggested or implied in all of the stress models taken in total, then the incompleteness of each particular model becomes apparent. Each model omits certain factors relating both to the external environment and to the organism that have been shown by the models to be important determinants of whether or not a given stimulus, event, or situation does or does not result in stress. This point can be illustrated by an analysis of Mechanic's model. We have chosen it because it is among the most comprehensive and clearly formulated of all of the available models. Mechanic describes four factors he believes determine whether or not a situation, event, or happening will be stressful to individuals. The model ignores, however, such important factors as the manner in which problems are formulated, the manner in which they are perceived by the individual, and how the individual deploys resources in order to solve the problems.

It is important to recognize that incompleteness is an attribute of most stress models even when we evaluate them from the perspective of the level of functioning to which they are intended to apply. Basowitz, for example, does not consider such factors as perception, personal experience, or general and specific resources that the individual may have at his command to use in dealing with problem situations. His model deals only with what are regarded as the likely effects upon individuals of situations obviously traumatic in character. It is not to be expected that all of the factors that produce stress will be taken into account in all studies. It is important, however, that these factors be explicitly recognized in the conceptual models upon which empirical studies are based. The fact that this is not the case is a major limitation of the stress models we have described.

Fifth, some stress models contain assumptions that are unjustified. The Basowitz model, to cite one, contains the implicit assumption that what is stressful for one person must necessarily be stressful for another. This same assumption is made by Janis, whose model does not explicitly provide for the possibility that persons in crisis situations may respond in a fashion that does not reduce their mental and intellectual efficiency. Others, such as the psychosomatic model and Wolff's formulation, contain the assumption that any stimuli perceived by the individual to be stressful will necessarily produce physiological and psychological consequences of a detrimental character. Mechanic and Dohrenwend are admirable exceptions in this regard, since both of them are careful to avoid making unnecessary and unwarranted assumptions.

Finally, it should be noted that a number of these models do not entirely explain the phenomena they purport to account for. This is especially true of Wolff's Protective Reaction Pattern model. Research based upon his model has produced a variety of physiological responses to stress. Examples are changes in gastric function, mucous membrane secretion, blood chemistry, cardiac functioning, and blood flow to the brain and extremities. These reactions are explained as inappropriate physiological responses by the organism to symbolic threats. For example, when a foreign object lodges in the eye, we flush it out by tearing; when we are confronted with threatening symbolic stimuli, we may also respond physiologically by tearing, as though to symbolically wash away the perceived threat. The major problem with this model, is, of course, that it does not explain why certain persons respond to noxious symbolic stimuli by tearing, others by intense mucous membrane secretion, others by hyperactive gastrointestinal activity, and still others with no apparent response at all. In addition to this problem, the experimental studies from which the model was derived are often tautological in design. A subject is exposed to what the experimenter defines as a traumatic event; exposure is continued until some visible physiological changes are produced. These changes are then interpreted as evidence for the operation of the Protective Reaction Pattern. If the subject does not manifest outward signs of stress, it is inferred that the stimuli are not sufficiently noxious, and so the experimenter simply intensifies them until something happens which he can measure.

In summary, we have identified six major limitations of existing models of stress. These are (1) referents for the concept of stress differ from one model to another; (2) the models are field-specific in the sense that they cannot be extended to all levels of human functioning without seriously distorting the phenomena at each level; (3) most of them fail to take into account nontraumatic but wearing events that produce psychological and physiological stress responses similar to those produced by traumatic events; (4) the models are incomplete in that they ignore critical factors that determine the nature of stress responses; (5) many of the models contain unwarranted assumptions as to the nature of traumatic stimuli and the likely responses of individuals to them; and (6) some of the models do not adequately explain the data upon which they are presumably based.

III. REQUIREMENTS OF A SATISFACTORY MODEL OF STRESS

Our discussion of these limitations leads us to consider the characteristics of an acceptable stress model. By the term "acceptable" we mean a model capable of integrating existing knowledge about stress into a single, unified framework. This framework should have the following characteristics: First, the referent of stress should be clearly defined, and formulated so as to distinguish between stress and related phenomena in a way that is both conceptually clear and empirically feasible. Second, the model should be capable of interpreting phenomena in a variety of environmental fields without unduly distorting the nature of any individual field. Third, the model must be able to account for both traumatic and nontraumatic events, while at the same time differentiating between degrees of wear and tear that may result from nontraumatic stimuli and situations. Fourth, an acceptable stress model must be capable of satisfactorily explaining the findings of all major relevant research. Fifth, it should be able to suggest new directions for research and especially research of a nonobvious nature. Finally, the model must be as complete as possible, taking into account the major factors that determine whether or not a given stimulus leads to the experience of stress. We have made an attempt to accomplish these diverse ends by formulating a comprehensive framework for the analysis of stress in the human organism. This framework relies heavily on the research and writings of the persons whose models we have discussed. In this section we present a revised formulation of the framework that we initially proposed (Howard and Scott, 1965).

The model we have developed is based upon an analysis of human functioning in problem-solving terms, and rests upon a set of complex assumptions about the character of the human organism. The most important of these assumptions is that each human organism tends to develop a characteristic level of activity and stimulation at which it most comfortably functions. The nature of this level varies tremendously among individuals: there are persons who require high and sustained levels of stimulation in order to feel comfortable and satisfied; there are others who require comparatively low levels of stimulation, and who feel most comfortable when demands made upon them are tightly dispersed around very low activity levels. Both genetic and behavioral factors determine variations in ranges of comfortable activity levels. A problem is defined as a stimulus or condition that produces demands on the human organism that require it to exceed its ordinary level of functioning, or that restrict activity levels below usual levels of functioning. This formulation suggests that a situation of boredom or of sensory deprivation are problem situations in much the same sense that crises, disasters, and acute insults to the integrity of the organism are problems.

Problems can be categorized into one of four types on the basis of the initial stimuli that introduce a threat to the organism: (1) problems posed to the organism from its internal physical environment; (2) problems posed to the organism from its external physical environment; (3) problems posed to the organism from its own psychological environment; and (4) problems posed to the organism from its sociocultural milieu.

Given the presence of a threat to the organism from one or more of its environmental fields, we can now consider the factors that determine whether or not it will master the threat. In considering these factors, it is necessary to distinguish between efforts at problem-solving and the actual resolution of a problem. We postulate five conditions that are necessary for successful problem-solving, or mastery. These conditions should be regarded as necessary but not sufficient conditions for mastery to occur.

The first condition necessary for mastery concerns the investment of energy. Here we must distinguish between general energy level of an organism and its specific energy level. The former refers to the overall energy potential the organism has; the latter refers to the amount of energy it has to expend for any particular problem. The energy potential of an organism, whether it be general or specific, is a product of both constitutional and environmental factors. The nature of an organism's experience within each of its environmental fields is an important determinant of its capacity to generate sufficient energy to resolve problems, and of its ability to allocate energy to specific environmental domains. Thus a person who has not been active over a period of time is more easily exhausted than someone who has been very active. Similarly, the repetitive performance of a specific task increases the capacity of the organism to perform the task and like tasks without exhaustion.

Second, mastery requires resources the organism can apply in working through a particular problem. A resource may be considered as anything that contributes to the resolution of problem situations. Resources are basically of two types: (1) general resources, such as intelligence, an intact neuromusculature, and the like; (2) specific resources, such as specialized skills, pertinent knowledge, and relevant tools or materials.

A third factor that determines whether or not an organism can master a problem concerns the way in which the problem is formulated, or the manner in which the threat is posed. Put simply, if an organism is to solve a problem, the problem must be solvable. Some problems by their very nature preclude mastery. Specifically, there are three ways in which this may be so. First, a problem may be open to possible solution, but solving it may involve demands that exceed the capacity of the organism; second, the problem may simply be without resolution; or third, the particular threat may be a part of a larger problem complex in which contradictory demands are made, and under such circumstances, the solution to one problem precludes the solution of another.

A fourth factor associated with mastery concerns the way in which the organism interprets a problem, and the corresponding "set" that develops. There is a growing body of research literature in the field of psychology that indicates that perception of a problem situation strongly determines both the nature and the extent of the response to it, and ultimately the probability of mastery. The importance of this factor is suggested by the research of Lazarus on psychophysiological responses to traumatic stimuli (Lazarus, 1963). Lazarus was able to substantially alter and diminish physiological responses of subjects to a traumatic stimulus by providing them beforehand with a variety of defense mechanisms against which to fend themselves from the trauma to which they were exposed. This research suggests that mastery depends in part upon how the organism defines the problem with which it is confronted; and the character of the physiological and psychological set it has at the time that the problem itself is introduced.

Fifth, mastery depends upon the way in which an organism responds to a problem. Three kinds of responses can be identified: an assertive response, a divergent response, and an inert response. An assertive response is one in which the organism meets the problem directly and attempts to solve it; a divergent response is one in which the organism diverts energy and resources away from the confronting problem; and an inert response is one in which the organism simply fails to mobilize its resources or to respond actively.

Mastery, then, depends upon an adequate source of energy, appropriate resources, the nature of the problem itself, the organism's "set" when the problem arises, and the manner in which the organism responds to the threat. Generally speaking, when mastery of a problem does occur, the state of the organism is superior to its state prior to the time of initial confrontation, in the sense that if the same problem arises again, the organism will be able to deal with it more efficiently than before.

Now we must consider what happens when mastery fails. To begin with, even when problems are successfully solved, a time gap exists between the initial provocation and the ultimate resolution. During the time in which the problem is being dealt with, the organism is in a state of greater or lesser mobilization, a state in which energy and resources are bound up so that the organism experiences tension. In cases of successful problem-solving, tensions are eventually dissipated and the organism returns to its usual level of functioning. When problems are not solved, however, tensions persist until mechanisms are found to cope with them. The failure to master threats therefore gives rise to a second-order problem; namely, that of dealing with unresolved tensions. In effect, failure in mastery requires the organism to use an excess of energy and resources in maintenance activities over what would have been required had mastery been achieved, and the necessity of excessive maintenance activity involves the organism in a state of continuous mobilization or tension. To the extent that excess maintenance tension exists, the organism can be said to be experiencing stress. In effect, stress is regarded as a state that results from the excess tensions produced by a failure of the organism to master threats from one or more of its environment.

Finally, there are two basic courses that can be taken by organisms experiencing undissipated tension. On the one hand, it may be necessary for the organism simply to live with the tension, as in the case of assaults to its physical integrity. This is ordinarily not feasible for long periods of time if the commitment of energy or resources committed to mobilization is great, because of the fact that it will ultimately cause the organism to become totally exhausted. Second, it may be possible to temporarily dissipate some of the accumulated tensions through a variety of physical, psychological, and social mechanisms of tension release.

IV. A RUBRIC FOR OTHER MODELS OF STRESS

It is not yet possible to judge the utility of the problem-solving model in terms of all of the relevant criteria identified in Section III of this paper. A substantial amount of research on stress needs to be formulated in terms of this model before it will be possible to evaluate its predictive power, the extent to which it avoids distortions of the diverse phenomena it seeks to explain, its completeness, and the new directions of research it suggests. In this sense the utility of the problem-solving framework cannot be immediately determined. It is possible, however, to evaluate the model in terms of the degree to which it adequately interprets the major models and research studies we have discussed. In this final section an effort will be made to reinterpret each of the eight principal stress models in terms of the conceptual framework we have proposed.

Mechanic describes situations that are capable of evoking discomforting responses in individuals. Such situations are, in our terminology, problem situations, since they constitute threats to the organism's integrity. His four factors that determine whether or not a situation, event, or happening produces discomforting responses are, in our terms, resources. It should be noted that the problem-solving model provides not only for the recognition of resources in the quest of mastery, but also the deployment of energy, the nature of the stimuli or problem situations, and the character of the organism's response to the provocation. Mechanic's concept of reversibility is analogous to the concept of mastery, or successful problem-solving. His concept of coping behavior is the equivalent of our concept of an assertive response aimed at the direct solution of a problem. Defense is synonymous with behavior aimed at solving the secondary problems that arise as a result of failure to master a provoking situation. Finally, Mechanic's definition of stress has two referents in our system. He uses the term to refer both to initial responses to provocative stimuli, and to subsequent discomfort from the failure to master them. Our definition of tension is equivalent to the first sense in which he uses the stress concept, while his second usage corresponds with our use of the term.

A fundamental notion contained in the Basowitz model is that of a continuum along which stimuli and situations fall. This continuum may be interpreted in two ways within the problem-solving framework. First, it expresses the probability that a given stimulus will or will not require resolution by a specific number of people in a specified situation. Certain stimuli, by virtue of their unique meaning to particular individuals, may pose problems only to them; other stimuli, by virtue of their commonly shared meaning, are likely to pose problems to a large number of persons. If we confine ourselves to the terminology that Basowitz suggests, however, it is only possible to deal with the stress evoked by symbolic stimuli. Alternatively, when viewed in a problem-solving framework these notions can be extended to other areas of functioning as well. In the physiological sphere, for example, only a few people in a given group may find the presence of dust or pollen to be a condition requiring resolution, whereas an epidemic of flu constitutes a problem for many more persons, and an outbreak of typhoid in an unimmunized population is a problem for a still wider range of people. A second interpretation of the Basowitz continuum focuses on the reversibility of problems. Stimuli may pose problems to a wide range of people, but there may be an equally wide distribution of knowledge, skills, and tools for solving them, while in other cases the stimuli may be such as to preclude resolution because of a lack of available means, or because the problems they pose are unsolvable. In the former instance the probability that stress will occur is minimal, whereas in the latter case it is quite high.

A second concept Basowitz employs is that of anxiety. In the problem-solving model, anxiety may be considered as the response of an organism to a circumstance that threatens its sense of mastery. It may be specific, in response to a particular situation, or generalized (free-floating), in response to an overall feeling of inadequacy. Such a response is to be expected when an individual is confronted with an unsolvable problem, or set of problems, or when he lacks confidence in the resources available.

The psychosomatic model can also be interpreted within the present framework without serious distortion to its meaning. In our terms, when a problem remains unsolved, for whatever reason (i.e., when mastery is not achieved), then the organism can be expected to experience tension in the form of continued mobilization. This gives rise to the second-order problem we have described, that of dissipating tension. Tension may be discharged in a variety of ways, in any of the environmental areas. Increased organic activity is one form that is likely to occur when various other possibilities within the symbolic environment are inadequate, or have been blocked. If we conceive of the organism as a whole system, however, the psychosomatic model can be expanded. By considering tension as a result of overmobilization, we can assert the plausibility of the reverse environment being discharged through symbolic channels. Here, too, then, the generality of a useful model is enhanced by translating it into problem-solving terms.

The Protective Reaction Pattern model corresponds in our framework to the process of mobilizing resources. What Wolff has pointed out is that while certain types of resources are effective for solving certain kinds of problems, the mobilization of these same resources are irrelevant (i.e., divergent responses) when the organism faces other kinds of problems. They have effectively demonstrated that the human organism characteristically overmobilizes its physical resources when confronted with problems originating in the symbolic environments, and that to the extent that these problems remain unsolved, a state of inappropriate mobilization is perpetuated, or in other cases recurs when the problem is brought to the awareness of an individual.

The apparent conflict between this and the psychosomatic model is easily resolved when put in these terms. Wolff's model focuses upon the response pattern to an unsolvable problem, and particularly the relationship of resources to the nature of the problem; the psychosomatic model focuses upon the failure in mastery itself and the resultant problem of dissipating tension. Both models are in fact consistent with our postulations, and the degree to which one would seem to fit particular data better than the other can be formulated in empirical rather than theoretical terms.

The three stages of the General Adaptation Syndrome that Selye has described—that of the alarm reaction, resistance, and exhaustion—can be related to the problem-solving model in the following way. The stage of alarm reaction corresponds in our model to the organism's mobilization of its general resources in response to a problem situation and of developing a "set." The stage of resistance corresponds to the mobilization of specific resources in response to the secondary problem of tension when the initial problem is unsolved. The stage of exhaustion corresponds to the depletion of energy and resources resulting from increased maintenance needs. When put in these terms, the applicability of the Selye model to behavioral as well as physiological phenomena is facilitated.

There are three key factors in the Janis model: the various phases of the disaster situation; the response to danger; and the determinants of these responses. In our terminology, disaster situations are unsolvable problems in the sense that there is little or nothing the individual can do to prevent their occurrence. Given that fact, the response that Janis proposes are of two types: divergent and inert. The responses he terms apprehensive avoidance and aggressive irritability are, in our terminology, divergent responses; those of stunned immobility, apathy and depression, and docile dependency we would term inert responses. The numerous situational and predispositional determinants he cites are, in our terms, tension-relieving mechanisms. They are devices by which to temporarily dissipate the tensions that accumulate from the continuous mobilization resulting from unsolvable personal crises or disasters.

Dohrenwend's adaptation of Selye's model is, like Selye's model, easily understood in problem-solving terms. As we saw, the basic sequence of stress responses as Selye has described them are readily understood in terms of our model. Dohrenwend's model consists of the additional concepts of internal and external constraints, and internal and external controls. The former describe characteristics of the problem situation, while the latter describe characteristics of the resources which persons have available for solving the problem. Dohrenwend's use of the concept of stress corresponds to our concept of tension; his concept of successful adaptation is similar to our concept of mastery; and his notion of maladaptation is akin to our concept of stress.

Finally, the mechanical model of stress can also be translated into problem-solving terms. The notion of the external load describes selected aspects of the problem situations; the concept of pressure is a general term that describes the tension of an organism generated by its efforts to solve problems; and the concept of strain is roughly similar to our concept of stress.

As empirical research continues, new stress models will undoubtedly emerge. Concepts will become more closely tied to operational procedures and we will be able to advance beyond the more or less heuristic frameworks that have been presented in this chapter. This must be an ever-present goal if we are to develop something worthy of being called "a theory of stress."

REFERENCES

ALEXANDER, F. 1950. *Psychosomatic Medicine, Its Principles and Application.* New York: Norton.

BASOWITZ, H., PERSKY, H., KORCHIN, S. J., and GRINKER, R. R. 1955. *Anxiety and Stress.* New York: McGraw-Hill.

BHARUCHA-REID, R., and RODABE, P. 1962. "The Internal Modulating System and Stress: A Neurophysiological Model." *Journal of General Psychology,* 66:147-58.

CAUDILL, W. 1953. "Cultural Perspective on Stress." *Symposium on Stress,* pp. 194-208. Washington, D.C.: Army Medical Service Graduate School.

DOHRENWEND, B. P. 1961. "The Social Psychological Nature of Stress: A Framework for Causal Inquiry." *Journal of Abnormal Social Psychology,* 62:294-302.

DUNBAR, H.F. 1947. *Mind and Body.* New York: Random House.

GRACE, W.J. 1950. "Life Situations, Emotions and Chronic Ulcerative Colitis." *Research Publication, Association for Nervous and Mental Disorders,* 29:679-91.

GRINKER, R. R., and SPEIGEL, J.P. 1945. *Men under Stress.* Philadelphia: Blakiston.

HOWARD A., and SCOTT, R.A. 1965. "A Proposed Framework for the Analysis of Stress in the Human Organism." *Behavioral Science,* 10:141-60.

JANIS, I. 1954. "Problems of Theory in the Analysis of Stress Behavior." *Journal of Social Issues,* 10:12-25.

KEPECS, J.G., and ROBIN, M. 1950. "Life Situations, Emotions and Atopic Dermatitis," *Research Publication, Association for Nervous and Mental Disorders,* 29:1010-15.

LAZARUS, R.S. 1963. "A Laboratory Approach to the Dynamics of Psychological Stress." *Administrative Science Quarterly,* 8:192-213.

LEVINE, S., and SCOTCH, N. 1967. "Toward The Development of Theoretical Models: II." *Milbank Memorial Fund Quarterly,* 45:163-74.

LINDEMANN, E. 1950. "Modifications in the Course of Ulcerative Colitis in Relationship to Changes in Life Situations and Reaction Patterns." *Research Publication, Association for Nervous and Mental Disorders,* 29:706-23.

MARGOLIN, S.G. 1950. "Variations of Gastric Functions during Conscious and Unconscious Conflict States." *Research Publication, Association for Nervous and Mental Disorders,* 29:656–64.

MECHANIC, D. 1962. *Students under Stress.* Glencoe, Ill.: Free Press.

RIPLEY, H.S. 1950. "Life Situations, Emotions and Glaucoma." *Research Publication, Association for Nervous and Mental Disorders,* 29:523–36.

SARBIN, T.R. 1962. "A New Model of the Behavior Disorders." *Gawein,* 10:324–41.

SCOTT, R.A. 1963. "Illness and Social Role Difficulties." Mimeog.

SELYE, H. 1956. *The Stress of Life.* New York: McGraw-Hill.

STEVENSON, I. P., and DUNCAN, C. H. 1950. "Alterations in Cardiac Function and Circulatory efficiency during Periods of Life Stress as Shown by Changes in the Rate, Rhythm, Electrocardiographic Pattern and Output of the Heart in Those with Cardiovascular Stress." *Research Publication, Association for Nervous and Mental Disorders,* 29:799–817.

WOLF, S. 1948. "Hypertension as a Reaction Pattern to Stress; Summary of Experimental Data on Variations in Blood Pressure and Renal Blood Flow." *Annals of Internal Medicine,* 29:1056–76.

WOLFF, H.G. 1948. "Changes in Form and Function of Mucous Membranes Occurring as Part of Protective Reaction Patterns in Man during Periods of Life Stress and Emotional Conflict." *Transactions of the Academy of American Physicians,* 61:313–34.

1950. *Life Stress and Bodily Diseases.* Baltimore: Williams and Wilkins.

1953. *Stress and Disease.* Springfield, Ill.: Charles C. Thomas.

11. Perspectives on Stress Research

SOL LEVINE AND
NORMAN A. SCOTCH

OUR DECISION as editors not to confine authors to a standardized definition of stress but to allow the common element to emerge from their attack on individual subject matter appears to have been justified. Each author found it necessary to develop his own working definition of stress in order to establish a conceptual base from which to approach his own subject matter. Once developed and operationalized, however, the stress concept serves as a selective and purposive guide to organize and systematize a wide range of data in a specific field. In this last chapter we will not attempt to summarize the major points of each of the preceding chapters, since each represents an intensive and, we believe, successful effort by each author to organize and systematize a specific substantive area. Instead, we shall point up and underscore some of the major common themes and emphases which run through all of the various chapters.

What, then, are some of the things we have learned from the

Sol Levine is chairman and professor, and Norman A. Scotch is professor, Department of Behavioral Sciences, The Johns Hopkins School of Hygiene and Public Health. They are co-editors of this volume.

attention each author has given to his subject matter? What is immediately apparent is that stress pervades many areas of life and that it
is a constant which individuals face daily. The task of managing or
coping with stress is an important determinant of the quality of
individual lives. For many the consequences of unremitting or un-
mitigated stress are considerable in terms of illness, pathology, or the
inability or incapacity to function adequately. The evidence for these
findings, while uneven and fragmentary, is convincing to all but the
most skeptical.

But the nature of stress is still difficult to comprehend. Thus, as we
have seen, the question of how stress operates, why it affects some
more than others, why in some cases it leads to particular consequences and not in others—all of this remains obscure, for here the
data are at best only preliminary and suggestive. It has been apparent throughout this book that at least two major barriers have prevented researchers from further penetrating the mysteries of the
stress phenomenon. The first barrier revolves around the lack of
conceptual clarity surrounding the phenomenon itself. This difficulty
is compounded by lack of agreement by various investigators on the
most fundamental—indeed elementary—questions as to whether the
process is lodged essentially in the nature of the stimulus, the way it
is perceived, or the manner in which it is managed. (Even further, as
pointed out by several of the authors, disciplinary provincialism
prevents investigators from viewing and appreciating the stress process except within a narrow framework as dictated by their range of
skills or the scope of their subject matter). The second major barrier
consists of numerous methodological problems concerning how best
to collect meaningful and valid data on stress.

INADEQUACY OF A SIMPLISTIC MODEL: COMPLEXITY OF SOCIAL STRESS

The various chapters in this book clearly illuminate the inadequacy
and incorrectness of a mechanical or simplistic stimulus-response
model to encompass the various phenomena in the stress continuum.
The picture of stress that emerges reflects the complexity of the
stress process so that we are presented with a more elaborate refinement and delineation of a number of specific components or dimensions of stress. These include such broad but delimited areas as (1)
the sources of stress, (2) the perception and meaning of the stress
stimulus to the individual, (3) the personality or response repertoire

of the person, (4) the individual's coping with or management of the stress stimulus, and (5) the ultimate outcome of the stress experience. Moreover, within each of these major areas the authors display considerable depth and sophistication and reject a simple stimulus-response relationship of two atomistic variables. Thus, for example, Croog, Gross, and the Dohrenwends do not merely count such atomistic events as death in the family or loss of job as sources of stress but sensitively analyze the structural and normative features of the family, the work situation, and the stratification system to explore and explain the complex operation of the stress process. In the process of delineating the complex and multidimensional aspects of the sources of stress, the authors broaden our perspective and increase our wisdom. Witness, for example, Croog's description of stress of the family's life cycle, as well as his repudiation of facile notions of the inexorable negative aspects of the conjugal family; Gross's view of organizations, on the one hand, as a means by which man manages threats and, on the other, as forces that generate and pose new problems for man; and the logical and systematic weighing and assessing of the literature on class and race by the Dohrenwends to ascertain the relative stress experienced by segments of the population differentially located in the social structure. Croog clearly delineates the role of the family as a mediator of stress from the role of the family in instigating and producing stress. He also carefully examines stresses arising from (1) the structure of the family, (2) differences between the structure of particular families and those that predominate in any particular social environment, (3) different aspects of the life cycle of families (early marriage, empty nest retirement, etc.), (4) role conflict (within and without the family), and (5) failure in interpersonal relationships. Similarly, Gross examines carefully and in some detail three major types of work stress: (1) stress of organizational careers (unemployment, poor pay, and lack of recognition), (2) task stress (job dissatisfaction, conditions of work and job content), and (3) organizational structural stress (social interaction, isolation and role conflict). In addition to examining all the foregoing as *sources* of stress, Gross further examines techniques within organizations that permit the worker to manage or attempt to manage stress. And the Dohrenwends describe differential kinds and amounts of stress within the class structure, the impact of which is mediated through a number of internal and external factors (resources, life duration, and availability of services).

Other chapters offer additional elaboration of the sources of stress.

282 PART FOUR : Conclusions and Implications

Notice, for example, the refinement offered by Jaco and his distinction between predisposing and precipitating factors in stress on the biological, psychological, and social levels. We encounter, for example, not only social predisposing factors, such as a marriage system, but also social precipitating factors, such as divorce. Similarly, our view of the sources of stress is enlarged when we consider Teeles emphasis on the perception of a hostile environment by many Negroes. Teele does not view this as an idosyncratic characteristic but as a pervasive feature of the psychic existence of large segments of the Negro community. The variables in this book, then, go beyond the usual epidemiological reliance upon age, sex, and social class to include such dynamic sources of stress as social isolation, role conflict, status inconsistency, disruption in modes of living, and the imaginative distinction by the Dohrenwends between stress involving security and stress involving achievement. In short, the various chapters cumulatively help to formulate a richer and more penetrating description of the social sources of stress.

COGNITION AND PERCEPTION OF STIMULUS

Another dimension clearly delineated and explicated throughout this book is the individual's awareness or perception of the stress stimulus. Whether a stimulus is likely to produce stress, pleasure, or a neutral emotional state depends largely upon the meaning it has for the individual. Granted that some stimuli are almost invariably interpreted as threatening and others as pleasurable by virtually everybody, most stimuli, by and large, are classified by the organism, and this classification process varies in terms of such factors as the context in which the stimulus appears and the number of times and how successfully such a stimulus was previously managed. Lazarus in Chapter Five of this volume deals with the importance of cognitive factors both in appraising a stress as threatening and in developing coping mechanisms. "Just how serious is the threat, how salient? Can I deal with it—what has been my past experience? Can I get help?" These and numerous other questions are quickly asked by the individual in preparing to mobilize his defenses and, more important, to select the appropriate course of action, whether this be fight, flight, or panic.

A man is fired from his job. How stressful is this? Inconvenience or disaster? The reaction to the firing depends a great deal on the man's social status, the number of alternatives he sees as available to him (full-employment or recession?), the extent to which he perceives there is group or institutional support (unemployment benefits, union benefits), and the perceived ultimate consequences it will have for him.

Or, caught by the police, the youthful "delinquent" assesses the possibility that he will land in jail. For Negroes and for lower-class members of society, the prospect is likely; for middle- and upper-class counterparts, it is less likely. Therefore, being apprehended will probably be more stressful for the former than for the latter—but, ultimately sent to jail, the experience will be considerably more threatening for the middle- and upper-class than for the lower-, who presumably know more of what to expect. Clearly, cognition and perception are important in determining the extent to which an event is stressful.

STRESS AS FAILURE OF ADAPTATION

Another theme that pervades this book is that stress is not to be viewed as occurring when this or that load, pressure, or stimulus is applied to the individual but instead when there is a failure of the individual's adaptive resources or capacities. In this respect the authors owe a heavy debt to the conceptualization of stress by Mechanic, whose contribution is acknowledged in a number of places. This is a distinctive emphasis and has important conceptual, substantive, and methodological implications. Gross (p. 59) offers the pithy definition of stress as the "failure of routine methods for managing threats." Cassel, leaning on the work of Hinkle, suggests that disease itself can be viewed as occurring when the adaptive responses of the organism to stressful stimuli are inappropriate in kind or amount or both. He argues for the need to learn the determinants of particular adaptive devices used by various segments of the population. Lazarus emphasizes that it is "necessary to separate processes involved in threat production from those involved in coping" and argues that stress reactions are reflections or consequences of coping processes intended to reduce threat. And the Dohrenwends focus on the distinction between adaptive and maladaptive responses. The organism's own response to the demands placed on it clearly constitutes an inextricable component of the stress experience.

The foregoing has profound implications for research on stress, especially when we consider the degree to which physiological indicators are often used as indices of stress. As Crider states (pp. 190-2), ". . . the physiological arousal characteristic of conflict situations, rather than representing a simple index of stress or a sign of debilitation, can be regarded as part of an active attempt by the subjects to cope with the 'problem' posed by the conflict." And

again, ". . . the behavioral and the physiological reactions to conflict
are independently organized systems. Indeed, it appears that physiological arousal plays an adaptive role in supporting the individual's
attempts to master or cope with aversive environments." Even more,
it must be remembered that physiological and emotional states do
not necessarily have a positive relationship to one another. As Cassel
cogently states, ". . . social processes may affect physiological
findings in the absence of any marked emotional disturbance. In fact,
there is suggestive evidence which would indicate that under certain
circumstances, marked alteration in affective states may be regarded
as an alternative response to social stresses and that the physiological
responses in such individuals may be less marked than those who do
not display such emotional responses." This underscores further the
necessity of relying on more than a single physiological indicator and
the need to study the organism over longer periods of time and not
only during scarce or short-term periods. It also points up the need
for researchers in this field to have greater familiarity with the physiological indicators they employ and not to place undue or unques-
tioned reliance upon them.

RELATIONS AMONG COMPONENTS

As we indicated in the first chapter, and as Jaco and Cassel attest, the
task of conceptualizing, understanding, and defining the dependent
variable or outcome component in the stress continuum (e.g., mental
illness, heart disease, etc.) remains a formidable problem. But perhaps the most crucial and overriding problem is that of linking and
describing the dynamic interplay among the various components of
stress. As Jaco says, " . . . while much literature includes the notion
of stress in its relationship to mental illness, little exists on the
precise connection between stress and specific forms of illness."
Stress, therefore, whether "external" or "internal" in existing psychological theories is lacking in specificity concerning its causal
linkage to specific mental illness. Jaco states that "many crucial
questions still remain concerning the precise contribution of stress to
the overall process of becoming mentally ill for an individual, such
as when stress occurs, how much stress is needed, as well as the
nature of those stresses that both predispose and precipitate a mental
aberration."

Cassel draws attention to a related question in his evaluation of
existing epidemiological data opposed to those obtained in labora-

tory studies. He points out that the "confusion which surrounds much of these data is largely attributable to the failure to specify or isolate a particular social process and in measuring them once they are pinpointed." Another major source of confusion, Cassel argues, is the failure of investigators to distinguish the consequences of social as opposed to psychological processes or personality factors. "Thus, it is not uncommon to find studies concerned with the relationship between various personality types and/or affective states and physical disease manifestations being advanced as evidence of the role of social factors as determinants of disease."

Despite the conceptual and definitional problems surrounding stress, and the equally difficult problem of measuring it, the field has generated a small body of consistent empirical findings. One of the major questions in the popular as well as the scientific literature is that of the relative stress experienced by different socioeconomic and racial groups in the society. The romantic notion that lower-class persons and Negroes in general fare more happily, are subject to less pressure than their counterparts in the society, and cope with their problems more successfully has gradually receded in the scientific literature. An examination of the various chapters in this book, especially those by the Dohrenwends and Teele, should serve to resolve this question further. Teele emphasizes the sense of alienation, isolation, powerlessness, and estrangement from the dominant society that blacks experience. He documents this in a number of ways, including the treatment of blacks by the popular media, their representation in the written history, and their exposure to violence, not only from the machinery of government but from white society in general. In his review of the Kerner Commission Report, as well as its supplemental studies, Teele underscores the relatively broad involvement of Negroes in the urban disorders and their widespread dissatisfaction and bitter frustration. He concludes that urban disorders can be understood largely in terms of the large degree of social stress Negroes have experienced.

Much of the value of the chapter by the Dohrenwends resides in their clear discussion of a wide range of data on differential stresses experienced by different class and racial groups. Even more impressive is how they succeed in ordering the diverse findings in the field by a conceptual model of their own under a number of explicit and clearly specified dimensions. As indicated previously, they distinguish between two types of stressors or disturbing events: those which are "achievement related" and those which are "security related." This distinction is refined further into "developmental" and "nondevelopmental" stressors. While the Dohrenwends report that lower-class members of society are more likely to experience more developmental achievement stressors, they also point out that other types of stressors appear to be distributed almost equally among all classes and that in some cases the higher-class groups are subject to more stressors. They indicate how difficult it is to weigh the different stresses experienced by the various class groups and conclude tentatively that "there is no firm evidence that the overall rate of stressors varies with social class." Examining variations by race, however, the authors are able to conclude more definitely that both middle- and lower-class Negroes are subject to stressors to a greater extent than their white counterparts.

Continuing their analysis of the stress experience of the two classes and the two races as guided by their conceptual scheme, the authors infer that with regard to internal and external mediating factors, lower-class persons are more disadvantaged than middle-class persons and Negroes are more disadvantaged than whites. A total assessment, considering all factors, permits the relatively firm generalization that "the severity of stress is lowest for middle-class whites and highest for lower-class Negroes." While this may not surprise many, it is illustrative of the type of definite empirical generalizations that can be explicated by a focused and systematic analysis of the data.

In recent years popular writers as well as political analysts have focused anew on the "broken family" or the "broken home"—because of its posited relationship to various forms of social pathology—in the hope of recommending some measures that might strengthen the family. The Moynihan report focused particularly on the phenomenon of the Negro family and the "tangle of pathology" in which it was enmeshed. Although Moynihan's analysis was mainly concerned with the lower-class Negro "broken family" and originally was an internal governmental report intended to expedite social measures to improve the plight of the Negro, it soon entered the public arena and became the object of controversy. The phenomenon of the broken family as a source of stress and as a contributor to the development of social pathology or social deviance is examined analytically and in some detail in the chapters by Teele and Croog. Teele points up the fairly consistent relationship between the broken home and delinquent behavior but emphasizes that the relationship is more complex than it might otherwise at first appear. For example, the effect of broken homes may hold more for girls than for boys when examined by different types of delinquency. The differential treatment by the courts and legal agencies of delinquent children from broken as opposed to unbroken homes must be considered. Then, too, the happiness of the home might be a more overriding feature than the broken home, per se. Finally, Teele emphasizes that one must consider other more dynamic components which may or may not be associated with the broken home structure.

Croog's analysis, while on a different level, is consistent with that of Teele and draws attention to a host of intervening and qualifying variables. In considering the effects of divorce, for example, Croog states: "It is not the simple fact of divorce alone which is stressful, but rather the particular total circumstances within which it occurs. The amount of stress experienced varies in relation to such factors as the age and sex identity of the divorced, the degree of family disapproval, the presence of children, and the level of ambivalence in the divorced person about the decision." He points to such mediating factors as the availability of other sources of support, the attitudes of significant others, and the availability of parental substitutes. Moreover, he emphasizes that when the family is "broken" it may be accompanied by such other stressors as poor parental role performance, unemployment, and interpersonal conflict. Examining the findings of mental health studies, he reminds us that the effect of the broken home on mental health impairment is higher for lower-class persons than their middle-class counterparts. Finally, Croog raises a question which, on a more general level, persists throughout the volume: the precise way in which the stressor, in this case the broken home, operates to yield negative consequences.

In analyzing and systematizing the literature on broken homes, the authors of this book expand our understanding of the various dimensions and complexities of this specific stressor phenomenon. Despite the need to bear in mind the subtle and manifold aspects of the broken home, and to recognize how far we have to go before we can describe exactly how it exerts its impact on behavior, the broken home appears to encompass a range of significant stress components and to be significantly involved in production of deviance and social pathology.

Stress is not an individual affair but must be viewed in terms of the social context in which it occurs. This is not an idle caveat but a basic characteristic of the human experience and, as Cassel relates, can also be demonstrated in animal behavior. Although this will immediately be recognized by those who have been exposed to behavioral sciences, it may not be sufficiently appreciated by all who are studying the stress experience. It is for this reason that it is useful to have as a departure Crider's clear review of the experimental literature. Crider cites a number of experiments which illustrate the differential responses to stress by individuals in various group situations as opposed to those who are alone.

Yet, as Cassel says, "Somewhat paradoxically some of the more convincing evidence concerning the role of social factors as determinants of disease comes from animal studies." Some of the established studies in the field indicate that physiological responses to stimuli vary with different group factors. Even more, animals living in groups begin to respond to the same stimuli in a similar manner. The role of one's group membership, one's relative position in a group, and the resources one can obtain from other group members emerge as likely factors to mediate the impact of specific stimuli upon the individual.

If group membership is an important mediating factor, a corollary finding—the negative impact of social isolation—runs through this book, particularly in the chapters by Jaco, Cassel, and Teele. Finally, while not stated explicitly or elaborated, the role of the dominant social forms and cultural patterns looms formidably. This is evident in many ways, ranging from the differential responses to experimental situations by persons from different societies to the role of institutionalized goals and means in alternately motivating, gratifying, and frustrating society's members.

Thus far we have emphasized some of the main conceptual themes in the book and have reviewed a few findings on social stress. We have deliberately refrained until now from discussing the chapter on "Models of Stress" by Scott and Howard because it is an organizing and integrative section of the book and should be treated separately. We believe the chapter makes several distrinctive contributions to our understanding of social stress, not least of which is its succinct review and ordering of the major conceptual models of stress. While most of the models Scott and Howard consider were useful and appropriate for the purpose for which they were developed, they tend to possess limitations in serving as a general integrative conceptual model or framework. Thus, from the vantage point of attempting to construct a workable overall integrative model, the authors examine and clearly describe the limitations of the major competing models in the field. These include the usual problems of definition and conceptualization; the models tend to be "field specific," making it difficult to move from one level to another; they tend to be restricted to acute and traumatic situations; they are incomplete in that they do not embody the various dimensions of the stress continuum; and they do not necessarily explain the phenomenon under consideration. Scott and Howard's critique is consistent with a number of observations made by other authors throughout this book.

The model the authors formulate attempts to overcome the limitations of other competing models and tries to integrate existing knowledge of stress into unified framework. As the authors indicate, their framework leans heavily on models developed by the writers they have studied. The model adduced by Scott and Howard views human behavior in problem-solving terms and assumes a characteristic level of functioning for each individual. It is difficult to summarize further their pithy, logically tight, and articulate elaboration of the problem-solving model. What is to be emphasized, however, is that they clearly explicate the various dimensions of stress and logically delineate specific components within each dimension. Thus, the authors distinguish among four classes of problems with which the organism may have to deal, five types of conditions which determine whether the organism can master the problem, and the two basic courses the organism may pursue when it experiences "undissipated tension." What is appealing in this model is that it succeeds in reformulating and embracing all the relevant dimensions and subdimensions of stress that appear in this book as well as in the other specific models of stress considered by the authors. Moreover, their model, while broad and encompassing, introduces further refinements that contribute additional analytic power to our understanding of stress. For example, they usefully classify the modes of response to a problem as consisting of an assertive response, a divergent response, and an inert response. Finally, and this is a significant step, the authors view the mastery of stress in dynamic terms; as they state: "Generally speaking, when mastery of a problem does occur, the state of the organism is superior to its state prior to the time of initial confrontation in the sense that if the same problem arises again, the organism will be able to deal with it more efficiently than before."

In assessing the utility of their problem-solving model, the authors appear to be successful in subsuming and reinterpreting the specific components of such other useful models as that of Mechanic, Basowitz, or Dohrenwend. The model developed by the authors seems to fulfill one of their dictums—that a satisfactory model not be "field specific" and that it not lose its value or relevance as one moves from one level of analysis to another, from the physiological, to the psychological, to the social.

Of course the usefulness of the model will be tested as it is employed by researchers and students. There is every likelihood that it will be refined, modified, and reformulated. For the present, however, it is a welcome addition to our conceptual armamentarium in that it integrates present knowledge and existing conceptual models and provides a thematic focus with which to approach stress phenomena.

Few subject areas in the social sciences are as amenable to and, indeed, require the knowledge and skills from a variety of disciplines as social stress. This is not to assert that all or most investigators should be interdisciplinary, but, in our judgment, it would advance the knowledge of the general field if individual investigators from different disciplines could, to the extent possible, be guided by a general conceptual model like that of Scott and Howard. At the very least we would hope that workers from different disciplines would explicate the specific dimensions they are studying and the level at which they are working. This would help one discipline to incorporate the findings of another.

The general conceptual rubric of stress, whatever its limitations, has provided students of the field with a searchlight for uncovering and systematizing diverse data. There is considerable agreement regarding the need for greater conceptual clarity and explication and more precise and dynamic linkage and explanation among the various components. We have also seen the existence of a few fairly firm empirical generalizations. Finally, workers in the field have shown sophistication in their effort to develop working definitions and conceptual models. Despite the problems that confront the student of social stress, conceptually and methodologically, progress is being made even while it remains a fertile and exciting field for study.

Index

291